The Essence of Islamic Philosophy

By

MASHHAD AL-ALLAF

(Ph.D. in Philosophy)

IIC - CLASSIC SERIES, USA

The Essence of Islamic Philosophy

By:

MASHHAD AL-ALLAF
(Ph.D. in Philosophy)

© Mashhad Al-Allaf 2003

To order please send an e-mail to:

iic_classic@yahoo.com

Islamic Information Center, USA.

Comments or suggestions please send e-mail to:

Mashhad9@yahoo.com
or
alallafm@slu.edu

Includes bibliography.

ISBN 0-9722722-1- 6

1. Islamic-Philosophy.
2. Religion-Philosophy
3. Medieval-Philosophy

I. Al-Allaf, Mashhad, 1957-

CONTENTS

CHAPTER TWO

CHAPTER FOUR

4. IBN SINA

Existence and the Task of Philosophy

Metaphysics

CHAPTER FIVE

5. AL-GHAZALI

Meta-Philosophy is the Task of Philosophy

Theory of Knowledge

Acknowledgments

I would like to thank scholars and publishers whose cooperation in giving permission to reproduce excerpts of previously published material was very helpful to achieve this work. I would like to give a special thanks to Fons Vitae publishing company for their copyright permission on al-Ghazali's *Deliverance From Error*, and their wonderful support.

My sincere thanks goes to Dr. Nicholas Rescher (Professor of Philosophy in the University of Pittsburgh) for his generosity in sending me some of his books on Islamic philosophy and Logic, and for giving me copyright permission to reproduce some of his writing.

A special thanks to my students who carefully studied and examined my work. Their suggestions were very useful.

I would like to thank my student at Washington University, Rouhullah Rahmani, the designer of the book cover. I think he expressed a quite impressive ability in art.

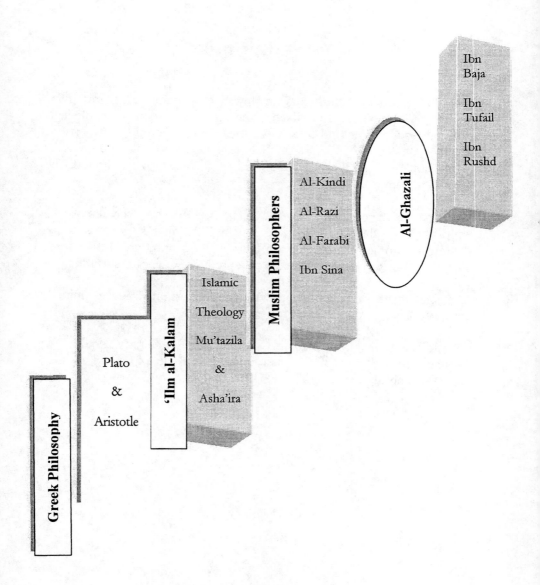

INTRODUCTION

What is The Essence of Islamic Philosophy?

1. Islamic philosophy has an essence that distinguishes it from other types of philosophies. Understanding this essence is the most suitable approach to understanding this area of philosophy. What is the essence of Islamic philosophy?[1]
Since Islamic Philosophy flourished within the environment and the domain of Islamic culture, its essence cannot be approached properly without touching on two themes: first, Islam as a religion and second, the Islamic civilization itself. The religion and the civilization are not the core subject of this book; however, I will touch on them in as much as it is needed to understand the essence of Islamic philosophy.

2. One might ask why we search for an essence of Islamic philosophy. A cultural advancement could be measured by the advancement of its philosophy. Philosophy itself might be the essence of any civilization or culture; a culture without philosophy is a culture without universal outlook. In fact some scholars support such a view; Albert Schweitzer in his book *Philosophy of Civilization*[2] holds that philosophy is essential in a civilization. He concludes that the decline of philosophy leads to the decline of the civilization. In order to justify his hypothesis and hold philosophy as the ultimate irreducible essence I think Schweitzer has to answer this question: Why does philosophy decline in the first place?

Answering this question in terms of "something else" makes that "thing" or that ultimate explanation more essential. In fact, the question

---

[1] The search for the essence (a*l-Mahiyyah*) in the question: "What is the essence of Islamic Philosophy?" coincides with the way in which we ask the question in Arabic language too: ماهي الفلسفة الإسلاميّة؟ (Mahiya al-Falsafah al-Islamiyya?) The word "Mahiya" in the question above refers to al- Mahiyyah الماهيّة (The Essence).

[2] Schweitzer, A (1949): see chapter one.

about the essence from which all of these aspects flows is still valid. What is it that underlies all aspects of a civilization?

We can answer this question by saying: the law, especially the Divine Law. The whole system of legislation underlies any civilization. Indeed, a civilization is nothing more than a law that elevates the individual and advances the society: elevation on the spiritual side, and advancement in both social and material life. This cannot be done unless we control the animalistic and savage side of human beings, and this cannot be accomplished without a strict law[3]. Therefore the legislative system has a two-fold function:

1- To establish what is important and beneficial for human existence.
2- To protect what is already established, by a set of laws, rules, regulations, and punishments.

Let us look at this example. An agricultural society of the ancient world is now considered more civilized than societies based on hunting or pirating. Agriculture represents prudence and more systematic thought than that of hunting and pirating. Forethought is what distinguishes a civilized society. Such systematic thinking and forethought manifest themselves clearly in the law of these ancient civilizations. If humans are left to their impulses, society will not achieve any progress. Furthermore, a civilized act requires using reason to think not only about this life, but also about the hereafter. This reasoning requires sacrifice.

3. So what is the essence of Islamic civilization?
Contrary to other civilizations such as Babylonian, Egyptian, Greek, Persian, Indian, and Western, where the names refer to geography or nations, Islamic civilization refers to Islam as its core. This core is spiritual and intellectual, and tends to be comprehensive. It is unlimited

---

[3] The validity, comprehension, applicability, and simplicity of the law are some factors that need to be considered in analyzing civilization. On the contrary to the man made legislative systems, the Divine Law stand as the most pragmatic through time, spatial dimensions, and cultural diversity.

in space and time. In fact, it does challenge spatial and temporal dimension of our life by emphasizing the immortal essence of man. It is not only for certain people; it is for the whole human race. This core is not for the Middle Ages or modern times; it is for any and all times.

Islam provides for humans a universal outlook (Weltanschauung): the origin of the universe, its essence, its goal, the meaning of life, values, the relationship between man and the whole universe, and the end of this life and what follows after.[4]

4. A question against this thesis:
An important question might be raised against our thesis: If law is the essence of civilization, why have some civilizations with an advanced systematic law declined?
The answer: they declined because the law itself became ineffective in their life for one of two reasons:

- It was not sufficiently comprehensive to fulfill the need of humans through space and time.
- The people themselves left the law and responded to their impulses; the law is active in itself, but they are not activating it in their life.

5. Beyond Orientalism
This book is an attempt to present Islamic philosophy from inside and within its own terms. In this age of beyond Orientalism this presentation is necessary and helpful not only to the understanding of Islamic civilization, but also to the very understanding of the roots of Western philosophy.
Let us now present the ideas of the Muslim philosophers in a chronological order.

---

[4] For a philosophical and theological introduction to Islam please see *Mirror of Realization* (2003).

CHAPTER ONE

"We ought not to be embarrassed of appreciating the truth and of obtaining it wherever it comes from, even if it comes from races distant and nations different from us.
Nothing should be dearer to the seeker of truth than the truth itself, and there is no devalue of the truth, nor belittling either of him who speaks it or of him who conveys it." **Al-Kindi**

AL-KINDI

Religion and The Task of Philosophy:

His Intellectual Life

What is Philosophy?

The Method of Philosophy

The Goal of Philosophy

The Task of Philosophy and Philosophers

Al-Kindi
(a. 185-256 A.H. / 805-873 A.D.)

Religion and The Task of Philosophy

1. His Intellectual Life:
Al-Kindi is the first philosopher in Islam. The word "philosopher" might not even do him justice. Al-Kindi was a mathematician first of all[5], physicist, astronomer, physician, geographer, plus an expert in music.
He wrote many books and treatises in many different fields of knowledge the sum of which is over 350 treatises, 11 of them on Arithmetic, 32 on Geometry, 22 on Philosophy, and the rest of his writing are on physics, astronomy, medicine, psychology, meteorology, topography, alchemy, and music.

In his classification of sciences Al-Kindi placed mathematics and logic as the first discipline, to be followed by physics, metaphysics, and theology.

Seeking truth was his first priority, regardless where truth comes from:

"We ought not to be embarrassed of appreciating the truth and of obtaining it wherever it comes from, even if it comes from races distant and nations different from us. Nothing should be dearer to the seeker after truth than the truth itself."[6]

---

[5] See Rescher, N. (1964): Al-Kindi: An Annotated Bibliography, includes reference to literatures on Al-Kindi's philosophy of mathematics. In spite of its date the book still has useful information that is very well organized.

[6] Al-Kindi (1948): p. 81. His book *On First Philosophy* was translated by Alfred L. Ivry. (see Ivry: 1974). However, I will retranslate some important passages because al-Kindi's philosophical language is even difficult for those who speak Arabic as a native tongue. In some other passages I will quote Ivry (1974).

Al-Kindi's love of wisdom led him to establish a solid background in Greek philosophy. His knowledge of the Aristotelian philosophy in specific made him more qualified in criticizing Greek philosophy when it contradicted the truth and the divine revelation of Islam.

Al-Kindi was known to the western medieval world as al-Kindus. Many of his books were translated into Latin by Gerard of Cremona (1114-1187), and made available to scientists and philosophers in the West. His work was very impressive, to the point that Cardan (Girolamo Cardano 1501-1576 an Italian Mathematician) considered him one of the twelve greatest minds.[7]

Al-Kindi's scientific achievements and his philosophy of science has influenced the medieval and modern western thought significantly. A good example to consider for the beginning of this intellectual dialogue and transition of Islamic knowledge to the west is Roger Bacon (1220-1292).[8] Bacon emphasized the importance of experimental method following the footstep of al-Kindi and al-Hasan ibnul Haitham (al-Hazen): "His contribution to scientific theory, like his empirical research, were confined largely to optics. With the aid of new source material from Alhazen and Alkindi, he was able to develop significantly many of Grosseteste's views concerning the tides, heat, and double refraction and to give the most mature expression to Grosseteste's theory that light (and all physical force generally) is transmitted in pulses like sound waves."[9]

2. Al-Kindi lived in Basra, Kufa, and Baghdad in Iraq where the religious environment and the caliphs (Muslim political leaders) were very supportive of the pursuit of knowledge, and searching for the truth regardless of its sources, following the first revelation of the Qur'an:

"Read! In the Name of your Lord Who has created (all that exist). He has created man from a clot (a piece of thick coagulated blood).

---

[7] De Boer, T.J. (1965): p.101.
[8] Bacon, R. (1962): Part VI.
[9] Wolter, Allan B. (1967): Vol.1. p. 241.

Read! And your Lord is the Most Generous.
Who has taught (the writing) by the pen.
He has taught man that which he knew not." (*Qur'an, 96: 1-5*)

The tradition of the prophet Muhammad (pbuh)[10] encouraged the search for knowledge and truth. The Prophet said: "seeking knowledge is obligatory on every Muslim (male or female)." In some narrations Muslims are encouraged to seek truth even if it is in China, because distance or cultural barrier should not prevent people from seeking the truth.

Muslim Caliphs encouraged the translation of the knowledge and wisdom of other civilization, with the strong belief that reason will confirm revelation and will not contradict it. Thus the House of Wisdom (Bait al-Hikmah) established by the caliph al-Ma'mun (reigned 813-833). In this institute Muslim and non Muslim scholars worked together to achieve one goal, i.e., wisdom, as in the Qur'an:

"He (Allah) granteth wisdom to whom He pleaseth; and he to whom wisdom is granted receives indeed a benefit overflowing; but none will grasp the Message but men of understanding." (*Qur'an, 2:269*)

The title of one of al-Kindi's books in philosophy is full of meaning. This book, which will be the focus of our study, is called: *Kitab al-Kindi ila al-Mu'tasim Billah fil Falsafah al-Ula (al-Kindi's Book for al-Mu'tasim Billah On First Philosophy)*.

This book is on metaphysics and was addressed to al-Mu'tasim Billah (The Muslim caliph at the time of al-Kindi who reigned 833-842). The caliph himself supported philosophizing.

---

[10] In Islamic religion if the name of the Prophet Muhammad or any other prophet is mentioned, then people should say: Peace and blessings of Allah be upon him (pbuh), in Arabic: صلى الله عليه وسلم. Salla Allahu 'Alaihi wa Sallam.

3. Some times al-Kindi is called "The Philosopher of The Arabs". But such a nationalist label is misleading and will be dismissed by us for two reasons:

First: because it diverts the attention away from his contribution to Islamic philosophy, and implies non-Islamic thought. Al-Kindi's philosophy is Islamic in essence, he strived to prove by reason many Qur'anic theses in opposing Greek philosophy. According to him the very role of philosophy from the very beginning is to know Allah (The God), as we will discuss later.

Second, such a label encourages ethnocentrism, which is a thesis rejected by Islam. People are equal in the sight of Allah; their preference in His sight is their obedience to Him, not their nationality. The Qur'anic teaching also emphasizes that good reasoning is the inheritance of all mankind.

4. What is Philosophy?
Al-Kindi ranked philosophy as the highest level and noblest of the human effort in dealing with and in understanding our existence. He defines philosophy as:

"Knowledge of the essence of things, insofar as is possible for man."[11]

This definition immediately causes us to the conclusion that philosophy according to al-Kindi must pass from the natural, phenomenological aspects of the existence to a more essential level that is the cause and the very essence of everything. In order to "understand" the truth rationally, we must know the meaning of "stand – under". That which stands under is the true cause of every thing that comes to be. Understanding the effects is only possible through knowing their causes, which, in turn, will help in achieving the truth, al –Kindi said:

---

[11] Al-Kindi (1948): p.77. Author's translation.

"It is impossible to find the truth that we are seeking without finding a cause."[12]

Natural sciences deal with causes and effects, and our understanding of the effects is enhanced by more theoretical descriptions and explanations of the causes. This type of knowledge is presented in physics, chemistry, biology, etc... But why is philosophy the highest in the search for truth and understanding than any other field of knowledge?

Al-Kindi's answer might be in three reasons:

1. Philosophy is a search for a universal cause and ultimate truth, not the particular causes. In physics, for example, we understand why physical objects fall down by understanding the cause through the law of gravity, but this law is particular. No matter how far you can extend it, it still does not help us to know why hydrogen and oxygen make water, or why we sometimes have a fever or why we die.

2. Philosophy is not only searching for the cause of existence, but also understanding the cause of continuation of the existence of everything, the cause that is the source of secondary causes and their effects. In this sense, knowing this cause, is knowing the essence of everything, and the ultimate truth.

3. Philosophy is the search for the one cause, the necessary one. If a cause is only a possible cause, then it is possible by something else. Thus it is not the necessary cause, and is not the ultimate truth.

Al-Kindi said:

"[T]he cause of the existence and continuance of everything is the True One, in that each thing which has a cause has truth. The truth, thus, necessarily exists in caused beings."[13]

---

[12] Al-Kindi (1948): p. 77.
[13] Al-Kindi (1948): pp. 77-78.

By the True One al-Kindi means Allah. But to what extent can we as philosophers, philosophize?

Al-Kindi said that we could go as far as our rational capability can go. In his definition of philosophy al-Kindi realized the limitation of the pure reasoning of the human mind. This point will be overlooked by al-Farabi and Ibn Sina; however, it will gain great importance and emphasis by al-Ghazali, and Ibn Taimia, who articulate this thesis in showing the limited domain of philosophy and bringing revelation as another level of reality.

Al-Kindi considered first philosophy or metaphysics the highest field of philosophy because it deals with the essence of everything. In his account Allah is the first cause. Thus he drew a conclusion that philosophy does not contradict religion, on the contrary philosophy will be the study of Divinity.

"The knowledge of the essence of things includes knowledge of Divinity, unity and virtue, and an entire knowledge of everything useful, and of the way to it; and a distance from anything harmful, with precautions against it."[14]

Thus he thought that philosophy would not only lead to Allah, but would also be a great proof of His unity. He thought philosophy would be manifested in virtuous action in the practice of truth. Since the messengers of Allah basically taught people these three things: knowing Allah, knowing that He is One, and good moral life.[15] Thus philosophy is necessary since it seeks the same goal on rational basis. In fact al-Kindi makes two points here:

First: that there is no contradiction between philosophy and religion.
Second: as a result, philosophy, as a way of seeking the truth, should not be dismissed from the circle of Islamic search for the truth, by claiming that it does not fit the core of Islamic belief. Ibn Rushd accentuates this thesis in his book *Fasl al-Maqal*.

---

[14] Al-Kindi (1948): p. 82.
[15] Al-Kindi (1948): p. 82.

---

5. The Scientific Method of Philosophy:

Philosophy is not mere reflection and speculation; it is an attempt to know by the aid of the mind and logical reasoning. As a scientist al-Kindi emphasized the role of mathematics and logic in philosophical inquiry, and wrote a treatise that mathematics is necessary for learning philosophy.[16]

In his classification of knowledge al-Kindi ranked logic and mathematics higher than any other field, including physics, metaphysics, and theology. This indicates that the philosophical speculation must be enhanced by scientific knowledge. Philosophy for him is no longer idealistic and utopian-like. Instead it is a skillful inquiry of the truth. In order to be consistent with his thesis, al-Kindi relied heavily upon mathematics in his process of philosophizing. Arguments presented in his metaphysics (*al–Falsafah al-Ula*) and in his natural philosophy, are the best examples, as we will see in studying his metaphysics.

Although logical reasoning is a useful method for developing philosophy, al-Kindi thought that "reason" couldn't be the "only" source of knowledge and truth. Al-Kindi made an initial attempt to criticize the pure reason. He also opens the door to make revelation accessible to philosophers. Unlike Greek philosophers al-Kindi himself introduced to philosophy, the concept of prophecy as a source of knowing the truth. Al-Kindi went even further to show the consistency between the truth of reason and the truth from revelation through prophets. He thought that knowledge came from the prophets, and through them is a level even higher than that of pure mind; since the mind is not infallible. This idea is stated in his treatise: *"Fi kammiyyat kutub Aristotalis, wa-ma yuhtaju ilai-hi fi tahseel al-falsafah"*.[17] *(On the quantity of the books of Aristotle and what is required for the attainment of philosophy)*. No one saw this point more clearly or made a good philosophical use of it, until al-Ghazali did in his books "al-

---

[16] See Ibn Abi Usaibi'ah (1884): The title of al-Kindi's treatise is: *"La Tunal al-Falsafa ella bi Elm al-Ryyadha."* (*The impossibility of attaining philosophy without mathematical science*).

[17] Al-Kindi (1950): pp. 362-374.

Munqidh" and "*The Incoherence of the Philosophers*" as we will see when we discuss al-Ghazali.

This contribution of al-Kindi in philosophy is important for two reasons:

First: it questions the power of reason as a sole source of knowledge capable of penetrating through reality. Most of the philosophers tend to think that anything that goes beyond the ability of reason is non-sense. This approach to reality reached its peak in positivist philosophy of the twentieth century.

Second: al-Kindi's contribution opposes the Greek conception of philosophy and reality that is based, to a certain extent, on their mythology. Greek philosophy misses an important conception of the role of revelation in the life of human beings as well as the spirituality of man.

6. The Aim and the Task of Philosophy: Knowledge ('Ilm) and Practice ('Amal).
Al-Kindi believes that the aim of the philosopher is divided into two related branches:

First, the theoretical goal: in which the philosopher must aim at knowledge for the attainment of the truth.

Second, the practical goal: in which he acts according to the truth.

Al-Kindi said:

"The aim of the philosopher is, in his knowledge, to attain the truth, and in his action, to act truthfully."[18]

Al-Kindi in stating the aim of the philosopher made a clear implication of one of the most important principle in the Islamic teaching; which is

---

[18] Al-Kindi (1948): p. 77.

the necessary connection between knowledge and practice (al-'Ilm wal 'Amal). This principle enhanced Islamic technology, as history progressed, by emphasizing the application of theoretical sciences. Theoretical knowledge should be sought only for the sake of its applications and the benefits that it will bring to the life of people on earth.

Al-Kindi's statement made a clear departure from the Greek approach to knowledge, which was theoretical and looked down on the practical side, and application as mere slavish work.

Since Allah is the most perfect, the all-knowing source of truth; the aim of the philosopher is to know the truth. Thus the aim of philosophy is to know Allah and to prove His existence and His unity, by logical reasoning. The task of philosophy being approached here is to reach the truth of religion and to harmonize with revelation.

Since Allah is the absolute good and absolute beauty, to know Him and His unity is to realize the value of beautiful and good things, accordingly the aim of the philosopher is also to know the virtues and establish them through practice:

"We ask Him Who examines our intentions, and who knows our conscientiousness in establishing the proof of His Divinity and the clarification of His Unity, and in defending (Him) against His opponents who disbelieve in that in Him by proofs which subdue their disbelief."[19]

---

[19] Al-Kindi (1948): p. 83.

Reading from al-Kindi on Defining Philosophy:[20]

"Indeed, the art of philosophy is: the highest of the human art in degree and it's rank is most noble. The definition of which is: knowledge of the essence of things, insofar as is possible for man.

The aim of the philosopher is, in his knowledge, to attain the truth, and in regard to his action, to act truthfully; not to act endlessly, for we abstain and the activity comes to an end once we have reached the truth.

It is impossible to find the truth that we are seeking without finding a cause, and the cause of the existence and continuance of everything is the True One [Allah], in that each thing that has a cause has truth. The truth, thus, necessarily exists in caused beings.

The noblest part of philosophy and the utmost in rank is the First Philosophy [Metaphysics], i.e., knowledge of the First Truth Who is the cause of all truth. Therefore, it is necessary that the perfect and most noble philosopher to be the man who entirely understands this most noble knowledge; for the knowledge of the cause is more noble than knowledge of the effect, because we know every knowable only when we have obtained full knowledge of its cause...

Thus, knowledge of the First Cause [Allah] has truthfully been called "First Philosophy", since all the rest of philosophy is contained in its knowledge. The first cause therefore, is the first in nobility, the first in genus, the first in rank with respect to that the knowledge of which is most certain; and the first in time, since it is the cause of time...

We ought not to be embarrassed of appreciating the truth and of

---

[20] From al-Kindi (1948): pp. 77-83. *Kitab al-Kindi Fi al falsafah al-Ula,* (Al-Kindi's Treatise On First Philosophy), the text is in Arabic language. I also used the translation (1974).

obtaining it wherever it comes from, even if it comes from races distant and nations different from us. Nothing should be dearer to the seeker of truth than the truth itself, and there is no devaluation of the truth or belittling either of him who speaks it or of him who conveys it. ...

The knowledge of the true nature of things contains the knowledge of Divinity, unity and virtue, and a total knowledge of everything useful, and of the way to it; and remoteness from anything harmful, with precautions against it. The acquisition of all this is what the true messengers brought from Allah great be His praise. For the true messengers, may Allah 's blessings be upon them, brought but an assertion of the Divinity of Allah alone, and an adherence to virtues, which are pleasing to Him; and the relinquishment of vices, which are contrary to virtues both in themselves and in their effects.

Thus, the acquisition of this precious possession [truth] is obligatory for people of the truth, and we must exert ourselves to the maximum in its pursuit....

We ask Him [Allah] who examines our inner intentions and who knows our hard work in establishing the proof of His Divinity and the clarification of His Unity, and in refuting His opponents who disbelieve in that in Him by proofs that suppress their disbelief. ..."

Al-Kindi

Theory of Knowledge (Ma'rifah)

Sense data and Reason

The Soul

Theory of Intellect (al-'Aql)

Aristotle's Theory of Soul and Intellect

Commentators of Aristotle and The Neo-Platonism

Prophecy and Philosophy

In Islamic philosophy it seems very difficult to separate the theory of mind from metaphysics and the discussion of existence. The epistemology of Muslim philosophers is tightly connected to their ontology. In fact, their metaphysics is epistemological in essence. However, for the sake of clarification I will present epistemology and metaphysics in separated chapters.

Al-Kindi
(a. 185-256 A.H. / 805-873 A.D.)

Theory of Knowledge

7. Sense data and Reason:

Al-Kindi's main goal of philosophy is to know Allah the creator of this world. A second goal that is related to the first is to prove in metaphysics *creation ex nihilo* (creation from nothingness), that the world is not eternal. But what sources of knowledge shall we use to achieve these goals?

Al-Kindi furnishes some epistemological premises to start with before getting into his metaphysics. He stated that human perception and knowledge are of two kinds:

1. Perception by the senses.
2. Knowledge through the intellect.

The existents are of two kinds:

1. Particulars, which are perceived by the senses, and
2. Universals, which exist in the mind.

The sensory perception is achieved through the contact of the senses with sensible particular objects. And since the sensible objects are in continuous motion and in a constant changing, therefore knowledge based on sensations is unstable and localized to the perceiver.[21]

The sensory perceptions take images of the sensory objects and send them to our mind, which establishes them in the area of imagination, then the imagination conveys them to the memory; and the sensible object is represented in our soul. For this reason sense perception is closer to the perceiver himself, and far from the essential nature of the

---

[21] Al-Kindi (1948): p. 85.

sensible object, also it is subjected to the contributing factors of making perception.

Another reason that sensory experience is not reliable because sensible materials exist in particular bodies, therefore sensory perception will relate to particular objects. According to al-Kindi knowledge of the particulars can not help to establish philosophical insights, since philosophy aims at knowing universal concepts, such as: species, genera, human soul, infinity, God, etc...

8. The mind, or the intellect is more qualified in establishing philosophical knowledge in dealing with universal concepts. This knowledge is superior to that of the senses, because it is possible to be validated and rendered certain by the intellectual principles that are necessarily true, such as the law of non-contradiction.[22]
Al-Kindi gave an example:[23]

If the universe is a body, then:
    Either it is infinite in quantity, or
    is quantitatively finite.
The universe cannot be quantitatively infinite,
(Al-Kindi will prove later on how actual infinity is impossible and contradictory)

Therefore, the universe is quantitatively finite.

Al-Kindi concluded from this form of reasoning that we reached the conclusion here with some kind of necessity. Its form does not exist in the soul as sense perception exists in it. In sensation there is no necessity only probability. Thus the intellect, but not the sensory perception, is more entitled to study the subject of metaphysics. Al-Kindi realized that there is a limited domain for sensation, which is the natural sciences, while in non-physical subjects or in mathematical sciences proves by demonstrative reasoning, is necessary. In

---

[22] Al-Kindi (1948): p. 87.
[23] Al-Kindi (1948): p. 87.

metaphysical subject we have to be rationalist in order to reach conclusions that are valid and necessarily true.

Al-Kindi's solution to the conflict between rationalism and empiricism came from his realization of the importance of physics, mathematics, and metaphysics to reach the truth.

His example mentioned is disjunctive syllogism of the form:

Either P, or Q
Not P

Therefore, Q

This form is only valid when one of the disjuncts is denied in the second premise. It is a deductive form of reasoning and its validity based on the necessary connection between the premises and the conclusion. Of course this form of reasoning has nothing to do with observation and sense experience thus it is formal and has certainty.

Al-Kindi said:

"[W]hoever examines things which are beyond nature, i.e., those which have no matter and are not joined to matter, will not find for them a representation in the soul, but will perceive them by means of intellectual inquiries."[24]

Al-Kindi thinks that different fields of knowledge since they have different subject matter must have different methods of study too. The perception and understanding of fields such as linguistics, physics, mathematics, and metaphysics, is different because their subject matter is not similar. Al-Kindi's methodological classification of sciences is based on the subject matter of each field of study:

"We ought, however, to aim at what is required for each pursuit, and not pursue probability in the science of mathematics, nor

---

[24] Al-Kindi (1974): p. 64.

sensation or exemplification in the science of the metaphysical; nor
conceptual generalization in the principles of the science of the
physical; nor demonstration in rhetoric, nor demonstration in the
principles of demonstration. Surely if we observe these conditions
the pursuits which are intended will become easy for us but if we
disobey this, we will miss the objectives of our pursuits, and the
perception of our intended objects will become difficult."[25]

9. The Soul and the Theory of Intellect (al-'Aql):
The theory of intellect is significant in Islamic philosophy for three
reasons:

First: it manifests the indisputable interest of Muslim philosophers in
reason and rationality.

Second: Its interaction with Islamic religion, especially the issue of
prophecy and philosophy.

Third: Its impact on philosophy in the Middle Ages especially Christian
philosophy.

Al-Kindi wrote treatises on the soul and one treatise on the intellect.
The soul according to him is a simple substance, non-material,
uncompounded, and imperishable. It has three powers: the rational, the
passionate, and the appetitive. While the last two functions to preserve
the growth and life, the rational power of the soul is that which controls
the other two, and seek perfection through the exercise of reason.[26]

Al-Kindi, as we discussed earlier, made a clear distinction between
sensational perception (faculty of sensation) and the knowledge
acquired by reason (faculty of reason). The first perceives what is
particular and material, while the rational power conceives the
universal, non-material, principles of knowledge such as the principle
of non-contradiction, species, and genera. The gap between these two
faculties is so big, however, al-Kindi linked both of them by another

---

[25] Al-Kindi (1974): p. 66.
[26] Al-Kindi (1950): Vol. 1. p. 255.

power in the soul that he called the representative faculty (al-Musawwirah also called takhaiyul or fantasia). This power is nothing more than an inner ability in the soul for imagination when the sensory object is absent. The senses cannot produce an image of a horse or an ox with wings, but the representative faculty can put together sense data of an ox and that of wings of a bird, producing an image that did not exist before in the data of senses. This faculty works best at two levels:

First, in sleep, when the power of sensation is almost not functioning, the representative power of the soul can pull some of the sensibles, which are stored in the memory, and produce a composite images that are not similar to objects in reality and might not be real at all, such as a dream about a winged ox, or a flying man. Some of the representation during sleep might be about the future, but the validity of these is contingent upon the strength and purification of the soul.

The issue of having future knowledge based on the power of representation will play from now on a major role in its relation to prophecy, and the superiority of philosophers to prophets in knowledge, especially with al-Farabi and Ibn Sina.

Second: in the time of pure and intense concentration, where the distraction of the outside sensible objects and their affect on the soul being reduced to the minimum, the inside power of imagination is more free to act,[27] as for example at the moment of aesthetic creativity.

10. The Theory of Intellect (al-'Aql).
Al-Kindi wrote a treatise *On Intellect (Fi al-'Aql)* was translated twice into Latin; one was by Gerard de Cremona.[28] Al-Kindi distinguishes four kinds of intellects:

1. The intellect is in act perpetually. It is not clear what al-Kindi meant by this first intellect, is it God, or the first intellect as a created intellect? It seems difficult to assume it is God, because the rest of his writings does not support.

---

[27] Al-Kindi (1950): Vol. 1. p. 284.
[28] Al-Kindi (1950): Vol. 1. pp. 351-352.

2. The intellect is in potency or potentiality. This intellect belongs to the soul. The soul is rational in potentiality, and any thing potential cannot move to actuality unless by something actual and perpetually acting[29], thus the first intellect is what brings the second intellect to actuality. This actualization happens when the soul is in connection with the active intellect and the intelligibles and forms become available to it. In this case this intellect and the intelligibles are the same thing, thus it is intellect that intelligizes and the intelligized itself; it is not like a thing in a vessel, nor as a likeness is in a body, because the soul is not a body.[30] When the soul actually acquires these non-material forms and intelligibles, it is called "acquired Reason" (al-'Aql al-Mustafad), al-Kindi said:

"For when the soul comes into direct contact with forms which have neither matter nor phantasm, ..., This form, then, which has neither matter nor phantasm, is the intellect acquired (al-'aql al-mustafad) for the soul from the first intellect."[31]

3. The intellect, which, in the soul, has already emerged from potentiality into actuality, and had already acquired by the soul and becomes one of its apprehended forms, but its action and application belong to the soul at will, whenever the soul wishes, it makes it appear, for example, writing in the writer.[32]

4. The intellect we call the emergent or appearing, after the soul brings it forth becomes known when the soul is in act, as in the act of man.[33]

The difference between the third and the fourth is that the third is something that was previously possessed by the soul and can bring forth at will whenever it wishes, while the fourth (al-Dhaher) is the one

---

[29] According to al-Kindi what is potential can not move to the state of actuality by itself, otherwise, if it has this ability, then it will be always in actuality.
[30] Al-Kindi (1950): Vol. 1. pp. 354-355. And McCarthy, R. (1964): p. 126.
[31] Al-Kindi (1950): Vol. 1. pp. 355-356. And McCarthy, R. (1964): p. 126.
[32] Al-Kindi (1950): Vol. 1. pp. 357-358. And McCarthy, R. (1964): p. 127.
[33] Al-Kindi (1950): Vol. 1. pp. 353-354. Also McCarthy, R. (1964): pp. 125-126.

that appears in the soul at the time it appears in action, such as the act of an actor on the stage is apparent to other.

These four kinds of intellects can be reduced to two: The intellect that is always in act. The soul, this soul is an intellect in potentiality. It becomes actual by the first intellect and is presented in two ways:

- When it becomes actual and acquires forms it is called acquired intellect (al-'Aql al-Mustafad), using this forms at will.

- When something appears in the soul the intellect is called apparent (al-Dhaher).

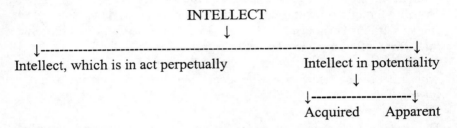

In order to understand the theory of intellect in Islamic philosophy we need to furnish a good background in the Aristotelian and Neo-platonic philosophy. Therefore, I will go through some details here about these two subjects, which will be useful in studying the rest of the philosophers.

11. Aristotle on the Soul and Mind.
Aristotle in his book *De Anima (On The Soul)* defines the mind as that part of the soul "with which the soul knows and thinks."(429a 10.) The Aristotelian conception of mind is not clear. In one sense this mind "can have no nature of its own, other than that of having a certain capacity. Thus that in the soul which is called mind (by mind I mean that whereby the soul thinks and judges) is, before it thinks, not actually any real thing." (429a 20)

This passage suggests that mind here is a mere capacity because it is not actual until it thinks. For this reason, Aristotle thought that it can not reasonably be regarded as blended with the body, in the sense that it does not have qualities or an organ like the sensitive faculty. It is "the place of forms". Aristotle is talking here about the relationship between sensation and mind; when we see a pen, for example, the sense of sight (eye) takes only the image of this object, not the material object, and sends it to the memory, thus the soul through this sense-perception takes into itself the form of this sensible object as perceived without matter. The mind will put together these forms or images and work on them in its process of forming ideas and opinions from these forms. This suggests that the potentiality of this mind cannot be actualized without the presence of these images in the memory.

Briefly, thought is impossible without experience, "the soul never thinks without an image." (431a 15) In this way Aristotle calls mind: "the form of forms and sense the form of sensible things." (432a 5) Aristotle seems to think about this mind as perishable. He thinks this is why we do not remember after death because this passive mind is destructible.

However, in the second sense, Aristotle presents another understanding of mind by saying:

"While there is another which is what it is by virtue of making all things: this is a sort of positive state like light; for in a sense light makes potential colours into actual colours. Mind in this sense of it is separable, impassible, unmixed, since it is in its essential nature activity." (430a 15)

This mind is not passive as the first one; on the contrary, it is active because its essential nature is pure activity. Its object of reasoning is its very activity of thinking, especially in abstraction, without connection to matter; "In every case the mind which is actively thinking is the objects which it thinks." (431a 15) This mind is engaged in continuous process of thinking. It is always knowing and "is not at one time knowing and at another not" (430a 20) as Aristotle said.

Aristotle thinks about this mind as imperishable, immortal, and eternal: "[T]his [mind] alone is immortal and eternal (we do not, however, remember its former activity because, while mind in this sense is impassible, mind as passive is destructible), and without it nothing thinks." (430a 20-25)

This passage is problematic and has been the source for disagreement among Aristotle's commentators. I will come back to it for further discussion later.

What Aristotle meant by these two conceptions, especially the second, is not quite clear. Interpreters of Aristotle made some effort for better understanding of his text. The question (s) raised is whether the active mind is a personal faculty of every single human soul, or an outside, unique, active intelligence for all mankind? Commentators took this matter as their task of philosophizing.

12. Alexander of Aphrodisias. (160-220 A.D.)

Alexander is one of the earliest Greek commentators who engaged in this problem. His commentary on the passive intellect is a distinction between passive mind as a state of potency and that of habitual. Alexander in his *De Anima* in (*Commentaria in Aristotelem Graeca, Supplementum II,* Berlin, 1887), said:

"The potential intellect, with which we are born, is twofold, each receptive of the other: The one is called hyle and is the materia intellect (for everything that receives something is that thing's matter); the other that comes about through teaching and habituation is the form and perfection of the first.

The first is physical and material with regard to whatever it has no experience of; this varies, according as some men are born with a good temperament and others not (in the sense that we say all men have an intellect).

The second is acquired and comes later. It is the form and habit and perfection of the physical intellect, not in everyone, but in those who strive and learn, in the way that sciences are learned.[34]

---

[34] Alexander of Aphrodisias (1887): pp. 81-82.

Thus Alexander thinks that intellect is of three kinds:

Intellect is potential or hyle. It is mentioned as hyle or material because it is similar to hyle as being always in potentiality and possible to move to actuality, which is quite acceptable in the Aristotelian terminology. But this does not mean that this intellect is matter. It is only a capacity or potentiality.

Intellect that intelligizes and acquires knowledge, which is habitual and comes later. This intellect is in actuality practicing and using knowledge. This intellect is nothing more than the first one after it is moved from potentiality to actuality through knowledge and the habit of intelligizing.

Active intellect, which is always in actuality, always thinking, not part of the soul, and none of its faculties or powers. Instead, it is an outside agent that makes the potential intellect actual by giving it intelligible forms. Alexander thought about this intellect as God Himself. The need for this actual, active intellect is the very Aristotelian reasoning that what the potential needs is an actual agent to actualize it.

However, the whole Aristotelian issue is related to the interpretation of his second concept or active intellect. Alexander seems to understand and thus interpret this active intellect as a cause that is able to activate everything from outside as an ultimate cause of activation. Alexander said:

"the first cause, which is the cause and principle of being for everything else; it is active also in the sense that it is the cause of being for everything intelligible... the first cause, which is intellect par excellence".[35]

Thus his understanding of this active intellect as an intellect separable, impassive, unmixed with matter, and immortal, is something that is identified with the first cause which means in Aristotelian terminology: God.

---

[35] Alexander of Aphrodisias (1887): p. 89.

This view leads to the idea that what is specific to every human's intelligence is passive intellect. In other words, our intelligence is nothing more than a capacity of being enlightened by the active intellect (God).[36] This also explains Alexander's reading of the statement from Aristotle:

"[T]his [mind] alone is immortal and eternal (we do not, however, remember its former activity because, while mind in this sense is impassible, mind as passive is destructible), and without it nothing thinks." (430a 20-25)

As follows: "without it nothing thinks" means to Alexander: 'without it (= the active mind) nothing thinks' and statements after the word "eternal" are in parenthesis. Alexander concluded from this reading that we couldn't actively think unless we are enlightened by God; without Him nothing thinks.

While it is still possible for others to read "without it nothing thinks" as continual description of the passive mind, as follows: "mind as passive is destructible and without it nothing thinks.'" Because if there is nothing to act upon (which is the passive mind here or the capacity) there will be no thinking subject for the active mind to exercise its activity.

Is Alexander's commentary on the Aristotelian active mind problematic? The answer relates to whether God is immanent or transcendent.

13. Is God immanent or transcendent?
If we seek consistency within the Aristotelian system of metaphysics, Alexander's reading poses some difficulties and stands problematic. Identification of the active mind with the first cause raises a problem

---

[36] Alexander also went further to suggest some platonic elements to the reading of Aristotelian intellect by saying that this active mind has the forms of everything and gives forms to matter and mind. This makes the process of knowledge and knowing opposite to the Aristotelian emphasis on the role of sense data in knowledge.

about the very Aristotelian conception of the first cause itself as presented in his book *Metaphysics* (1072a 15-20 and 1074b 30-35). In this book Aristotle presents the first cause or God as the Unmoved Mover who is busy intelligizing himself, "and its thinking is a thinking on thinking", and thus, knowing only himself, his ultimate causal activity to the world is that of attraction. While in *De Anima* (according to Alexander's reading), Aristotle presents the active intellect as an intellect that is actually imparting knowledge in man and not just passively attracting. God is presented in *De Anima* as immanent in man. Thus, God is in actual[37] Motion and being busy enlightens human passive mind, while in *Metaphysics* God is presented as more of a transcendental being.

14. Ross disagrees with Alexander's interpretation.
Contemporary Aristotelian scholar Sir David Ross thinks that it would not be necessarily inconsistent on Aristotle's account to speak of God's immanence in the *De Anima*, and of His transcendence in the *Metaphysics*, and it might be possible for these two books to represent different Aristotelian views of God.[38]

Although Ross's reading of the two divergent views of Aristotle on God dismisses Alexander's interpretation, it does not offer a solution to this problem and it does not justify why it would not be necessarily inconsistency between these two minds.

If we reject Alexander's interpretation, then we have to face another philosophical question: If the Aristotelian active intellect is not to be identified with God, then is it an intellect that exists in every single man? Or is it more like an identical principle that exists in all humans?

15. Gilson's Fallacy in supporting Alexander's interpretation.
Contemporary scholar of medieval Christian philosophy Gilson in his article on *The Greek-Arabic Sources of Augustinism Influenced by Avicenna* 1929, reached a conclusion regarding Aristotle's active

---

[37] According to Aristotle nothing can come from potentiality to actuality unless by something actual. Potential can not actualizes another potential.
[38] Ross, Sir David (1930): p153.

intellect very similar to that of Alexander of Aphrodisias. Gilson argues in different way:

If we put Aristotle's passage from *De Anima* (430a 15-25) about the active intellect beside other passages from other of Aristotle's books: *Metaphysics* (1072, and 1074) and his book *Nicomachean Ethics* (1177b) we can easily conclude that the active intellect that Aristotle talked about in *De Anima* is nothing more than God Himself.[39]

Gilson's argument begs the question; because the whole issue which is in dispute here is whether Aristotle's first cause active intellect, mentioned in his *Metaphysics* as a transcendent intellect, is the same as that intellect mentioned in *De Anima* as immanent in man. What Gilson did is nothing more than an assumption that Aristotle's talk in these three books is identical and related to each other without proving how. To assume something to be true that needed to be proven to be true is called begging the question fallacy in logic.

16. Clarification: The Aristotelian Concept of the Soul
The soul according to Aristotle is the form of the body. It gives a natural body actuality. The soul's connection to the body is that of form to matter. Aristotle said in *De Anima*: "Hence the soul must be a substance in the sense of the form of a natural body having life potentially within it. But substance is actuality, and thus soul is the actuality of a body as above characterized." (412a 20-25) Soul is the first grade of actuality of a natural body having life potentially in it. It is related to organized body. The soul also is the final cause of the body (415b 15).
The soul has some powers: "the psychic powers…are the nutritive, the appetitive, the sensory, the locomotive, and the power of thinking." (414a 25-30) The plant has the nutritive only. Other orders of living have more; man has in addition the power of thinking, i.e., mind.

---

[39] Gilson, E (1929): p 12.

In the *Nicomachean Ethics* Aristotle mentioned that the soul has some irrational elements such as those of vegetative and appetitive, and the rational element, which is mind. (1102b 25-30)

The soul has tools for perception which are the five senses that exist in the body. Through them the soul receives perceptions of objects which are images of the material things, but not the things themselves. The mind is a higher level that deals with these perceived images. It is uses the soul as a tool. In this sense it is the tool of the tools; like a hand with tools, it is a tool for them.
This is also presented in the *Nicomachean Ethics* as a source of contemplation, which is the complete happiness of man. "[T]he activity of reason, which is contemplative, seems both to be superior in serious worth and to aim at no end beyond itself" (1177b 15-20)

Aristotle's account of mind in these three books was inconsistent, probably due to the lack of clear conception about it; Aristotle's philosophy of intellect was not fully developed. His conception of mind in *Metaphysics* by itself is problematic, and that of the *De Anima* is even more problematic, and the sum of both is confusing. Aristotle himself declare lack of knowledge regarding this mind:

"We have no evidence as yet about mind or the power to think; it seems to be a widely different kind of soul, differing as what is eternal from what is perishable; it alone is capable of existence in isolation from all other psychic powers. All other parts of soul ...are...incapable of separate existence." (413b 20-30)

There are two things here worthy of notice: "different kind of soul" and "alone" both suggest that Aristotle was trying to at least single out this mind without clearly knowing what it is, "it seems to be an independent substance implanted within the soul and to be incapable of being destroyed." (408b15-20). The word "seems" reflects his uncertainty about this mind. The word "implanted" suggests that this mind is not a mere internal power of the soul. How is it implanted? Aristotle himself has no answer. Also, what Aristotle said about this mind as incapable of being destroyed does not mean in this context something eternal. He simply meant it is not like sensitive faculties; if the old man could recover the proper kind of eye, then he will see like the young man, "The incapacity of old age is due to an affection not of the soul but of its vehicle, as occurs in drunkenness or disease. Thus it is that in old age the activity of mind or intellectual apprehension declines only through the decay of some other inward part; mind itself is impassible." (408b 20-30)

From both passages above it seems that Aristotle is still talking about a mind as something somehow related to the soul and implanted in it in a way Aristotle himself knows not how. It is also presented as an independent substance, but Aristotle here is also quite puzzled about how independent this mind is.

This problem also appears in Aristotle's passage on the active mind, in which he mentioned three words that might indicate a better understanding of these two different intellects, i.e., the word "alone", "while" and "passive". Again what Aristotle said:

"[T]his alone is immortal and eternal (we do not, however, remember its former activity because, while mind in this sense is impassible, mind as passive is destructible), and without it nothing thinks." (430a 20-25).

The word "alone" mentioned as a way of pecularization of the active mind as immortal and eternal. The word also mentioned in the context of comparison with another intellect through the word "while" the other intellect mentioned as being passive and destructible. This is the first time for Aristotle to call the mind which is pure capacity or potentiality as "passive", this might suggest that mentioning passivity instead of capacity is only because the word passive is in best comparison with active.

Before I go any further in the discussion I would like to present some other commentators ideas on this issue.

17. Themistius (317-388 A.D.)

His interpretation of the active intellect made through the process of acting upon the mind as a capacity to produce habitual intellect, in his *De Anima*, in *Commentaria in Aristotelem Graeca*, Themistius said about the intellect in act: "It takes hold of the intellect in potency and leads it to act, thus producing the habitual intellect, in which universal notions and sciences abide."[40]

The active intellect as presented by Themistius is the maker and supplier of thoughts and forms. Thus it is more identified or comparable with God since God is the provider of everything. He used this interpretation as an explanation for the fact that many people could have the same ideas, which means they have no individual role in forming their own ideas.

This might suggest that Themistius is thinking about the active intellect as an outside principle for all humans, but this seems to be more a Platonic[41] reading of an Aristotelian text presented to justify the Christian belief of an intervening God based on Platonic reading of forms. As a result of the above interpretation Themistius had to face the issue of the immortality of the soul; because what is left for man from the Aristotelian text is the passive perishable intellect that contradicts clearly the claim of the immortality of the soul.

Themistius presented special reading of this Aristotelian passive mind. He thought that what Aristotle meant by destructible and perishable passive mind is the composite matter of it but not mind itself. Thus, the composite matter is perishable, but the passive mind is unmixed with the body. So both intellect active and passive intellect are separable from matter. However, this interpretation faces two difficulties:

Aristotle himself said that this passive mind is destructible, not in matter, has no qualities, and has no organ like that of the sense faculty. It is not a composite of matter but is still perishable.

It makes the description of the passive intellect very similar to that of the active mind especially being non-material, non-destructible, and immortal. But this is not a matter of interpretation because this is not

---

[40] Themistius (1900): P. 98.
[41] Although Themistius was not a Christian thinker, he worked for Constantine the Christian emperor. Themistius could be considered as a Neo-platonic philosopher who tends to reconcile Plato and Aristotle.

how Aristotle himself talked about the passive mind emphasizing clearly its perishability. When the text is clear there is no room for commentary.[42]

19. John Philoponus (Yahya al-Nahawi) (6th century)
In the sixth century John Philoponus presented a good summary of the opinions of Alexander of Aphrodisias who mentioned three kinds of intellects: the passive or potential intellect, the habitual intellect, and the active intellect.[43]
John Philoponus seems to agree with Alexander's classification of three intellects, but he disagrees with him about the active intellect is being an outside cause. Philoponus thought that the word "separable"[44] in Aristotle's language does not mean separated from, which he took as still meaning that this intellect is not an outside agent. Rather, it is part of the soul itself. In this sense, Aristotle's passage mentioned above is not so problematic, and both intellects are internal. Thus, he dismissed the word "alone" without justification.

20. Prophecy and Philosophy.
The issue of intellect raised a more complicated problem in Islamic philosophy related to the issue of acquiring knowledge. Especially knowledge of the future and prophecy. Is it possible for the intellect of

---

[42] **[18]** Simplicius also commented on this issue. Simplicius was an Athenian philosopher who lived in Athens. When Justinian closed the philosophical schools in Athens in 529 A.D., Simplicius traveled to Persia and lived there for four years, then went back to Athens in 533. As a Neo-Platonic philosopher, Simplicius had difficulties with this problem of the perishability of the passive intellect. He raised the question:
"How can it be an intellect and be corrupted, if it is immaterial? For every intellect is said to be without matter, and for this reason every intellect is intelligible." Simplicius (1882): p. 247.
His answer might not seem very convincing; however it reflects the intellectual environment at that time. He thought that this passive intellect is corrupted, but not ceasing existence or non-being. It is corrupted by being raised to a higher existence or being through activation of a separate entity of the soul.
[43] Philoponus, John (1897): p. 520.
[44] Philoponus, John (1897): p. 534.

the philosophers to gain knowledge similar to that of a prophet? There
is nothing in al-Kindi's writings to suggest that he held the philosopher
in a higher position than that of the prophet, or to suggest that
prophethood is a human faculty. On the contrary, al-Kindi thinks that
prophethood is a mere divine inspiration, and nothing comes from the
human (prophet) himself, whether a divine law, or prediction of the
future, or even just answering a question. In his book *"Fi kammiyyat
kutub Aristotalis, wa-ma yuhtaju ilai-hi fi tahseel al-falsafah"*.[45] *(On
the quantity of the books of Aristotle and what is required for the
attainment of philosophy)* al-Kindi distinguishes between human
knowledge and divine knowledge. The divine knowledge such as that
of the prophets it is not acquired by any human effort or by logic or
mathematics, or in time; it is eternal received from divine inspiration.
While the human knowledge such that of the philosophers does need
human effort, and is based on mathematics, logic, and experience, and
thus it is in time. Being in time, the knowledge of the philosophers is
first limited to its source, i.e., reason, second, it is not certain. To make
the comparison clear, al-Kindi quoted some answers of the prophet
Muhammad (pbuh) and some verses from the Qur'an to show that these
answers are outside the domain and the ability of human knowledge. It
is divine knowledge:[46]

To the question: who will give life and resurrect these decayed bone
after they have become dust, as some one asked the Prophet
Muhammad. Al-Kindi said that the answer revealed from God to the
prophet is:

**"He will give life to them Who created them for the first time! And
He is the All-Knower of every creation!"** (Qur'an: 36: 79)

Al-Kindi thinks that the best philosophical minds will not be able to
answer this question in such a clear and precise way. Al-Kindi said that
putting things that already exits together is easer than bringing
something from nothing, since God created human from nothing then, it
will be easer to resurrect man.[47]

---

[45] Al-Kindi (1950): p. 359.
[46] Al-Kindi (1950): p. 373.
[47] Al-Kindi (1950): p. 374.

Also al-Kindi brought the issue of creating something from its opposite, like fire from green tree, as a sign of Divine ability:

"He Who produces for you fire out of the green tree, when behold you kindle therewith.
Is not He Who created the heavens and the earth, Able to create the like of them? Yes, indeed! He is the All-Knowing Supreme Creator." (Qur'an: 36: 80 and 81)

Al-Kindi concluded that the human mind in its best philosophical ability is absolutely incapable of offering such an answer as short and accurate as that which God gave to his messenger.[48]

---

[48] Al-Kindi (1950): p. 376.

Reading from al-Kindi on Epistemology[49]

"...Indeed the human existence is of two kinds:

One of which is nearer to us and further from nature.

This is the existence of the senses which we have from the beginning of our development, ... Our existence with the senses, through the contact of the sense with its sensible object, takes neither time nor effort, and it is unstable, due to the motion and flux of that which we contact, its changed in every case by one of the kinds of motion. ... Thus it always occurs in continuous motion and uninterrupted change. It is that the images of which are established in the imaginary [part], then conveys them to the memory; and it [the sensible object] is represented and portrayed in the soul of the living [being]. ... it is very near to the perceiver.

The other is closer to nature and further from us, being the level of the intellect.

It is true that the existence is [nothing more than] two kinds: perceptional existence and intellectual existence, since things are universal and particular. By "universal" I mean the genera of species and the species of individuals, while by "particular" I mean the individuals of species. And the particular, material individuals fall under the senses, while genera and species do not fall under the senses nor are they perceptionally dependent; but they fall under one of the faculties of the perfect soul, i.e., human soul, that which is termed the human intellect.

... Every [universal] concept of species, and that, which is above the species, however, is not represented to the soul, for all representation is

---

[49] Al-Kindi (1948): pp. 84-87, and al-Kindi (1974): I found Ivry's translation of chapter two from page 61, is appropriate and I used some of his translation with some modification based on my reading of the original Arabic text of al-Kindi (1948).

sensible, rather, it is proven true in the soul, validated and rendered certain through the validity of the intellectual principles which are known necessarily, as that "it is" and "it is not" cannot both be true. ...

This is an [intellectual] existence for the soul which is not sensory, [but] is necessary, [and] does not require an intermediary; and an image will not be represented for it in the soul, since it has no image, having neither color, sound, taste, odor, or anything palpable; it is, rather, a nonrepresentational apprehension. ...

[W]hatever has no matter and is not joined to matter is not represented in the soul at all, and we do not think that it is a representation. We acknowledge it only because it is a necessity to affirm it, as when we say that outside the body of the universe there is neither void nor plenum i.e., neither emptiness nor body. This statement is not represented in the soul, for "neither void nor plenum" is something which the sense has not apprehended, and is not attached to a sense, so that it could have an image in the soul, or be believed to have an image. It is something which only the intellect necessarily perceives, in accordance with the premises which will be set forth.

For we say, in the investigation of this, that the meaning of "void" is a place without any spatial object in it. Now "Place" and "a spatial object" are in that type of relation where one does not precede the other, so that:

> If there is place there is, necessarily, a spatial object, and
>
> If there is a spatial object there is, necessarily, place.
>
> It is therefore not possible for place to exist without a spatial object; whereas by "void" a place without a spatial object is meant.
>
> It is not possible, therefore, for an absolute void to exist..."

Al-Kindi

Metaphysics

Al-Kindi's Mathematical Philosophy:
Creation, Eternity, and Infinity

Al-Kindi's Natural Philosophy:
Matter, Motion, and Time are Finite

The Existence of God:
Kalam argument
Essence and Generation or
(al-Mahiyya wal-Hudooth)

This chapter covers the field traditionally called "Metaphysics", in Arabic language called: "Ma ba'ad al-Tabi'ah" or "al-Ilahiyyat."

Al-Kindi
(a. 185-256 A.H. / 805-873 A.D.)

Metaphysics

21. Al-Kindi's metaphysics has a special place in Islamic philosophy for four reasons:

First, contrary to Greek philosophy, al-Kindi's metaphysics introduces ideas of "creation", "creation from nothingness" and the idea of the "creator". His philosophical discourse opens the door for philosophers to consider religious concepts philosophically.

Second, contrary to Greek philosophy, al-Kindi introduces concepts of "revelation" and "prophecy" in the discussion of knowledge and reality.

Third, his metaphysics does not only introduce new ideas, but also stands in direct opposition to traditional Greek philosophy, especially to the idea of the eternity of the world.

Fourth, al-Kindi establishes a case of precedence in the domain of the relationship of monotheistic theology to matters of reason. Muslim, Christian, and Jewish philosophers will later follow this precedence.

22. Al-Kindi's metaphysics is comprehensive and holistic, as it encompasses mathematics, logical consistency, natural sciences and religion. It utilizes concepts such as infinity, quantity, space, time, physical magnitudes, logical inconsistency, self-contradiction, possibility, necessity, soul, intellect, and God.

The first thesis in al-Kindi's metaphysics is that the world is created by Allah. As an implication, his main thesis is to prove first that God is the only eternal being and the ultimate cause of existence, and second to prove, as a result, that the world is not eternal.

23. Al-Kindi: New approach to Metaphysics:

Al-Kindi in his metaphysics insisted on offering a consistent opposition to the Aristotelian metaphysics, especially the philosophical issue of the eternity of the world. Aristotle thought the world is eternal, and its motion and time are eternal too. Aristotle himself did not offer good arguments to prove his point. Aristotle thought that infinity could not exist in actuality; however, he contradicted himself and stated that the actual existent world is eternal and thus is infinite.

Aristotle's first cause is a pure intellect that is self-centered. It has no concern about the rest of the universe and only busy in intelligizing itself. Then how can everything in this universe take place and operate? How is the first cause controlling this world? These and other questions are very hard to answer within the Aristotelian scheme.

Al-Kindi did not find Aristotelian metaphysics appealing at all, in spite of the fact that he admired Aristotle very much as a man with great wisdom.[50]

Al-Kindi was a mathematician and Aristotelian cosmology lacks mathematical foundations and suffers from inconsistency; therefore, al-Kindi's opposition to Aristotle in metaphysics reflects the independency of al-Kindi's philosophical reasoning and his emphasis on his identity. The core emphasis of al-Kindi's philosophy is Islamic in essence, which reflects the teachings of the Qur'an and the tradition of the Prophet.

24. The Eternal and The Only Eternal

Al-Kindi's philosophy emphasizes that the world is not eternal, and contrary to Aristotle, al-Kindi states clearly the following Islamic themes:

A- The world is created.

---

[50] Actually al-Razi, as we will see in the next chapter, also expressed no interest in the Aristotelian philosophy. Al-Kindi criticized Aristotelian metaphysics; while al-Razi criticized Aristotelian physics especially motion and the static world.

B- The world is created from nothing.

C- Allah is the Creator of this world.

D- Allah created the world in time (at a specific time), thus the world has a beginning in time.

E- Allah created the world in time by his will.

F- The world not only has a beginning in time, but also will have an end in time, and that end is based on the will of its creator to end it.

To prove these points, al-Kindi tried to show that matter, motion and time are inseparable from each other. If one of them is eternal, then the rest are eternal as well. Al-Kindi presented some arguments to prove that the eternity of any of these three is "impossible" and in fact, self-contradictory.

The definition of eternity causes contradiction when the concept of actual infinity is applied. The eternal is the necessary in the sense that it must never have been a non-existent being, and "before" does not apply to him because in an actual infinity "before" and "after" make no sense. The eternal has no cause, has neither subject nor predicates, and the eternal is imperishable.

Al-Kindi said:

"The eternal is that which must never have been a nonexistent being, the eternal having no existential "before" to its being; the eternal's subsistence is not due to another; the eternal has no cause; the eternal has neither subject nor predicate, nor agent nor reason, ...The eternal has no genus, for if it has a genus, then it is species, ...The eternal does not perish, perishing being but the Changing of the predicate, not of the primary substratum; as for the primary substratum, which is being, it does not change, for the perishing of a perishable object does not involve the being of its being. ... A perishable object therefore has a genus, and if the eternal is corruptible, it has a genus. However, it has no genus, this is an impossible contradiction, and therefore it is impossible for the eternal to perish.

Motion is change, and the eternal does not move, for it neither changes nor removes from deficiency to perfection. Locomotion is a kind of motion, and the eternal does not remove to perfection, since it does not move. Now the perfect object is that which has a fixed state, whereby it excels; while the deficient object is that which has no fixed state, whereby it may excel.

The eternal cannot be deficient, for it cannot remove to a state whereby it may excel, since it cannot ever move to (a state) more excellent, nor to (a state) more deficient, than it; the eternal is, therefore, of necessity perfect.

Now, inasmuch as a body has genus and species, while the eternal has no genus, a body is not eternal."[51]

25. Al-Kindi's Mathematical Metaphysics:
Al-Kindi uses infinity to disprove the eternity of the world. His first step can be summarized in his statements as follows:

"It is not possible, either for an eternal body or for other objects which have quantity and quality, to be infinite in actuality, infinity being only in potentiality."[52]

What he is saying is: **Actual infinity is impossible.** Why? And how?

Al-Kindi constructed an argument that is heavily based on mathematics:

First, he thought it is necessary to appeal to some of the axioms in mathematics. He called these axioms: "the true first premises which are thought with no mediation." By this he probably meant that the mind could grasp their truth immediately, without demonstration or need of proof. These premises need no mediation because they are self-evident,

---

[51] Al-Kindi (1974): pp. 67-68.
[52] Al-Kindi (1974): p. 68.

and these we can call axioms. He stated the axioms that he needs to disprove the eternity of the world as follows:[53]

1. **All bodies of which one is not greater than the other are equal;**
2. **Equal bodies are those where the dimensions between their limits are equal in actuality and potentiality;**
3. **That which is finite is not infinite;**
4. **When a body is added to one of equal bodies it becomes the greatest of them, and greater than what it had been before that body was added to it;**
5. **Whenever two bodies of finite magnitude are joined, the body which comes to be from both of them is of finite magnitude, this being necessary in (the case of) every magnitude as well as in (the case of) every object which possesses magnitude;**
6. **The smaller of every two generically related things is inferior to the larger, or inferior to a portion of it.**

26. Al-Kindi's Arguments Against Eternity of the World

After stating his thesis as: an actual infinity is impossible, and after supporting it with six mathematical axioms that their truth is self-evident, al-Kindi tried to present his refutation of Aristotelian thesis that the world is eternal in a logical argument which is closer to a mathematical theorem. The following is the argument as Al-Kindi stated it:

"Now, if there is an infinite body, then whenever a body of finite magnitude is separated from it, that which remains of it will either be a finite magnitude or an infinite magnitude. If that which remains of it is a finite magnitude, then whenever that finite magnitude which is separated from it is added to it, the body which comes to be from them both together is a finite magnitude; though that which comes to be from them both is that which was infinite

---

[53] Al-Kindi (1974): p.68.

**before something was separated from it. It is thus finite and
infinite, and this is an impossible contradiction."[54]**

Structuring al-Kindi's argument:

If there is an infinite body, then after separating a finite magnitude from
it, the remaining of it will:

> A- either be a finite magnitude, or
> B- an infinite magnitude.

Al-Kindi refutes both of them as necessarily contradictory. Let us start
with A.

A. The remaining is a finite magnitude.

Al-Kindi thinks that:

1. If the remaining is a finite magnitude, then whenever that finite
magnitude (which is already separated from it) is being added back to
it, then the body, which comes to be from both of them together, is a
finite magnitude. (axiom # 5)

2. However, that which comes to be from them both (the remaining
plus the separated together) is that which was infinite before something
was separated from it.

----

3. Therefore, it is finite and infinite,

4. We know from the axiom # 3 that that which is finite is not infinite,

5. Therefore, a finite infinity is an impossible contradiction.

6. Thus, actual infinity is impossible.

7. Therefore, the existence of an infinite body in actuality (such as an
 eternal world) is self contradictory.

----

8. Therefore, the world is not eternal.

---

[54] Al-Kindi (1974): pp 68-69.

Let us move now to the second part of the argument (part B). Al-Kindi refuted this part as follows:

B. The remaining is an infinite magnitude.

If the remainder is an infinite magnitude, then whenever that which was taken from it is added back to it, it will:

> B1-either be greater than what it was before the addition, or
> B2-equal to what it was before the addition.

B1- To be greater than what it was before the addition.

1. If it is greater than what it was before the addition, then that which has infinity will be greater than that which has infinity.

2. However, according to axiom # 6: the smaller of two things is inferior to the greater, or inferior to a portion of it.
   Therefore, the smaller of two bodies which have infinity is inferior to the greater of them or inferior to a portion of the greater (if the smaller body is inferior to the greater, then it most certainly is inferior to a portion of it) and thus the smaller of the two is <u>equal</u> to a portion of the greater.

3. However, according to axiom # 2: two equal things are those whose similarity is that the dimensions between their limits are the same.

4. Therefore, the two things possess limits, and they are both finite.

5. Thus, the smaller infinite object is finite, and this is an impossible contradiction. One of them is not greater than the other.

6. Therefore, the remainder cannot be an infinite magnitude.

7. Therefore, actual infinity is impossible.

8. Therefore, the world is not eternal.

B2- To be equal to what it was before the addition.
1. If it is equal to what it was before the addition, then this means that a body has been added to a body but has not increased anything,
2. However, premise one contradicts axiom # 4.
3. Also, the whole of this addition is equal to it alone and to its own part, then the part is like the whole, and this is an impossible contradiction.
4. Therefore, the remainder cannot be an infinite magnitude.
5. Therefore, actual infinity is impossible.
6. Therefore, the world is not eternal.

Al-Kindi concluded:

"It has now been explained that it is impossible for a body to have infinity, and in this manner it has been explained that any quantitative thing cannot have infinity in actuality."[55]

27. Similarities between Al-Kindi and David Hilbert on Infinity:
From his conclusion we can say that al-Kindi aimed at a mathematical contradiction in the heart of the issue of actual infinity. In other words, actual infinity is self-canceling, and the only thing left is infinity on the potential level. Consider this example for the sake of simplification: when we count from number 1 to number 2, we can count fractions in between such as: 1.1, 1.11, 1.12, 1.13, 1.14, ... 1.2, ... 1.3, ... 1.9, 1.91, 1.92, ...1.99, 1.999, 1.9999, and we can count $1.9n$ as many as we can count to almost infinity (of course, without reaching it), but no matter how many $1.999999n$ we can count, we know that the actual end is number 2, and we are only <u>potentially</u> going between [1-----and-----2], and what <u>actually</u> exists is the finite limit of number 1 and that is number 2. The counting of $1.99999n$ to infinity is unachievable and is actually impossible to reach; however, we can potentially assume the process of counting to go evermore.

---

[55] Al-Kindi (1974): p. 69.

Al-Kindi's notion of mathematical infinity is what relinquished Aristotelian cosmology as contradictory. Bodies that exist in actuality have a finite magnitude, and if we think about a body as infinite, that is only because it happens on the level of ideas but not in reality. Natural objects are necessarily finite.

Al-Kindi's appeal to pure mathematics in refuting this metaphysical notion is an attempt to establish belief in God. Al-Kindi's work might be considered as one of his most significant contributions to Islamic philosophy. Aristotle mentioned the idea that actual infinity is impossible. However, al-Kindi's contribution resides in his ability to use an Aristotelian premise in order to go beyond Aristotelian cosmology itself and to establish a totally different cosmos in which God is the creator. Al-Kindi also appealed to the notion of infinity in order to support religious belief by scientific knowledge, assuming that the truth is one and could be reached by reason and revelation with no contradiction. Al-Ghazali, from a similar perspective, will offer similar arguments in his book *The Incoherence of The Philosophers,* which we will later discuss.

Al-Kindi was able to single out the notion of infinity in order to dwell on it mathematically, naturally (its application in natural sciences), and philosophically in his metaphysics. Since the time of al-Kindi, no many philosopher or mathematician followed up as deeply on the notion of "infinity" until the twentieth century when a great mathematician, David Hilbert, published his paper "On The Infinite" 1925, in which he said:

"[T]he definitive clarification of the *nature of the infinite* has become necessary, not merely for the special interests of the individual sciences, but rather for the *honor of the human understanding* itself."[56]

Hilbert discussed infinity in both fields, the microphysics and the macrophysics. After he mentioned physics and the divisibility of atoms,

---

[56] Hilbert, D (1925): pp. 370-371.

particles, electrons, quanta, and how it is that none of these permits infinite division in an absolute and unrestricted way, he said:

"And the net result is, certainly, that we do not find anywhere in reality a homo-geneous continuum that permits of continued division and hence would realize the infinite in the small. The infinite divisibility of a continuum is an operation that is present only in our thoughts; it is merely an idea, which is refuted by our observation of nature and by the experience gained in physics and chemistry."[57]

The infinite can not be actually found "anywhere in reality" especially in physics. It exists only on the level of potentiality, "in our thoughts"; it is an idea. A physical object that exists outside the mind is finite. Thus, the body of the world that exists outside is finite, and thus it can not be eternal. At the end of his paper Hilbert said:

"The final result then is: nowhere is the infinite realized; it is neither present in nature nor admissible as a foundation in our rational thinking-a remarkable harmony between being and thought."[58]

28. Al-Kindi's Natural Philosophy:
The Simultaneous Existence of Matter, Motion, and Time:
Al-Kindi proved the impossibility of the existence of an actual infinite body by asserting that bodies are quantitative objects, and then proving that any quantitative thing couldn't have infinity in actuality.
Time and motion are quantitative; thus, it is impossible for both to be infinite in actuality. Therefore, they are finite and time has a beginning.

Let us now follow al-Kindi's way of proving that motion and time are finite:[59]

" if there is a body, then there must of necessity either be motion or not be motion. If there is a body and there was no motion, then either there would be no motion at all, or it would not be, though it would be

---

[57] Hilbert, D (1925): p. 371.
[58] Hilbert, D (1925): p. 392.
[59] Al-Kindi (1974): p. 71.

possible for it to be. If there were no motion at all, then motion would not be an existent. However, since body exists, motion is an existent, and this is an impossible contradiction and it is not possible for there to be no motion at all, if a body exists. If furthermore, when there is an existing body, it is possible that there is existing motion, then motion necessarily exists in some bodies, for that which is possible is that which exists in some possessors of its substance; as the (art of) writing which may be affirmed as a possibility for Muhammad, though it is not in him in actuality, since it does exist in some human substance, i.e., in another man. Motion, therefore, necessarily exists in some bodies, and exists in the simple body, existing necessarily in the simple body; accordingly body exists and motion exists.

Now it has been said that there may not be motion when a body exists. Accordingly, there will be motion when body exists, and there will not be motion when body exists, and this is an absurdity and an impossible contradiction, and it is not possible for there to be body and not motion; thus, when there is a body there is motion necessarily."

29. Premises in supporting his Arguments:

Al-Kindi, before presenting his arguments, started by offering a few premises and conclusions of previous mathematical demonstrations that are clear. Therefore they need no further proof. Some of them are:

1.The actual body of the universe is finite, and it is quantitatively finite.

2. Things that are predicated of a finite object are necessarily finite, such as: place, time, motion, and quantity.

3. If there is motion, there is of necessity a body. (I will complete this statement after al-Kindi proves it, as we will see later).

4. Motion is not only spatial (from place to place), but also some different kinds, such as: change (internal motion as chemical or biological), alteration, and the change of an object's substance, which is generation or corruption.

5. Every change or motion is a counting of the duration of the body; thus, every change and motion is temporal.

6. It is not necessary for the whole to be in motion in order to say that whole body moves. The motion of some of the parts (and the possibility of other parts to move) is enough of an indication that the whole exists in motion.

30. Structuring his argument on Motion:
Now let us go back to section 28 in order to examine and reconstruct al-Kindi's argument on Motion. What he is saying is this:

1. The existence of a body has one of these two possibilities:

> -It exists with motion.
> -It exists with no motion.

2. Al-Kindi thinks that if a body exists, then it must be of necessity that it exists with motion. Going from nonexistence to existence is motion.

3. Now, if you take the second possibility and claim that a body exists with no motion, then you have to clarify further that:

> a.   either there would be no motion at all, or
> b.   it would not be, though it would be possible for it to be.

Al-Kindi disproves A (there would be no motion at all):
1. If a body exists and there is no motion at all, then that means that motion does not exist.

2. However, since a body exists, motion is an existent too. (According to premise # 2, motion is one of the things predicated of the finite body.)

3. Therefore, to say that there is a body (an actual existent body) with no motion at all is an impossible contradiction. (According to # 4, motion is of many different kinds).

4. Therefore, it is impossible for a body to exist and be without motion at all.

Clarification:
The very concept of an actual finite existing body means, by definition, an object with motion. For example, a wooden chair came into existence by the act of a carpenter who made it out of various material things, came into existence through motion. The coming into being itself is motion.

A newborn baby (as a finite actual being) came into existence in a process (motion) of being born and growing up, and thus existence (coming into being) by definition is motion.

Al-Kindi disproves B (motion would not be, though it would be possible for it to be):
1. If you claim that a body exists with the possibility to be in motion and not to be in motion, then, its motion is possible to be and not to be.

2. Al-Kindi says: "when there is an existing body, it is possible that there is existing motion, then motion necessarily exists in some bodies."[60]

3. However, "that which is possible is that which exists in some possessors of its substance."[61] For example, "writing which may be affirmed as a possibility for Muhammad, though it is not in him in actuality, since it does exist in some human substance, i.e., in another man."[62]

4. Motion, therefore, necessarily exists in some bodies, and exists in the whole body.

5. Therefore, motion exists necessarily in the whole body; accordingly, a body exists and motion exists.

---

[60] Al-Kindi (1974): p. 71.
[61] Al-Kindi (1974): p. 71.
[62] Al-Kindi (1974): p. 71.

6. Therefore, it is impossible for a body to exist and motion not to exist.

7. Therefore, as al-Kindi said: "when there is a body there is motion necessarily."[63]

This last conclusion will be added to premise #3 in section 29. Thus 3 will read as a modified premise-proof statement of the simultaneous existence of matter and motion as follows:

If there is motion, there is of necessity a body, and when there is a body there is motion necessarily.

Remember that al-Kindi is not only trying to prove that an actual finite quantitative body necessarily has a finite motion, but also he is trying to prove that matter and motion simultaneously co-exist.

31. Is it Possible for a Body with no Motion to Start Moving?
Al-Kindi did not stop at the previous proof, but he went further to raise certain difficulties regarding matter and motion. He said:

"It is sometimes assumed that it is possible for the body of the universe to have been at rest originally, having the possibility to move, and then to have moved."[64]

Al-Kindi thinks that this opinion is necessarily false. His argument is:[65]
If the body of the universe was at rest originally and then moved, then:

    A. either the body of the universe would have to be a generation from nothing, or
    B. it is eternal.

---

[63] Al-Kindi (1974): p. 71.
[64] Al-Kindi (1974): pp. 71-72.
[65] Al-Kindi (1974): p. 72.

Al-Kindi disproves A: (The universe is a generation from nothing)

1. If it is a generation from nothing, then its "becoming", or its coming to be, is prior to motion.

2. But, according to premise # 4 on previous classification of motion, generation is one of the species of motion.

3. However, becoming a body is not prior to motion, since motion is the essence of "becoming" (according to # 4 and modified # 3 above).

4. Therefore, the generation of a body can never precede motion.

5. It was said, however, that the universe has been originally without motion.

6. Thus it was, and no motion existed, and it was not, and no motion existed, and this is an impossible contradiction.

7. Therefore, it is impossible, if a body is a generated from nothing, for it to be prior to motion.

8. Therefore, the assumption that the universe originally existed in a motionless state and then started moving is contradictory and necessarily false.

Al-Kindi disproves B: (The universe is eternal having rested and then moved.)

1. If the body of the universe is eternal, having rested and then moved, then the body of the universe, which is eternal, will have moved from actual rest to actual movement.

2. However, that which is eternal does not move (according to what was already explained about the eternal in section 12.)

3. Therefore, the body of the universe is then moving and not moving, and this is an impossible contradiction.

4. Therefore, it is not possible for the body of the universe to be eternal, resting in actuality, and then to have moved into movement in actuality.

5. Motion, therefore, exists in the body of the universe, which, accordingly, is never prior to motion. A motionless universe is impossible.

Al-Kindi concludes from previous arguments:

"Thus if there is motion there is, necessarily, a body, while if there is a body there is, necessarily, motion.
It has been explained previously that time is not prior to motion; nor, of necessity, is time prior to body, since there is no time other than through motion, and since there is no body unless there is motion and no motion unless there is body. Nor does body exist without duration, since duration is that in which its being is, i.e., that in which there is that which it is; and there is no duration of body unless there is motion, since body always occurs with motion, as has been explained. The motion of the body counts the duration of the body, which is always a concomitant of the body, which is (also) always a concomitant of the body. Body, therefore, is never prior to time; and thus body, motion and time are never prior to one another."[66]

To put al-Kindi's account of natural philosophy in its historical context, i.e., the 9th century, al-Kindi seems to present an advance philosophy of time, motion, and matter.

Al-Kindi offers another account to prove the impossibility of a static motionless universe; he said that giving another account "shall add to the skill of investigators of this approach."[67]

---

[66] Al-Kindi (1974): pp. 72-73.
[67] Al-Kindi (1974): p. 73.

We are not going to examine these arguments for two reasons: first, what we presented is sufficient in serving our purpose, and second, according to modern science and the first principle of Newton's physics, i.e., the principle of inertia: matter is in a constant state of motion.

32. Al-Kindi's Cosmos between Aristotle and the Qur'an.

Should we wonder why al-Kindi overemphasized the relation of matter and motion within a finite universe?

We can probably offer two reasons:

1. Qur'anic concepts. Qur'an offers a cosmos in which everything is in a constant state of motion: the earth, the moon, the sun, the stars, the heavens, and the total universe. Allah said in the Qur'an:

"And a sign for them is the night. We withdraw therefrom the day, and behold they are in darkness. And the Sun runs on its fixed course for a term (appointed). That is the Decree of the All-Mighty, the All-Knowing. And the moon, we have measured for it mansions (to traverse) till it returns like the old dried curved date stalk. It is not for the Sun to overtake the moon, nor does the night outstrip the day. They all float each in an orbit." (Qur'an, Ya-Sin (36): 40)

2. Aristotelian physics is static. Aristotelian cosmos is based on his main principle of physics, which states that everything exists in a state of no motion or motionless, and they do not move until they are forced by something else or an agent to move them. This principle left two difficulties in philosophy that burdened the medieval philosophers:

First, in physics, it had a negative impact on the development of physics in the Middle Ages. Al-Razi criticized this principle, as we will see later.

Second, in metaphysics, it led to the introduction of unnecessary agents, (47 of them or 55 as Aristotle mentioned in his *Metaphysics*

1074a 5-15) and metaphysical entities as auxiliary forces in order to initiate motion in the first place.

This point led Aristotle himself to some inconsistencies regarding his first cause (which is pure form) and its relation to the motion of physical bodies: in specific, the need of intermediate intellects to transfer the force of motion from the pure form to the material objects, in the sublunary region, by an unjustified chain of intellect that goes gradually through 47 or 55 minds until it reaches earth.

Al-Kindi probably thought that Aristotle's concept of mathematical infinity is problematic in metaphysics and lead to self-contradiction regarding the eternity of the world, in other words, Aristotle said that actual infinity is impossible, however, the actual world is eternal (infinite). Now, if Aristotle was not consistent in his philosophy, so why did al-Kindi admire him?

Probably the admiration was based on the work of Aristotle in logic, and this is what al-Ghazali is going to warn philosophers and people from: that the success of the philosophers in logic does not necessarily guarantee their success in other fields especially in metaphysics.

33. Al-Kindi Disproves the Eternity of Time
(It is impossible for time to be infinite in actuality, neither in the past nor in the future):

Al-Kindi offers another argument to disprove the eternity of the world based on the concept of time, as follows:

"Before every temporal segment there is [another] segment, until we reach a temporal segment before which there is no segment, i.e., a segmented duration before which there is no segmented duration. It cannot be otherwise--if it were possible, and after every segment of time there was a segment, infinitely, then we would never reach a given time--for the duration from past infinity to this given time would be equal to the duration from this given time regressing in times to infinity; and if [the duration] from infinity to a definite time was known, then [the duration] from this known time to temporal infinity would be known, and then the infinite is finite, and this is an impossible contradiction."[68]

34. Structuring the Argument that Time is Finite (in its past)

1. Before every period of time there is another, until we reach a temporal period of time before which there is no period of time and this is the end.

2. Al-Kindi thinks that it cannot be otherwise, i.e., you cannot go back in regression to infinity (actual infinity is impossible).

3. Now if you think it were possible, and before every period of time there is another to infinity, then you should also think that after every segment of time there was a segment, infinitely, and thus we would never reach a given time.

4. Why would we never reach a given time? Because the duration from past infinity to this given time would be equal to the duration from this given time regressing in time to infinity;

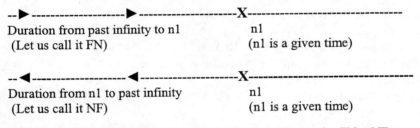

--▶----------------------▶--------------------X------------------------------
Duration from past infinity to n1   n1
(Let us call it FN)   (n1 is a given time)

--◀----------------------◀--------------------X------------------------------
Duration from n1 to past infinity   n1
(Let us call it NF)   (n1 is a given time)

Duration from F to n1 = Duration from n1 to F   or simply: FN = NF

5. But if the duration from infinity to a definite time (n1) were known (finite), then the duration from this known time to temporal infinity (F) would be known (finite) too.

6. Thus, the infinite is finite, and this is an impossible contradiction.

---

[68] Al-Kindi (1974): p. 74.

7. Therefore, time cannot have an actual infinity in its past.

8. Therefore, time is actually finite.

9. Since time is nothing more than numbers counting motion, motion is finite too.

10. And since finite motion cannot exist unless it is a motion of a finite body, then the body is finite too.

Another Argument: (time is actually finite, in its past, and the world is not eternal) al-Kindi said:
"Furthermore, if a definite time cannot be reached until a time before it is reached, nor that before it until a time before it is reached, and so to infinity; and the infinite can neither be traversed nor brought to an end; then the temporally infinite can never be traversed so as to reach a definite time. However, its termination at a definite time exists, and time is not an infinite segment, but rather is finite necessarily, and therefore the duration of a body is not infinite, and it is not possible for a body to be without duration.
Thus, the being of a body does not have infinity; the being of a body is rather finite, and it is impossible for a body to be eternal."[69]

35. Time is Actually Finite (in its future), the World is not Eternal:
Structuring the argument in al-Kindi's language with some changes when it is needed for clarification:[70]
1. It is not possible for future time to have infinity in actuality. Why?

2. It is impossible for the duration from past time to a definite time to have infinity (according to previous proof).

3. Also times are consecutive, one time after another time, and then whenever a time is added to a finite, definite time, the sum of the definite time and its addition is definite too (according to axiom # 5 in section 26).

---

[69] Al-Kindi (1974): pp. 74-75.
[70] Al-Kindi (1974): p. 75.

4. If, however, the sum was not definite, then something quantitatively definite would have been added to something else quantitatively definite, and the result was something quantitatively infinite assembled by them (But this contradicts axiom # 4).

5. But time is a continuous quantity, i.e., it has a division common to its past and future. Its common division is the present, which is the last limit of past time and the first limit of future time.

6. Every definite time has two limits: a first limit and last limit. If two definite times are continuous through one limit common to them both, then the remaining limit of each one of them is definite and knowable (according to the previous proof above in section 29).

7. It has, however, been said that the sum of the two times will be indefinite; it will then be both not limited by any termini and limited by termini, and this is an impossible contradiction.

8. It is thus impossible, if a definite time is added to a definite time, for the sum to be indefinite; and whenever a definite time is added to a definite time, all of it is definitely limited, to its last segment.

9. It is, therefore, impossible for future time to have infinity in actuality.

36. Conclusion:
Since body and motion are finite, thus they are not eternal. They have a beginning in time, and they came into existence at a certain time and will perish at a certain time, too. Thus, they are created, and therefore, the world, as a constitution of objects in their motion, is created too, and is created in time since time is the number of motion.

37. A Question
If someone raised the question that although the world has a beginning in time, it does not mean it is created by God; it just came into existence by itself. To this question al-Kindi has the following answer, which I will discuss under the proofs of the existence of God.

Proofs of the Existence of Allah (The God)

38. Al-Kindi presented three kinds of proof for the existence of God:

1. The proof of Essence and generation of the universe (coming into existence).
2. The proof for unity and multiplicity.
3. The proof from design.

I will emphasize in my discussion the first argument because it represents a new argument that did not exist before in the Aristotelian philosophy. This argument is deeply related to Islamic scholastic theology ('Ilm al-Kalam). However it was developed by al-Kindi and al-Ghazali. It represents the Islamic cosmological arguments that that proves the existence of cause (God) through the effect, which is the generation of the universe or the created existents. This argument is based on causation.

The second argument for unity and multiplicity is more about proving that this cause is one than proving its existence.

39. The Kalam Argument

Kalam argument is derived from the teaching of the Qur'an. The Qur'an advises people to understand the Creator through observing His miraculous act of creation. To reach an understanding of the cause by reflecting upon the effects, Allah says:[71]

"Have you seen what you ejaculate? Did you create it, or are We the Creator? It was We that decreed death among you. We will not be outstripped that We will charge you and cause you to grow again in a fashion you do not know. You have surely known the first creation. Why then, will you not remember! Consider the soil you till. Is it you that sow it, or are We the Sower? If We will, We would make it broken orts and you would remain wondering.

---

[71] In some verses in the Qur'an the pronoun "We" is used as a reference to Allah (The God = The One). This is perfectly acceptable in the Arabic language. This "We" is sometimes called the royal we.

(Saying:) `We are laden with debts! Rather, we have been prevented!' Consider the water which you drink. Is it you that send it down from the clouds or We? If We will, We would make it bitter, why then do you not give thanks? Consider the fire which you kindle. Is it you that originated its tree, or are We the Originator?" (Qur'an, 56:58-72)[72]

The conclusion presented in the Qur'an in a form of challenging question, Allah says:

"Is there any doubt about Allah, the Creator of the heavens and the earth?" (Qur'an, 14:10)

Same guidance for reasoning is mentioned by the prophet Muhammad saying:

"Do not reflect upon the essence of God, instead, reflect on the creation of God."

---

[72] More verses from the Qur'an refer to the same form of reasoning:
"Have We not made the earth a cradle and the mountains as pegs? And We created you in pairs, and We made your sleep a rest, and We made the night a mantle, and We made the day for a livelihood. And We built above you seven strong ones, and placed in them a blazing lamp and have sent down from the clouds pouring rain that We may bring forth with it grain and plants and luxuriant gardens." (Ch.78: 6-16).
Another verse:
"Assuredly in the creation of the Heaven and of the Earth; and in the alternation of night and day; and in the ships which pass through the sea with what is useful to man; and in the rain which Allah sends down from Heaven, giving life by it to the earth after its death, and by scattering over it all kinds of cattle; and in the change of the winds, and in the clouds that are compelled between the Heaven and the Earth; are signs for those who understand."
Allah also says:
"Have you not seen how Allah created the seven heavens one above the other, setting in them the moon as a light and the sun as a lantern? Allah has caused you to grow from the earth, and to it He will return you. Then He will bring you forth." (Ch.71:15-18).

Muslim theologian (Mutakallimun) followed the Qur'anic teaching in proving the existence of God through cause and effect, going from creation and the created things to the Creator Himself.

There are some different forms of this argument. The one that is most suitable and serves our purpose here is the one presented by Imam al-Ghazali (1058-1111) in his book *Ihya' Ulum al-Deen (Revival of the Religious Sciences)*. Al-Ghazali said:

"[B]y way of preparation and following the example of the learned theologians, we say: One of the obvious logic of the mind is that:

1. an originated phenomenon cannot come into existence without a cause.
2. Since the world is an originated phenomenon,
3. it cannot come into existence without a cause."[73]

We can clarify this argument further as follows:

    1.   Everything that is originated (has a beginning in time) cannot come into existence without a cause.
    2.   The world is an originated thing (began to exist in time).
----
    3.   Therefore, the world cannot come into existence without a cause.

The conclusion of this argument negates the possibility of an effect to exist without a cause. This argument is valid and consists with the rules of syllogism. Since one of its premises is negated, the conclusion has to be negated too. The argument is logically valid.

The first premise states that whatever begins to exist in time must have a cause. It establishes philosophically the principle of causality as a category of pure reasoning, also it has been established by scientific knowledge that if you do not have fever and fever began to exist then

---

[73] Al-Ghazali (1987): Vol. 1. p.126.

there must be a cause of such happening (which is the effect), and if there was no rain and rain began to exist there must be a cause, and if there was no death and occur then death must be an effect of a cause, same thing if there was no life and life came to be, then there must be a cause of it.

This premise only establishes the factual statement about the way things are, but it does not support the necessary connection between the cause and the effect in regard to the future. In other words, it does not claim that the future happening will resemble by necessity the past experience, in fact al-Ghazali was aware of this problem and criticized it in his book *The Incoherence of The Philosophers* when he devoted a chapter to the issue that three is no necessary connection between cause and effect. We will discuss this later with al-Ghazali. This issue also discussed after al-Ghazali by Malebranche and David Hume.

Thus the first premise is only stating metaphysical principle of the connection between cause and effect, but it not stating anything about the very nature of this connection; it does not claim that the medication that you use today and causes recovery is going to *necessarily* recover you after ten years, the premise is only stating that if you recover in the future, then this happing must be caused by *a cause*.

Al-Ghazali explained the first primes by saying:

Regarding the first premise: an originated thing cannot come into existence without a cause, because every originated phenomenon belongs to a certain definite time the precedence or the subsequence of which may be assumed. Its being definite in time and distinct from what preceded it and what succeeded it, will naturally require one who renders things definite, and this is the cause.[74]

As in regard to the second premise: that the world is an originated phenomenon and began to exist, seems more difficult because we can easily say: who said so? Or how do you know that the universe began to exist?

---

[74] Al-Ghazali (1987): Vol. 1. p. 126.

Al-Ghazali presented an extensive argument to prove it.[75] However, I will try to use a proof for the second premise that is related to al-Kindi's previous argument on the impossibility of actual infinity. This proof shows that the opposite of the second premise is a logical contradiction.

---

[75] Al-Ghazali (1987): Vol. 1. pp. 126-127. In this book al-Ghazali said in regard to the second premise: that its proof is found in the fact that:
> Bodies are not independent of motion and rest.
> Both states (motion and rest) are originated phenomena;
> Whatever is not independent of originated things is itself originated.

This proof consists of three claims:
In the same book, same page, al-Ghazali gave more elaboration to prove the second premise in his argument that the world is an originated phenomenon and thus it is not eternal.

The first is that bodies are not independent of motion and rest. This is readily understood and requires neither meditation nor thinking, for he who conceives of a body being in neither the kinetic state nor in the static state is both ignorant and foolish.

The second assertion is our saying that both motion and rest are originated phenomena, the proof of which is found in their alternation and in the appearance of the one after the other is gone. This is true of all bodies, those that have been seen as well as those that have not been seen. For there is not a static object the potential motion of which is not required by the mind, and there is no moving object the potential rest of which is not required by the mind. The sudden is originated because of its immediate occurrence and that which has gone is also an originated matter since it is no longer due to the fact if it is proven it is eternal it will obligate that it does not turn to nothing.

The third assertion is our statement that whatever is not independent of originated things is itself originated. Its proof lies in the fact that if it were not so, then there would be, before every originated phenomenon, other originated phenomena which have no beginning (infinite); and unless these originated phenomena come to an end in their entirety, the turn for the present originated phenomena to come into being immediately would never arrive. But it is impossible for that which has no end, which is infinite, to become actual.

Therefore the conclusion is that the world is not independent of originated phenomena, and that which is not independent of originated phenomena is itself originated. And when its being as an originated phenomena has been established, its need for an Originator becomes a necessity through obvious comprehension.

1. If the universe never began to exist (has no beginning in time), then the universe is eternal.
2. If the universe is eternal, then a series of actual infinite events has been elapsed.
3. But we know that actual infinity is impossible.

----

4. Therefore, the universe must have a beginning in time.

This presentation of the Kalam argument shows the connection between Islamic scholastic theology and al-Kindi's mathematical philosophy.[76]

If someone raised the question that the universe has a cause but it is caused by itself, al-Kindi replies by this following argument.

40. Al-Kindi's Proof of Essence and Generation.
(It is impossible for a thing to be the cause of the generation of its essence)
Al-Kindi already proved that the idea of the eternity of the world is self-canceling, and it is a contradiction on both mathematical and logical levels. Thus al-Kindi proved that the world is not eternal, in some other words it came into existence, or its existence is generated.

In the third chapter of his book *On First Philosophy,* al-Kindi went beyond that to prove that the world, as an originated phenomenon, cannot be the cause of its existence (its essence), and thus must be brought into existence by something else other than itself: God.

Al-Kindi's argument:
It is not possible for a thing to be the cause of the generation of its essence, its becoming a being is either from something or from nothing. Thus, we have four possibilities:[77]

---

[76] The Islamic Kalam argument has been borrowed and utilized by Christian theologians to prove the existence of God. This argument is well presented and defended in the writings of William Lane Craig in his books *The Kalam Cosmological Argument* (1979) and *Reasonable Faith* (1994).

First: a non-existent thing and its essence is non-existent.
Second: a non-existent thing and its essence is existent.
Third: an existent thing and its essence is non-existent.
Fourth: an existent thing and its essence is existent.

The first is impossible, because it is nothing and its essence is nothing. "Nothing" is neither a cause nor an effect, (cause and effect are predicated only of something).
Therefore, it is not the cause of the generation of its essence.

The second, of course, with a similar proof, is impossible.
The second is also impossible by another proof based on the law of identity. Al-Kindi said:[78]

1. If it is non-existent and its essence is existent, then its essence is different from the thing.

2. Thus, its essence would not be it (it = the thing).

3. However, the essence of everything is that thing itself.

4. Therefore, a thing would not be itself and it would be itself, but this is an impossible contradiction (according to the law of identity).

5. Therefore, a thing cannot be the cause of the generation of its essence.

The third is impossible (an existent thing and its essence is non-existent) for the same reason above based on the law of identity.

The fourth (an existent thing and its essence is existent) is also impossible, al-Kindi said:[79]

---

[77] Al-Kindi (1974): p.76.
[78] Al-Kindi (1974): p.77.
[79] Al-Kindi (1974): p.77.

1. If the thing is an existent thing and its essence is existent, and it were the cause of the generation of its essence, then its essence would be its effect.

2. But the cause is different from the effect.

3. Therefore, it would be the cause of its essence while its essence would be its effect.

4. Thus, its essence would not be it (it = the thing).
However, the essence of every thing is that thing itself (according to the law of identity).

5. But from this argument it follows that it would not be itself, and that it would be itself. This is an impossible contradiction.

6. Therefore, a thing cannot be the cause of the generation of its essence.

41. Clarification:
Let us take gold as an example. If the essence of gold is its atomic number in the periodic table in chemistry which is 79°, then the thing which is gold with its physical and chemical characteristics such as yellow in color, malleability...etc, cannot generate and give existence to its essence which is the atomic structure, in fact the atomic structure itself is what gives gold its characteristics, and if this essence changed to more or less than 79, then deferent thing with different qualities will appear. Therefore a thing cannot generate its essence, otherwise the existence of the "thing" will be prior to its existence which is contradictory.

Another example is that humans cannot generate their own existence, if we are the cause of the generation of our existence, then we will not die (because we can give ourselves existence), but we know that we die and perish, therefore we are not the cause of our own existence.

41. Conclusion:

Al-Kindi concluded from previous arguments that the world is not eternal and cannot come into being on its own. The world cannot be a cause of the generation of its essence. Thus it came into existence by a cause other than its essence and that cause is Allah who created the world from nothing.

CHAPTER TWO

Al-Razi
(a. 251-313 A.H. / 865-925 A.D.)[80]

What is Philosophy?

1. His Life and the Necessity of Spiritual Medicine

Abu Bakr Muhammad Ibn Zakariya al-Razi was born in Raiy, Khurasan. In Raiy, he studied mathematics, logic, natural philosophy, and medicine. He eventually became a physician (Tabib) and the director of al-Ray hospital in his early thirties. He then moved to Baghdad, in Iraq, where he was the head of the Baghdad Hospital, in addition to his practice and career as a physician.

Al-Razi is the greatest physician in the Middle Ages and modern time, (if not of all times as some scholars think). His insight and contribution in medicine transcend the treatment of the physical body to that of the soul. His holistic approach and contribution in psychology could be found in his book *al-Tibb al-Ruhani (The Spiritual Medicine)[81]* in which he thinks that the health of the body related to that of the soul, and the harmony between the soul and the body must be established in order to achieve health and happiness. By correctly diagnosing the connection between soul and body, al-Razi was able to refer to what we call today as psychosomatic illness.

Although al-Razi was mainly a physician and a psychologist, he was also, to a lesser degree, an alchemist, scientist, logician, and a philosopher. His most famous work in medicine was his book *al-Hawi*, also known as *al-Jami'* or *Compendium of Medicine*. This book was a

---

[80] The Islamic classical sources give different dates about his birth and death. According to Ibn Abi Usaibi'ah al-Razi died 320 A.H., while al-Biruni gives 313 A.H., and al-Safadi 311 A.H. However, I lean toward the dates given by al-Biruni.

[81] Translated as: *"The Spiritual Physick"* by A.J. Arberry (1950).

main textbook in the Western Universities until the eighteenth century. In 1279, this book was translated into Latin by the Sicilian Jew Faraj ibn Salim (Farragut) under the title *Continens*. Al-Razi was known to the Latin as the "Rhazes". Another masterpiece in medicine is his treatise *On Smallpox and Measles*. This book translated and printed many times until 1866. The rest of al-Razi's writing (the sum of which is around 200 books and treatises) is on issues in natural philosophy such as space, vacuum, time, matter, and some commentaries on logic, and commentary on Plato's Timaeus. Others were written on *Refutation of the Mu'tazilah*, one on *al-Sirah al-Falsafiyyah (On Philosophical Life)* and one *On Prophecy*, which is the most disputed.[82]

2. Non-Aristotelian

In philosophy al-Razi developed no interest in the Aristotelian philosophy. On the contrary, he authored some works to criticize Aristotelianism. He found Plato's natural philosophy more appealing, and utilized some of the Socratic and Pre-Socratic ideas.

As a physician his empirical clinical practice in medicine seems to shape and color his metaphysics. His approach to philosophy is more naturalistic and his methodology emphasizes empiricism, as we will see when we discuss his metaphysics.

3. What is the goal of philosophy?

Al-Razi's absolute trust in the rational faculty made him think that philosophy is superior to revelation. In fact, he went further to present philosophy as the salvation of man. Al-Razi thought that the soul has a continuous desire to attach itself to bodies and unite with matter to enjoy sensuous pleasure. God created the intellect to make the soul awake from its slumber and enable it to detach itself from matter and to enjoy intellectual pleasure. Thus, by philosophization, man can teach himself the truth, and overcome the sadness and the pain of the material changeable physical world. After all, philosophy teaches that this material world is not real and the real existence is that of a soul without

---

[82] Al-Biruni wrote a bibliography on the quantity and classification of al-Razi's writings counting a total of 184 titles. A contemporary publication was done on the treatise of al-Razi by Paul Kraus called al-Razi Philosophical Treatises, found in al-Razi, Zakariya (1939).

matter. When all souls philosophize, they will attain liberation from this material world and they go back to their real world. At this stage, the whole material world will dissolve and vanish, and matter, which is now deprived of this spiritual essence, will return to its original state as primeval matter.[83]

4. Is evil more than good in the human life?

As a physician al-Razi saw enough suffering from illness and other defects in the physical existence of the material body and human life. This made him more a pessimistic philosopher who thought that the existence of evil outweighed the existence of good, to the point that he defines pleasure negatively as nothing more than the relief from pain. Thus, pain and suffering were the key factors in his philosophical outlook. His ideas were criticized by Muslim and non-Muslim scholars; Sa'ed al-Andalusi in his book *Tabaqat al-Umam* criticized al-Razi as being shallow in philosophy and never delved into theology. Al-Razi criticized some philosophers and Mutakallimun without well understanding them. This is why his ideas, as Sa'ed thinks, are absurd and lack philosophical depth.[84]

---

[83] Naser Khusru: Zad al-Musafreen p.115 and A'laam an-Nubowwah, p.51.

[84] Al-Razi's idea about the existence of evil was also criticized by the Jewish philosopher Mosa Ibn Maimoon (Maimonides) (1135-1204) in his book *Dalalat al-Ha'ereen (Guide to The Perplexed)* Part III, Chapter 12, p.496. Although Maimonides derived the main ides of his philosophy from Muslim philosophers, he thinks that al-Razi's idea present major ignorance about observing the goodness of existence.

Al-Razi
(a. 251-313 A.H./ 865-925 A.D.)

Metaphysics

5. The Five Co-Eternal Principles
In metaphysics, al-Razi presents an independent approach that is
neither known to the Islamic teaching, nor to that of Greek
Philosophers like Aristotle. Al-Razi believes in five co-eternal existent
principles. In his treatise, *Maqalah Fi al-Qudama' al-Khamsah
(Discourse On The Five Eternal Elements)*, al-Razi mentioned them as
follows:
1. The Creator.
2. The Universal Soul.
3. The Primeval Matter. (Absolute Matter or al-Hayoula al-
   Mutlaqah)
4. The Absolute Time.
5. The Absolute Space.

Some Muslim scholars such as Fakhr al-Deen al-Razai and ash-
Shahrastani think that his philosophy of the five eternal principles is
borrowed from the Sabi'an thinkers of Harran.[85] Al-Razi himself
admitted in his *Kalam al-Ilahi* that he derived these ideas from the
Harranians, however, sometimes he refers to Pythagoras, Empedocles,
Anaxagoras, and Democritus as a source of his non Islamic
metaphysics.

6. Al-Razi Against the Aristotelian Principle of Motion
In order to prove the eternity of matter, al-Razi has to prove that its
motion is intrinsic and based on internal principles. Otherwise,
something else will cause its motion, and hence it is not eternal. Thus,
al-Razi has to reject from the beginning the Aristotelian static principle
of motion; i.e., material bodies are at rest and they need a mover to
move them. Al-Razi offered an opposing and alternative physics by

---

[85] See al-Razi, Fakhr al-Deen (1323 A.H./1905 A.D.): p. 86.

writing *A Treatise Showing That Bodies Move by Themselves and That Movement Belongs to Them Essentially*. In this book he maintained the idea that all bodies move intrinsically downward toward the center of the world, opposite to Aristotle who thought that they move upward and downward depending upon their composition. For example, vapor goes up and stone goes down. Al-Razi's principle of the intrinsic movement of bodies is very close to what we call today the principle of inertia. However, matter can not move in a universe that is full of matter, thus there must be a room or void in the universe for matter to move, and vacuum seems to be necessary for motion. With this reasoning al-Razi found himself again opposing two Aristotelian concepts in natural philosophy; first, the concept of void, and second, that of place. Aristotle thinks that there is no void in the universe, and he criticized Democritus who thinks vacuum is necessary to the motion of atoms. Aristotle's idea of the void is related to his concept of place that he defined as: "the boundary of the containing body at which it is in contact with contained body."[86] According to this definition, Aristotle left no void between bodies. Al-Razi needed the void not only for bodies to move but also, on the atomic level, for the indivisible atoms as the ultimate constitution of matter.

7. Eternity and Coming into Existence

Because of the lack of systemization in al-Razi's philosophy, it is very difficult to understand his ideas on the eternity and creation. There are two versions to his theory, I will present them as A and B:

A. The five principles co-exist eternally; however, first thing to mention is the primeval matter or absolute hayoula (hyle) which is a simple (non-compound) pure spiritual light (noor). This hayoula is the source of the individual souls, which are also simple, spiritual and their substance is light (noor) too. The pure spiritual light, or the absolute hayoula, could be called reason or light that emanates from the overflowing light of God. The light of the absolute hayoula is followed by shadow, and from this shadow the animal soul is created as lower level for the service of the rational soul mentioned above.

---

[86] Aristotle (1941): Physics. IV. 212 a5.

However, co-eternally and simultaneously with the existence of the absolute hayoula, body exists, but it is not simple. Rather it is a composite existent. This body has a shadow too from which the four characteristics came: warmth and cold, dryness and moistness. From these four qualities the four elements came into existence: fire, air, water, and earth. And, from these four elements all heavenly and earthly bodies formed.

Since God is eternally active, the process of coming into existence is eternally occurring.   Therefore, there was no beginning in time of such process, and hence, no creation from nothingness or coming into existence at a specific time.

B. The five principles co-exist eternally; however, the soul, motivated by its desire to unite with matter, materializes itself in order to produce and practice sensuous pleasures. In this stage, the soul was ignorant. As a result, the soul failed to achieve this desire. The Creator, out of his mercy and knowledge, helped the soul to create this world (knowing that the soul will come back to its own world regretting such sensuous happiness and material attachment, since the soul is at a higher level than matter). Thus the hayoula of man was created and the soul attached to it. In this human form the soul slept, and the Creator sent the intellect (al-'Aql) to awake the soul from sleep and guide it back to its real world and genuine destiny. Thus, the more work of the intellect is the more awareness of the soul about its essence (as a higher level of intelligible), reality, and its happiness. More philosophy (as an act of the intellect) means more freedom from the regretted material attachment (which is also freedom from suffering) and a move toward the real happiness.   Philosophy is thus prescribed by al-Razi as a painkiller by which the soul can escape the material pain and earthly pressure of capturing it. All souls will stay in this material world until they liberate themselves by philosophy. At this stage the material world will vanish and dissolve, while the soul will go back to its original state as a pure universal soul with no attachment to matter, and the absolute hayoula will go back to its original state of being as a primeval matter deprived of all spiritual forms.[87]

---

[87] This version based on the account given by Abu Hatim al-Razi in his book *A 'lam al-Nubowwah.*

However, this salvation by philosophy might not be possible to achieve within a period of one lifetime. Thus, whoever could not philosophize, his soul will come back to existence and rejoin matter again and again until this soul learns the virtue of philosophizing and purifies itself by reasoning, and thus can free itself and be part of the intelligible world.

From both accounts, we can say that creation was meant to be the act of "enforming" (giving forms to) a formless matter, but this led to the presupposition of three existents: The Creator, a formless matter, and the forms themselves, the last one never mentioned by al-Razi. Either he assumed it, or he took individual souls as a representation of them.

8. Al-Razi's Light and Shadow, and the Islamic Creed
By adhering to five co-eternal principles al-Razi first stands against his Islamic faith, which teaches the belief in Allah (The Only God), and second, stands with no evidence or logical argument against the teaching of the Qur'an in regard to the Oneness of Allah. Allah said in the Qur'an:

"Say: "Allah is the Creator of all things; and He is the One, the Irresistible." (Qur'an, 13:16)

Also the Qur'an offers logical arguments on the oneness of Allah:

"Had there been therein (in the heavens and the earth) aliha (gods) besides Allah, then verily, both would have been ruined. Glorified is Allah, the Lord of the Throne, (High is He) above all that (evil) they associate with Him!" (Qur'an, 21: 22)

The form of this Qur'anic argument is:
Premise 1: If there were gods in the heavens and earth besides Allah, then they (heaven and earth) would be destroyed and collapsed (every god seeking power and control)
Premise 2: But they are Not collapsed (the universe is systematically working)

Conclusion: Therefore, there is only one God.

This argument is logically valid. It worth mentioning here that the Islamic religion is offering a logical argument in the Qur'an, while al-Razi's philosophy is lacking logical reasoning. In other word, religion is presenting itself rationally while philosophy presenting itself allegorically.

Al-Razi's account on eternity in version A could be reduced to two principles: light and shadows, which is levels of darkness. This might strengthen the criticism made by Fakhr al-Deen al-Razi and ash-Shahrastani about the Harrani sources of al-Razi's non-Islamic belief. Also, this duality of light and shadow might suggest a rational attempt made by al-Razi to present the old Persian Mani's religion (which is based on the belief of two principles, light and darkness (al-noor wal-dulmah), good and evil (al-Khair wal-Sharr or Ahreman and Ahoramisda) in a form of novel philosophy instead of an ancient religion.

The belief in these two principles also condemned by the Qur'an, which rejects any association of any partner with Allah. Since God is the absolute power, He does not need partners.

"And Allah said (O mankind!) "Take not ilahain (two gods in worship). Verily He (Allah) is (the) only One Ilah (God). Then fear Me (Allah) much." (Qur'an, 16:51)

Al-Razi's ideas on prophecy are similar to those of Brahmanism, which appeals to reason only and thinks of no need for revelation and prophecy. In fact, al-Razi attacked all religions in addition to prophecy and wrote some books on this subject such as *Makhariq al-Anbiya'* and *Hiyal al-Mutanabi'een*. He thought since God gave the light of reason to every single soul then there is no need for any prophet to mediate between God and human mind. Every mind is capable of knowing the truth and reaching salvation by reasoning. Al-Razi also thought that religions are the main cause of problems and warfare in the human life.

His ideas on prophecy are criticized by Abu Hatim al-Razi (d. 933) in his book *A'laam an-Nubowwah.*

9. Questions:

There are many questions left with no answers in al-Razi's metaphysics, such as how the shadow of the absolute hayoula came into its eternal existence. It presupposes the existence of something else, and how the individual soul (light) as a simple substance attached to the compound bodies. Are these five co-eternal principles worth the same value? Should they be worshiped? And how? How do laymen deal with concepts such as absolute space and absolute time? How do people who cannot philosophize reach their salvation? Should they suffer because they are not philosophers? And whose philosophy is better in reaching salvation?

If al-Razi thinks that people of reason and philosophers should rule the society, the question still remains: Whose philosophy should we follow? What makes the Platonic approach better than the Aristotelian one? What makes both of them better than the Divine Law? All of these problems were left in al-Razi's philosophy without answers.

Probably because of this lack of consistency and lack of pragmatic solutions in dealing with the complexity of philosophical issues in their relation to the life of Muslims, we found no Muslim philosopher carried on al-Razi's ideas in the Islamic intellectual history.

CHAPTER THREE

Al-Farabi
(259-339 A.H./ 872-950 A.D.)

What is Philosophy?

1. Intellectual Life
Abu Nasr Muhammad ibn Muhammad ibn Tarkhan al- Farabi was born
in Farab, Transoxiana year 259 A.H./872 A.D. He studied in Baghdad,
Iraq. Al-Farabi developed great interest in logic. While he was studying
in Baghdad with his Christian teacher Yuhanna ibn Hailan, al-Farabi
manifested an incomparable ability in mastering logic, especially
Aristotelian, to the point that scholars called him the "Second Master"
(al-Mu'allim al-Thani), and Aristotle was the first.

Al-Farabi moved to Aleppo, Damascus, (Syria). This region was ruled
by Sayf al-Dawla al-Hamdani from 333-357 A.H./944-967 A.D., a
brilliant ruler who respected and supported the intellectual life, and he
himself was a poet. Although al-Farabi was very much respected by the
ruler, he lived a quiet and simple life in Aleppo, where he worked as a
garden keeper. This was a job that gave him a life of solitude, and
more time for reading and reflection. He moved back to Baghdad where
he studied logic again with another Christian teacher, Matta ibn Yunus.
He then traveled to Egypt and then returned to Aleppo where he died at
the age of eighty around 339 A.H./950 A.D.

2. His Writings
Al-Farabi's writings in philosophy are comprehensive; he covers all
traditional fields of philosophy with special emphasis on logic, on
which he wrote many commentaries on Aristotelian logic and found his
own way to link logic to the Arabic language and linguistics. Al-Farabi
presented novel work in the field of classification of sciences in his
book *Ihsaa' al-Ulum (Classification of the Sciences)* in which he added
sciences that were not known to Greek culture such as theology,
jurisprudence (fiqh). In political philosophy, al-Farabi wrote his most

celebrated book *Mabadi' 'Ara' Ahl al-Madinah al-Fadilah (The Perfect State)* in which he rejects much of the Platonic political philosophy and establishes Islamic concepts for this field. However, in his metaphysics al-Farabi was captured by Aristotelian metaphysics that positioned him in a direct conflict with Islamic teaching, especially the issue of the past eternity of the world. In spite of his ability in logic al-Farabi failed to implement and utilize the logical argument from the Qur'an. In fact, he did not even spend any effort on that. Philosophy was to him superior to religion and a philosopher was higher than a prophet in the rank of knowledge. From this perspective al-Farabi made the relationship between Islamic religion and philosophy quite problematic. This approach to the conflict of religion and philosophy was quite destructive, especially to the effort already made by al-Kindi to reconcile them.

Al-Farabi was also a musician, and authored influential books in this field such as *Kitab al-Musiqa al-Kabir (The Great Book on Music)*.

3. "Thy neighbour is thy teacher."
Henry Farmer in his book, *Al-Farabi's Arabic-Latin Writing on Music*, quoted the above Arabic proverb to refer to the dialogue and to bridge the intellectual relationship between the East and the West, saying that al-Farabi's work on Arabic music "enables us to see how far our Muslim "neighbours" in Spain and elsewhere were our "teachers".[88]

The impact of al-Farabi on the philosophers who came after him was great especially on Ibn Sina (Avicenna) who articulated and systemized many of al-Farabi's ideas. However, the impact of al-Farabi on the west was even greater. The Latins knew him by the names Alpharabius and Abunaser. Christian and Jewish philosophers relied upon his writing on the existence of God, essence and existence, Divine attributes, the problem of the universals, and possibility and necessity. Some of the philosophers such as Albertus Magnus (1193-1280) and his student St. Thomas Aquinas (1225-1274) were acquainted with his writings and certainly borrowed ideas from al-Farabi as Rev. Robert Hammond proved.[89]

---

[88] Farmer, Henry G. (1934): Preface.
[89] Hammond, Robert (1947): pp. 11, 55.

Regarding modern philosophers, Saeed Sheikh suggested that there is an impact from al-Farabi's political theory and deductive system on Spencer, Rousseau, and Spinoza.[90]

Farmer said: that "hundreds of treatises which were translated out of the Arabic into Latin to become the text-books of schools of Christian Western Europe."[91] Al-Farabi's writings were translated into Latin. His most famous book, *Ihsaa' al-Ulum (Classification of the Sciences)*, was translated twice in the twelfth century, once by John of Seville and again by Gerard of Cremona, both under the title of *De scientiis*. Farmer said that the book was already known in the Jewish school, since Moses ibn Ezra (d.c. 1140) used it. Also there was a condensed Hebrew version of this book made by Qalonymos ben Qalonymos (d.c. 1328). Farmer himself possessed a copy of this condensed version.[92]

4. Does the Study of Philosophy Need Anything to Precede it?

Al-Farabi answers: yes. In fact he went further to state some requirements are necessary for anyone who wants to start studying philosophy. In his treatise *Ma yanbaghi Ta'alumohu qabal Ta'alum al-Falsafa (What must Precede the Study of Philosophy)*, al-Farabi mentioned these requirements as follows:[93]

1. Natural sciences. It is required before studying philosophy and one should be well acquainted with it.

2. Mathematics. It helps the mind with exact demonstrations; also it helps in the process of abstraction by moving from the sensory to the more abstract or the intelligible.

3. Logic. It is a means of distinguishing valid reasoning from fallacious one, and knowing what is true and what is false.

---

[90] Sheikh, Saeed M. (1982): p. 58.
[91] Farmer, Henry G. (1934): p. 16.
[92] Farmer, Henry G. (1934): p. 6.
[93] Al-Farabi (1907): p. 61-62.

4. Moral conduct. It is the ability to control one's character and instincts, so his mind can grasp the abstract and the perfect instead of staying attached to the sensory and the material.

5. Philosophy and its Subject Matter
The purification of the soul should serve as a requirement of any act of philosophizing; also, the very result of philosophy is a satisfied pure soul. The love of the truth and wisdom must be the prime motivation of any person seeking knowledge.

Since philosophy is an attempt to understand the universe and our existence through rationalization, the philosopher should begin this career by studying logic and mathematics, especially geometry. These are pure sciences that cohere very well with rationality of man and help in processing valid reasoning, and at the end they help in making sound judgments.

Since sciences take their importance from the subject matter of the study, thus studying nature must be always under the provision of reason.

Natural sciences deal with the particular, changeable, perishable existents, as in biology and chemistry, physics, and other fields, while logic and metaphysics deal with the non-corporeal, unchangeable, universal, and eternal.

The eternal, the unchangeable, the universal is better than the particular. Thus philosophy ranked as the highest field of knowledge; its subject matter is not the existent individuals, but the very existence itself.

6. Al-Farabi Shifting the Concern of Philosophy
I should comment here that al-Farabi from this point is shifting the subject matter of philosophy from knowing the Creator, to the study of the "existence" (al-wujood) as such. As a result of this shift, the sole task of philosophy is no longer restricted to knowing Allah. Al-Farabi clearly diverted his attention and study from that of al-Kindi and Islam to an Aristotelian approach to philosophy which is studying being qua being.

7. The Divisions of Philosophy

Al-Farabi's division of the fields of philosophy is presented through a larger scheme called division of sciences. His theory of the classification of the sciences is presented in two of his books, *Ihsa' al-Ulum (Classification of the Sciences),* and *Al-Tanbih 'ala Sabil al-Sa'adah (Reminder of the Way of Happiness)*. In these books, al-Farabi establishes the division into: logic, theoretical sciences; and practical sciences with their subdivisions. Thus the parts are as follows:[94]

1. Logic.
2. Theoretical Sciences: Mathematics, Natural Sciences, and Metaphysics.
3. Practical Sciences: Ethics, and Politics.

8. The Task of Philosophy

The task of philosophy is to present us with a universal outlook that helps us to understand our existence, ourselves and the entire universe. In other words, philosophy is the science of sciences, and also has a practical task to purify our soul. It makes us rationally fulfill our purpose of existence by achieving our essence in practicing reason to its full capacity, so that we can be closer to the Divine, the Most Perfect. Al-Farabi thinks that what philosophers do is to imitate God as much as possible within the power of man.[95]

9. The Aim of Philosophizing

The goal is to know Allah, and to know that he is One, immovable, and is the cause of the existence of all things. Finally the goal is to know that He is the organizer of this world by His wisdom and justice.[96]

I should comment here that God according to al-Farabi is the cause of the universe. However, the universe is eternal, which means that this God is no longer the creator of the universe. According to al-Farabi God and the universe both eternally co-exist. This is contradictory to the Qur'anic teachings. This issue will be clarified when we study his metaphysics.

---

[94] Al-Farabi (1968): p. 16-17.
[95] Al-Farabi (1328 A.H./1910 A.D.): P. 13.
[96] Al-Farabi (1328 A.H./1910 A.D.): P. 13.

Al-Farabi
(259-339 A.H. / 872-950 A.D.)

Theory of Knowledge

The Active Intellect and the Human Mind

10. Human Soul and the Faculty of Reasoning:

The human soul is an essential existent in the sublunary system. The human body as a corporeal existence can achieve its perfection and completeness only through the soul. The soul has some divisions and faculties or powers as al-Farabi elaborates:

> "Once man comes to be, the first thing to arise in him is the faculty by which he takes nourishment, namely the nutritive faculty-, then afterwards the faculty by which he perceives the tangible, like heat and cold and the other tangibles, and the faculty by which he perceives the objects of taste; and the faculty by which he perceives scents; and the faculty by which he perceives sounds; and the faculty by which he perceives colours and all visible objects like rays of light. Together with the senses another faculty arises which consists in an appetition towards the objects of perception so as to desire or to dislike them. Then afterwards another faculty arises in him by which he retains the imprints of the sensibles in the soul when these sensibles are no longer perceived, this being the faculty of representation. By this faculty he connects some of the sensibles with each other and disconnects others in different connections and disconnections, some being false, some true. An appetition towards the objects of representation is joined with this faculty as well. Then afterwards the rational faculty arises in man; by it he is able to know the intelligibles and by it he distinguishes good and evil and by it he grasps the arts and sciences. An appetition towards the objects of reasoning is joined with this faculty as well."[97]

---

[97] Al-Farabi (1985): p 165.

Thus:

- First of all is the nutritive power or faculty (An-nafs al-Ghadhia), by which man takes nourishment.[98] The main power of this faculty is in the heart.

- The second power of the soul arises in him is (An-nafs al-Hassa) the faculty or the power of sensation and perceiving the tangibles, the objects of taste, scents, sounds, colors, and visible objects. Together with the senses another faculty arises which has appetition toward the objects of perceptions so as to desire or to dislike them. The main power of sensation is in the heart, while its auxiliaries (the five senses) are distributed in the human body.

- Then, afterwards the faculty or power of representation (al-Quwwa al-Mutakhayyila) arises, which is a power by which he retains the imprints of the sensibles in the soul when these sensibles are no longer perceived. By this power man can connect the sense data and sensibles with each other, and disconnect them in many different ways. Some of these are true and some are false connections or disconnections.[99] This power is also in the heart.

Then afterwards the rational power or faculty arises (al-Quwwa al-Natiqa). This faculty is divided into two forms:

The theoretical reason, by which man becomes aware of the intelligibles (which are not an action or production of human being).

The practical reason, by which man becomes aware of the present and future particulars.[100]

By the functionality of both the theoretical and the practical, the rational faculty can help man to perform some activities as rational being:[101]

---

[98] Al-Farabi (1985): p. 164.
[99] Al-Farabi (1985): p. 164.
[100] Al-Farabi (1985): p. 218.
[101] Al-Farabi (1985): p 164.

- he can rationalize and know the intelligibles. (Logic and pure reasoning)
- he can make a distinction between good and evil. (Moral judgments)
- he can distinguish the beautiful from the ugly. (Aesthetic judgments)
- he can possess and grasp the arts and sciences. (practical reasoning as an application of his knowledge)

- The appetitive faculty (al-Quwa al-Nuzu'iyya), by which man can desire or dislike things, is the faculty which makes the will arise. This power can act upon the previous faculties. By the power of will we can accept or reject things that come from sense perception or from representation or from the reasoning. This appetitive power is dependent on the ruling faculty of senses and the faculty of representation and reason, as heat exists in the fire and dependent on the substantiality of fire.[102] Appetition might be towards knowing a thing or doing a thing. This power is in the heart, too.[103]

Al-Farabi summarizes his theory about the soul of the human and his body as follows:

" Then first organ which comes to be is the heart, then the brain, then the liver, then the spleen. They are, then, followed by all the other organs. And the activity of the organs of reproduction starts later than the activity of all other organs."[104]

Humans come into existence by the combination of form and matter; the womb in the female is that organ that serves the heart in providing the matter, while the organ which serves the heart in providing the form is the organ which generates the semen.

The human body is corporeal, and imperfect, and what makes man reach a higher level of existence is the soul by an epistemological

---

[102] Al-Farabi (1985): p174.
[103] Al-Farabi (1985): p 170.
[104] Al-Farabi (1985): p. 186, Author's translation.

process through which it moves from the particular sensible objects to more universal concepts and intellectual entities. This intellectual progress within the human soul can be made possible only by means of the power of representation.

Although the soul represents the completeness of the human body, the mind is that which gives the soul its completeness or entelechia. Man is nothing more than an intellect ('Aql), according to al-Farabi.

11. The Theory of 'Aql and the Intelligibles

Al-Farabi in his *Risala fi al-'Aql (Treatise on The Intellect)* discussed four kinds or stages of intellects based on their nature and essence:

1. The potential or material intellect,
2. The intellect activated by first principles,
3. The acquired (mustafad) intellect, and
4. The active intellect; sometimes called by Qur'anic name Roh al-Qudus (spirit of holiness). This intellect is also the giver of forms.

The mind exists in the soul of the child as a mere capability or potentiality, and it becomes actual mind through experience, in the process of its apprehension of the forms of bodies and material things, by means of the senses and the representative faculty.[105] The human mind is called by al-Farabi al-'Aql al-Haulani.[106] This intellect ('Aql) is only potentially intellect.

The intelligibles, which are impressed on the rational faculty of man (an-nafs an-Natiqa), are of two kinds:[107]
-   Actual intelligibles (intelligized) which also are actual intellects in their very essence.
-   Non actual intelligibles, which are the material things that are non intellects; they are only intelligibles in the potential sense.

---

[105] Al-Farabi (1895): pp. 43-44.
[106] From the Greek word "Hyle" means matter, this word is an Aristotelian term transliterated into Arabic as "Al-hayoulaa."
[107] Al-Farabi (1985): pp. 196 and 198.

Since the human mind, which arises in man early in his life, is a disposition in matter prepared to receive the imprints of the intelligibles, it is only a faculty capable of receiving and then knowing. In other words, it is not active, thus not actual but mere potentiality.

If the human mind is potential and the intelligibles are potentials too, then how can man acquire knowledge and proceed from sensation to a higher level of knowledge? In other words, how is it possible in the first place for the human intellect to move from potentiality to actuality?

Al-Farabi has an answer to this problem:

Neither the intelligibles nor the rational faculty in man has the power to become of itself actual. The potential intelligibles become actual when they become a process of thought or intelligized by an actual intellect, but they are in need of something else to transfer them from potentiality to a state in which the intellect can make them actual.

For the human mind to become an intellect in actuality, and be able to intelligize the intelligibles, it also needs something else to transfer it from potentiality to actuality. The existent that performs this transfer and affect, the human mind is the Active Mind (al-'Aql al-Fa''al) whose essence is an actual intellect, incorporeal, and separated from matter.

12. The Relationship between the Active Intellect and the Human Mind

The relationship of the active intellect to the human mind is like the relation of the sun to the sight of the eye. The eyes have the potentialities and capabilities to see, but the actual seeing of bodies and material objects happens through the light of the sun.[108] The sun provides the light to our eyes to see, and thus affects us.

Only by this kind of relationship between the active intellect (incorporeal) and the rational faculty of man (which is material) human knowledge becomes possible, and the intelligibles arise at the same time in the human mind from the sensibles which are preserved in the faculty of representation. By this process we know the first intelligibles

---

[108] Al-Farabi (1985): p. 202.

which are common to all men as, for example, the whole is greater than the parts. These common first intelligibles are of three kinds:[109]

-   The principles of the practical productive skills.
-   The principles by which man distinguishes between good and evil within the human action.
-    The principles which are used for knowing the existents that are not a production of man and not within the domain of action of man, such as the heavens and the first cause and the other primary principles and their rank in the level of existence.

Gaining knowledge of the common principles makes human mind (the acquired intellect) gain its first perfection. However, this knowledge is supplied to him and made possible only by the active intellect ('Aql al-Fa''al) in order to be used to reach the human ultimate perfection, which is felicity, meaning that his soul reaches its ultimate happiness. This is a state of being in which man becomes in no need of matter for its support, since man at this stage becomes one of the incorporeal and immaterial substances, and he needs to maintain his soul in order to remain in this state continuously for ever.[110] Of course, the voluntary good actions and the virtues will help in attaining this level of ultimate happiness. Thus, they need to be sought for this end; they are not good for their own sake, but for the sake of felicity only.

"The presence of the first intelligibles in man is his first perfection, but these intelligibles are supplied to him only in order to be used by him to reach his ultimate perfection, i.e. felicity. Felicity means that the human soul reaches a degree of perfection in (its) existence where it is in no need of matter for its support, since it becomes one of the incorporeal things and of the immaterial substances and remains in that state continuously for ever. But its rank is beneath the rank of the Active Intellect.

That aim is achieved only by certain voluntary actions, some of which are mental and others bodily actions, and not by indiscriminate actions

---

[109] Al-Farabi (1985): p. 204.
[110] Al-Farabi (1985): pp. 204, 206.

but by defined and determined actions which arise out of definite and determined dispositions and habits, since there are voluntary actions which are an obstacle to felicity. Felicity is the good which is pursued for its own sake and it is never at any time pursued for obtaining something else through it, and there is nothing greater beyond it for man to obtain. The voluntary actions which help in attaining felicity are the good actions; and the dispositions and habits from which these actions proceed are the 'virtues', these being goods not for their own sake but goods for the sake of felicity only. But the actions which are an obstacle to felicity are the bad things, namely the evil actions, and the dispositions and habits from which these actions arise are defects, vices and base qualities."[111]

No matter how incorporeal the human soul is going to be, it is still ranked beneath the level of the active intellect. Also the active intellect itself is not going to be active continuously because its effectiveness is limited by its material. The only eternally active and completely incorporeal is God; thus, God will be the real Active Mind. Al-Farabi summarizes his idea about reasoning and the actualization of the intelligibles as follows:

"The potential intelligibles become actual intelligibles when they happen to be intelligized by the intellect in actuality, but they are in need of something else which transfers them from potentiality to a state in which [the intellect] can make them actual. The agent, which transfers them from potentiality to actuality, is all existent. Its essence is an actual intellect of a particular kind and is separate from matter. It is that intellect which provides the material intellect' which is only potentially intellect with something like the light which the sun provides to the sight of the eye, since its relation to the 'material intellect' is like the relation of the sun to the Sight of the eye. For eyesight is a faculty and a disposition in matter and is, before it sees, potentially sight, and the colors are potentially seeable and visible before they are seen. But neither is the faculty of sight in the eye itself sufficiently qualified to become actually sight nor are the colors

[111] Al-Farabi (1985): pp. 205,207.

themselves sufficiently qualified to become actually seen and viewed. It is the sun, which gives light to the sight of the eye, joining the two, and which gives light to the colors, joining it to them. Thus sight becomes through the light which it acquires from the sun actually seeing and actually sight, and the colors become through that light actually seen and viewed after having been potentially seeable and visible. In the same way this 'intellect in actuality' conveys to the 'material intellect' something which it imprints on it, which is in relation to the 'material intellect' the same as light in relation to sight. Sight sees, through light itself, the light which is the cause of its ability to see and the sun which is the cause of light, and by this very light it sees the things which are potentially seeable and visible so that they become actually seen and viewed. In the same way the 'material intellect' becomes aware of that very thing which corresponds to the light in the case of sight, and through it comes to know the 'intellect in actuality' which is the cause of having that thing imprinted on the 'material intellect'; and through it the things which were potentially intelligible become actually intelligible, and the 'material intellect' in its turn becomes actually intellect after having been potentially intellect. The action of this 'separate' intellect upon the 'material intellect' is similar to the action of the sun upon the sight of the eye. It is therefore called 'Active Intellect' ranking tenth among the 'separate' things below the First Cause which have been mentioned, whereas the 'material intellect' is called 'Passive Intellect'. When, then, that thing which corresponds to light in the case of sight arises in the rational faculty from the 'Active Intellect', intelligibles arise at the same time in the rational faculty from the sensibles which are preserved in the faculty of representation."[112]

It seems from the above quote that the human mind, through its connection with the active intellect, transfers the sense perception to a universal meaning, by which the soul can realize more. However, it also seems that these universals already exist in the active intellect itself who gives them to, or imprints them on, the human mind (material intellect). This passage raises some question about an

---

[112] Al-Farabi (1985): pp. 199, 201,and 203.

essential issue in the medieval epistemology called the problem of universals.

13. The Problem of Universals

Universals such as man, whiteness, and motherhood (could be called "concepts," too) have relationship to the particulars. To us it seems that the universal concept such as whiteness, or motherhood is a concept that is derived by abstraction from many particulars, such as many individual mothers or many white things that all share whiteness or motherhood. However, the relationship between the universals and these particulars is one of the deep metaphysical issues in the history of philosophy. Plato thought that these universals exist by themselves regardless of the existence of their particular instances. Aristotle denied such independence of the Platonic forms, emphasizing the existence of the particulars first. But al-Farabi, who is well acquainted with both Plato and Aristotle, seems to be neither Platonic, nor Aristotelian regarding the issue of universals. What kind of relationship is al-Farabi holding between particulars and universals?

Al-Farabi answers:
"The universal in reference to the particular is like the genus and species in reference to individuals."[113]

The universals are substantial because they are permanent and subsistent; however, they are not the type of things that exist in themselves, because their existence depends on the existence of the individuals. Al-Farabi said:

"The universal is the one found in many and affirmed of many. The inference is that the universal has no existence apart from the individual."[114]

But the existence of the universals "is accidental in the sense that they are subject to the existence of individuals. That does not mean,

---

[113] Al-Farabi (1907a): pp. 95.
[114] Al-Farabi (1907a): p. 94.

however, that universals are accidents, but merely that their existence in actuality can take place only per accident."[115]

Although the universal exists in the mind as a concept, al-Farabi thinks that the particular also exists in the mind. Thus, its existence is not accidental in the outside objects but also has an actual existence in the mind. The mind has the ability to build universals after surveying the whole particulars by means of generalizations and abstractions.

It is very difficult to summarize al-Farabi's idea about the problem of the universals. However, three things might be said:

1. The universal needs the particular in order to exist. It has an actual existence in the particular; therefore, al-Farabi is not a nominalist.

2. The universal exists after the existence of the particular by means of abstraction.

3. The universal exists by itself before the existence of the particulars and independent from the existence of these particular instances. In this sense, it exists only in the active intellect that is going to give it to the human mind in as much as sight occurs by both eyes and light; the active mind is the light to the human mind.

But this raises another problem about acquiring knowledge, which makes the process of knowledge more an issue of illumination and closer to the experience of a mystic. The process of knowledge, according to al-Farabi, could be of three kinds:
- sense perception,
- rational knowledge, and
- illumination. In this type the active intellect emanates universal meanings and true knowledge to the human mind that devotes its life to philosophical reflection in an attempt to separate itself

---

[115] Al-Farabi (1907a): p. 96.

from material things as much as possible in order to achieve this connection with the active mind which is pure and separable from matter. This connection helps the philosopher reach his ultimate goal: happiness. In this last kind of knowledge the human mind, through the philosophers, becomes capable of knowing the future and the intellects above the sublunary system.[116] This is problematic too because it makes the philosopher equivalent to prophets. To this problem we will spare the following section.

14. Philosophy and Prophecy

The faculty of representation being intermediate between the faculty of senses and the rational acts upon the sensibles which the senses bring to it and imprinting on it. Thus, it will be kept busy by this kind of action as well as in serving the rational faculty at the same time by supplying the appetitive when these faculties are in the state of their first perfection. For example during sleep, the faculty of representation will be on its own and free from the fresh imprints of the sensibles, since senses do not work during sleep, and also relieved of the service of the rational and the appetitive faculties. Thus, it will turn to the preserved imprints of the sensibles and will act upon them by the act of association. By putting together or separating them from each other, a

---

[116] Al-Farabi used many different names to refer to the human mind as follows:

- Human Mind (al-'Aql al-Insani), a rational faculty existing in man.
- The Rational Faculty or Power (al-Quwwa al-'Aqila)
- An-nafs al-Natiqa, distinguishing human from animal by the power of speech and sound reasoning.
- Al-'Aql al-Heulani, because it is corporeal and exists in matter, and not pure incorporeal intellect. From the Greek word Hyle.
- Al-'Aql al-Mustafad, since the human is receptive in its relation to the Active Mind, thus it is also called (al-'Aql al-Mustafad) because it is gaining the benefit of knowledge from something else which is the Active Mind.
- Potential Mind, as a possibility or mere capability to receive affection or to be affected by the Active intellect in order to be an Actual Mind.
- Actual Mind, after receiving the influence from the Active Mind.

third activity will be displayed as a result in the representative faculty. This activity is called reproductive imitation (al-muhakat). The faculty of muhakat is capable of imitating the sensibles and the intelligibles and the nutritive faculty and sometimes it even imitates the appetitive faculty. It also has the ability to imitate the temperament in which it happens to find the body.[117]

Since the faculty of representation is closely connected with the rational faculty, what the rational faculty obtains from the active intellect emanates sometimes from the active intellect to the faculty of representation. In this sense the active mind acts in some way upon the faculty of representation as well by providing it sometimes with the intelligibles whose proper place is in theoretical reason, and sometimes by particulars in the form of sensibles whose proper place is in practical reason.[118]

It receives the intelligibles by imitating them with those sensibles which it puts together, and receives the particulars sometimes by representing them as they are and sometimes by imitating them with other sensibles. Those particulars reach the faculty of representation without the intervention of deliberation.

From this relationship with the active intellect, two things result in knowledge in the human mind:

> True visions arise from the particulars, which the active intellect gives to the faculty of representation in dreams;

> Divination concerning things divine arises from the intelligibles provided by the active intellect, which it receives by taking their imitations in instead.[119]

This type of knowledge could occur to man in sleep as well as in waking life. However, their occurrence in waking life is rare and happens among very few people. The occurrence of the type of knowledge in sleep concerns particulars, while few concerning

---

[117] Al-Farabi (1985): pp. 210,212.

[118] Al-Farabi (1985): p. 220.

[119] Al-Farabi (1985): p. 220.

intelligibles occur only when the faculty of representation is extremely powerful in man and developed to perfection and when the sensibles which reach it from the outside do not overpower it so as to absorb it completely. It does not work in the service of the rational faculty. Thus, its state in waking life is like its state during sleep when it is relieved of other activities.[120]

Al-Farabi continues that:

"If it happens that the faculty of representations imitates those things with sensibles of extreme beauty (al-Jamal) and perfection (al-Kamal), then man who has that sight comes to enjoy overwhelming and wonderful pleasure, and he sees wonderful things which can in no way whatever be found among the other existence.
It is not impossible then that when a man's faculty of representation reaches its utmost perfection he will receive in his waking life from the active Intellect present and future particulars of their imitation in the form of sensibles, and receive the imitation of the transcendent intelligibles and the other glorious existence and see them. This man will obtain through the particulars which he receives 'prophecy' (super natural awareness) of present and future events, and through the intelligibles which he receives prophecy of things divine. This is the highest rank of perfection which the faculty of representation can reach."[121]

I should comment here that al-Farabi at this point departs from the essence of Islamic religion, by equating the level of prophecy with that of philosophy, and making prophecy as a pure human intellectual process rather than a divine inspiration.

In his book *Sharh Risalat Zenon al-Kabeer al-yunani (Commentary on the treatise of the great Zeno of the Creec)* al-Farabi said under section four on prophecy:

---

[120] Al-Farabi (1985): p. 222.
[121] Al-Farabi (1985): pp. 223, 225, Walzer's translation with some modifications by the author.

"And the holy prophetic soul, at the beginning of its rationale, at the beginning of its enthrallment, receives emanations in one strike [Daf'ah wahida], without any need of a syllogistic order [of reasoning], and the soul that is not holy receives intuitive knowledge by an intermediary, and [this soul] receives other knowledge by way of syllogistic reasoning.

The prophet legislates traditions *(sunan)* and Divine laws *(sharâ'i')* and leads the nation [Ummah] to follow [the Divine law] by desires and fears, explaining to them that they have a just God, who will reward them according to their deeds, rewarding goodness and punishing evil, and not demanding of them any knowledge that they are incapable of. Indeed this rank, i.e., the rank of knowledge, is higher than the reach of everyone." [122]

Here al-Farabi made the point clear that there are few differences between the prophet and the philosopher:

First: The prophet receives his knowledge, as whole, from the active intellect in one shot, without a personal effort in logical reasoning or philosophical reflections.

Second: The prophet legislates things through the Sunnah and the Divine law that regulates the benefits of people through regulation of rights and duties.

Third: The prophet leads the people to apply the divine law in their lives in order to achieve their happiness.

---

[122] Al-Farabi (1349 A.H.): p. 8. This treatise was published in Haydar Abad, India, and I compared this copy with two manuscripts:
1.   Awqaf manuscript, Baghdad, Iraq: number 39/7071.
2.   National Museum manuscript, Baghdad, Iraq : number10922/A
This treatise was also translated into English Language by Dr. J. Kenny. However, I had to retranslate it or correct the translation according to the correct reading of these manuscripts.

Fourth: His method is practical by mentioning the absolute justice of God, Who reward goodness and punishes evil.

Fifth: The prophet does not demand of the public any knowledge that they are incapable of.

Al-Farabi continues explaining the revealed law and the task of the prophet

> "The prophet obliges on them instructions regarding deeds, such as salat and zakat. For salat includes a state of humble prayer, purification and preparation to receive the emanation of [overflowing] mercy and remembrance of Allah and his Prophet.
> Zakat includes justice, equity and care for the poor; by which the universal order of the world remains preserved. The rest of observed acts of worship include good morals, detachment of soul, avoidance of obstacles, and other benefits; it would require a long discourse to explain the wisdom of any one of them."[123]

15. Al-Farabi's Philosophical Religion and Religious Philosophy

Al-Farabi's main concern was to reconcile Islamic religion with Greek philosophy. According to him, truth must be one. This is why he tried to reconcile Aristotle and Plato in the first place in his book *al-Jam'*. He also thought that the task of philosophy is to achieve a universal outlook. However, Islam itself presents such a comprehensive and practical outlook, thus al-Farabi thought that the truth of both, Islamic religion and philosophy must be harmonious and not contradictory.

To achieve this reconciliation al-Farabi tried three ways:

First, to understand Islam as a religion in a more general sense without dealing with its details. For example, his emphasis on Allah as an efficient cause was in order to match the Aristotelian first cause,

---

[123] Al-Farabi (1349 A.H.): p. 8.

without considering seriously the issue of Divine eternal will in Islam, which is contradictory to Aristotelian first cause.

Second, to find one source for both of them. According to him, the active intellect is the source of knowledge for both the prophet and the philosopher. Thus, Aristotle and Muhammad (pbuh) are equivalent in this sense. This is clearly contradicts the Islamic faith. The knowledge of the prophet in Islam is mere revelation and is not philosophical mediation.

Third, to interpret the Qur'anic language in a way that serves the philosophical understanding. For example, the Arabic word "Ibda'" which strictly means in Arabic: *creation* from nothingness without a previous form, meaning that both the universe and its form were created. Al-Farabi took the word "Ibda'" to mean *eternally* coming into existence.

Al-Farabi thought that philosophy and religion expresses one truth in two different methods; the language of the Qur'an is more precise and specific because it is addressed to the public, while the language of the philosophy is more abstract and demonstrative because it is addressed to the elite. What al-Farabi is saying is that religion is for those who are not intelligent enough; thus, the prophet will deal with them in a simple, sometime symbolic and figurative language (the language of the scripture), while the philosophers as elite are exempt from these religious obligations and there is no need for them to follow the teaching of the prophet, which is the Islamic teaching.

This theoretical thesis of al-Farabi will be the practice of ibn Sina, who is going to drink alcohol (which is prohibited in Islam), justifying that because he is intelligent and knows when to drink and why to drink. The philosophers held the ability of their intellect superior to that of God. Allah made the consuming of alcohol prohibited in Islam because the human intellect is one of the five necessities in the Islamic Divine Law and must be preserved in order for the society to achieve a better level of living and happiness. Thus to make alcohol permissible is contradictory to reason itself. We know that reason (human intellect) is going toward more restriction in legislating the consuming of alcohol.

The thesis of al-Farabi will find application with Ibn Baja and Ibn Tufail, but will be criticized by al-Ghazali and Ibn Taimia.

Al-Farabi
(259-339 A.H./ 872-950 A.D.)

Metaphysics

The Existence of God

16. The Contingency Argument:

"The Possible" and "The Necessary"

Al-Farabi's main argument is based on two essential concepts: "the possible" (al-Mumkin) and " the necessary" (al-Wajeb). The possible is everything that has existence not from its essence.

The existence of every existent is either necessary or possible. The necessary existent is either necessary by itself and by its essence, or it is necessary by something else other than itself – if it is necessary by something else other than its essence, then it is called "possible."[124]

Premise 1: The possible by definition, is only possible by something else; thus it must be preceded by a cause in order to exist (a cause by which it came into existence).

Premise 2: Since it is unreasonable to trace the chain of causes and effects to infinity (without reaching an end),

----

Conclusion: Therefore, there must be an existent being, whose existence is necessary,[125] and this Being is uncaused, most perfect, and actual eternity.

Al-Farabi clarifies the second premise that possible causes cannot go to infinity because cause and effect are connected in a relation or chain. Each of them is an intermediary being caused regarding one aspect and

---

[124] Al Farabi (1890): p. 57.
[125] Al-Farabi (1890): p. 57.

a cause in regard to another. Everything that is intermediary must have a limit and a limit is an end. Possible things must depend on the existence of a necessary existent that is unaffected by causes, whether material, formal, final or efficient.[126]

17. The "Possible" Cannot be the Cause of its Essence

Al-Farabi argues in an attempt, similar to that of al-Kindi on essence and generation, to say that the possible existent cannot be the cause of its existence for the following reasons:

First: The "possible" cannot be the cause of itself, since a cause essentially precedes its effect. For example, if we say that A is a cause of B, we mean that the existence of B is actually proceeds from the existence of A. The conclusion is that the existence of the cause precedes the effect, and a thing cannot have two existences, one which precedes and is a cause, and the other which is after and is an effect. Therefore a thing cannot be the cause of itself.[127]

Second: The cause is essential to the existence of the effect. If the possible were the cause of its existence, then the essence of a thing has two existences: in one it gives cause and in the other as receiving effect. But an essence cannot have one giving essence and the other a non-essential receiving effect.[128]

Third: Causation is an asymmetrical relationship; if A is the cause of B, then B cannot be the cause of A. Thus, the possible cannot be the cause of itself. If B is the cause of A and A is the cause of B, then B is the cause of itself, and that thing's existence must precede its existence which is unsound.[129]

---

[126] Al-Farabi (1349 A.H.): pp. 4-5.
[127] Al-Farabi (1349 A.H.): p. 4.
[128] Al-Farabi (1349 A.H.): p. 4.
[129] Al-Farabi (1349 A.H.): p. 4.

18. God is One
This necessary Being must be one and unique in its substance, and it is impossible for anything else to have the existence that the necessary has:[130]

The very meaning of being "necessary" is being one and only one with no partner.

If there were two necessary beings they would have to be:

The same which means one identity, hence one essence only,

Or different from each other, so that in which they differ would not be the same as in that which they share.
That part of the difference would be a part of that which sustains the existence of both. That which they have in common is the other part. Thus each one of them would be divisible. The two parts would be the cause of the subsistence of its essence.
Therefore, it would not be self-subsistent, thus another cause must be the first and necessary cause for both. Yet none of them is the necessary Being.[131]

Or partly alike and partly different, which means the identity and the simplicity of each is destroyed, thus none of them is perfect.

Therefore the most perfect being must be one and only one.[132]

---

[130] Al-Farabi (1985): p. 58.
[131]Al-Farabi (1985): pp. 59-60.
[132]Al-Farabi (1985): p. 60. This paragraph from al-Farabi (1349 H.) might give a simpler version of the argument: He must be one, since in any pair one is first and the other is second. There is a natural precedence of one over two, even if they are together. For they would either share in everything, and in that case there would be no duality between them, or they would differ, and in that case one of them would have to be the reason for the other, since one of them would be necessary existent. If the other were necessary existent, neither of

19. Al-Farabi and The Qur'anic Logic

I should comment here that though al-Farabi was a Muslim philosopher, he did not utilize any of the logical arguments in the Qur'an on the Oneness of God to reach his conclusions. However, the Qur'an does offer many arguments on the topic of the unity of God. The following are two examples from the Qur'an:

1- **"Say: if there had been (other) gods with Him, - as they say - behold, they would certainly have sought out a way to the Lord of the Throne!"** (*Qur'an, 17:42*)

2- **"Had there been therein (in the heavens and the earth) aliha (gods) besides Allah, then verily, both would have been ruined. Glorified is Allah, the Lord of the Throne, (High is He) above all that (evil) they associate with Him!"** (*Qur'an, 21: 22*)

The logical form of the second Qur'anic argument is:

Premise 1: If there were gods in the heavens and earth besides Allah, then they (heavens and earth) would be destroyed and collapsed (every god seeking power and control)

Premise 2: But they are Not collapsed (the universe is systematically working)

Conclusion: Therefore, there is only one God.

The argument has this valid form that we call Modus Tollens:
If P......, then ..... Q
Not Q

Therefore, Not P

---

them would be distinguished and identified as necessary existent, but would be distinguished by something else. But there is no problem for something to be necessary existent if its existence is one as far as the meaning of its essence is concerned.

20. The Divine Attributes

This necessary Being is what al-Farabi calls Allah, Who is One, Eternal, and everlasting in its substance and essence. He is the first cause, uncaused, self-sufficing, and does not change from one state of being to another. Allah is Neither matter nor is he all sustained by a matter or a substratum, nor does he have form. A form according to Al-Farabi can exist only in matter,[133] and if God is a form then he would be composed from both form and matter, and its essence would be sustained by two things that stand as causes to its existence;[134] therefore, God is simple, Uncompounded, and very difficult to define.[135]

This Being is the absolute Mind and absolute Goodness, the absolute thinking, and the ultimate subject of its own reasoning (He is the thinking and the thought in one). God thinks his own essence, and thus he actually becomes thinking and intellect and as a result of his essence thinking it (ta'quluhu). God becomes intelligized, (He is 'Aql , 'Aaqel, and Ma'qool in one.)[136] His thinking essence is the very essence that is thought by Him as an intellect as one undivided, the most perfect, and the most complete.

God is the absolute and transcending beauty and the absolute and transcending love, and He possesses the most complete internal happiness, whose being is his very essence, in whose truth and reality coincide.[137]

Humans usually call the Divine by the noblest names as a reference of the most honored. Some of these names are reference to the essential nature of the Divine, and others are names that are reference to the relation of the Divine to the universe. These two approaches look at the divine attributes but do not affect the unity of his essence.[138]

---

[133] In actuality, form and matter are always together and cannot be separated. A form can potentially exist without matter.
[134] Al-Farabi (1985): p. 58.
[135] Al-Farabi (1890): p. 4.
[136] Al-Farabi (1985): p. 70.
[137] Al-Farabi (1985): p. 72, 74.
[138] Al-Farabi (1985): p. 76.

According to al-Farabi, these attributes need to be understood metaphorically, and the essence is not understood, unless according to a feeble analogy.

To know the necessary Being with these attributes, we must strive and purify the soul and train the mind to know the non-material or the abstract. Al-Farabi is saying we do not have a clear grasp of knowledge about the very essence of God since the divine attributes are understood metaphorically.

Mutakallimun thought that we could possess knowledge about the creator by searching and reflecting upon the creation and created things instead of focusing on His essence, even though al-Farabi was not stating the same thing. Al-Farabi thinks the very essence of God is beyond knowledge.

In regard to the indefinable attribute of God, al-Farabi seems to manifest the Qur'anic attribute of God; however, al-Farabi as a result of believing in the eternity of the world, did not consider Allah as the Active Creator (al-Khaliq) who created everything from nothing by His power of will. In the Qur'an Allah clearly stated that He is the Creator of heavens and earth (Badi' al-Samawat wal Ardh). Also al-Farabi neglected how Allah describes Himself in the Qur'an as nothing like Him:

"(He is) the Creator of the heavens and the earth: He has made for you pairs from among yourselves, and pairs among cattle: by this means does He multiply you: there is nothing whatever like unto Him, and He is the One that hears and sees (all things)." (*Qur'an, Al Shura:11*).

Notice that attributes of the Divine are mentioned in this verse in both negation and affirmation. Al-Farabi was describing the God of the philosophers as pure intellect more than describing the God in the Islamic religious sense.

21. The Theory of Emanation and the Eternity of the World

Al-Farabi's theory of mind is a clear manifestation of the non-Islamic elements in his philosophy. His theory is based on a serious mistake: Al-Farabi could not make a distinction between the knowledge of God and the will of God.[139] According to him, the absolute knowledge of God is the very source of existence, thus there is no will to control or to initiate the coming into existence. The existence of the world follows necessarily from the absolute knowledge of the Divine.

From this mistake al-Farabi proceeded to a more serious position in Islamic philosophy which is the eternity of the world. His ontological conclusion is based on a mistake in his epistemological premises. Both al-Farabi's premises and conclusion stand clearly against the Islamic teaching.

His argument goes as follows:
God's knowledge is the very cause and source of the existence of every thing. Since the knowledge of God is eternal and absolutely perfect, the forms and types of all existent things exist eternally in God. Therefore, they are eternal.[140]

Since God is the Eternal Being, and the types and the forms of the existents eternally co-exist, their coming into existence (eternally) is a necessary act. Al-Farabi said:

"...and the First [The Necessary Being] is that from which existents brought [into existence], and since ever the First exist, the type of existence that is specific to Him [which is eternal], it implies necessarily that all other existents, whose existence can not be brought up by man's will and choice, will follow from Him."[141]

---

[139] Al-Farabi (1890): p. 6.
[140] Al-Farabi (1890): p. 6.
[141] Al-Farabi (1985): p. 88, author's translation, what is in parenthesis is mine.

22. How are Things Eternal and Still Come into Existence?

In order to answer this question I have to go through al-Farabi's theory of Emanation (Nadhriyyat al-Faidh), which represents his cosmology. For the sake of simplification, I will divide his theory into two parts:

First: The becoming of the Celestial System, which is divided into:
      A. The becoming of the Intellects.
      Bathe becoming of the Celestial (Heavenly) Bodies.

Second: The becoming of the Sublunary System.

First: The "Becoming" of the Celestial System:
A. The Cosmology of the Intellects:

From God (and His absolute knowledge, His generosity and His perfection,) eternally emanates or overflows and proceeds an Intellect that is similar to Him (as an image of Him). Al-Farabi called this "the second", which means the second existence and "the first 'Aql or intellect". As far as existence, it is a second level of existence and God's existence is level one. As far as comparing it with spirits and intellects, it is the first 'Aql or spirit.

This First intellect or 'Aql (al-'Aql al-Awwal) is incorporeal substance and it is not in matter.[142] This intellect ('Aql) involves into two types of intellectual activity:

First: It thinks its own essence, and as a result of its substantification in its own essence the existence of the First Heaven (al-Sama' al-'Ula) follows necessarily.[143]

Second: It thinks the Necessary (the First, God), and from this activity a third level of existence comes into being, which is going to be the second 'Aql.

This first intellect (al-'Aql al-Awwal) (which is the second existent) is in charge of the motion of the outermost celestial sphere (al-Falak al-Akbar)[144] or First Heaven (al-Sama' al-'Ula).

---

[142] Al-Farabi (1985): p. 100.
[143] Al-Farabi (1985): p. 100.

The intellect ('Aql) in the third level of existence is also not in matter. It's substance is intellect and has also two intellectual activities:

First: it thinks its own essence, and as a result of its substantification in its own essence, the existence of the sphere of the fixed stars follows necessarily.

Second: it thinks of the First (the Necessary Being = God). As a result of this thinking a fourth level of existence follows and comes into existence, which will be the third intellect or 'Aql.[145]

By these two intellectual activities and in the same logical and ontological succession, the rest of the intellects ('Uqool) and heavenly bodies come into existence. Each intellect follows necessarily from the activity of that intellect in thinking the Necessary (the First), and the heavenly bodies follow necessarily from the activity of that 'Aql in its thinking its own essence, and as result of its substantification in its own essence.

This process of intellectualization continues until it reaches the existence of the Eleventh, which is also going to think its own essence, and it thinks the First (the Necessary). However, with this intellect (The Eleventh) this kind of existence of intellects (which is pure intellectual in no need of matter or substratum) will come to an end, and the process of coming into existence of these transcendent entities, which are in their substances intellects and intelligible, will stop.
The coming into existence of The Heavenly bodies is also going to come to an end with the sphere of the Moon (Kurat al-Qamar) which cames into existence as a result of the activity of the Tenth intellect thinking its own essence.
Below the Sphere of the Moon is our world of four elements (Fire, Air, Water, and Earth), or the material world, the existence of composition of form and matter.

---

[144] Al-Farabi (1890): p. 7, and (1985): p. 100.
[145] Al-Farabi (1985): p. 100,102.

All these intellects ('Uqool) are transcendent entities, non-material and in no need of matter and substratum. They think the First and their own essence. Each one thinks its own essence, and as a result one of the celestial bodies follows.[146]
The most excellent of these immaterial intellects is the Second. All others follow according to rank and order until the Eleventh is reached.

Allah = The First
(The Necessary Being)

The following emanated from Him

First Intellect ('Aql) (Second existent) First Heaven, (al-Sama' al-'Ula)

Second Intellect   Fixed Stars, (Kurat al-Kawakeb)

Third Intellect   Sphere of Saturn (Zuhal)

Fourth Intellect   Sphere of Jupiter (Al-Mushtari)

Fifth Intellect   Sphere of Mars (Al-Marreekh)

Sixth Intellect   Sphere of the Sun (al-Shams)

Seventh Intellect   Sphere of Venus (Al-Zahra)

Eighth Intellect   Sphere of Mercury ('Atared)

Ninth Intellect   Sphere of the Moon (Kurat al-Qamar)

Tenth Intellect   (Eleventh existent)

No Heavenly bodies exist from the tenth intellect. What exists below this is the world of four elements and change: earthly bodies or the earth.

---

[146] Al-Farabi (1985): p. 100.

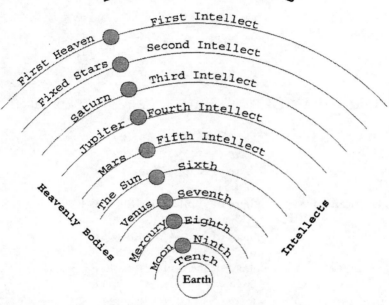

Al-Farabi
Theory of Emanation

* The first intellect ('Aql) that was emanated represents a second
level of existence. God is the First level of existence.
The tenth intellect will be the eleventh existent,
or the eleventh level of existence.
This last intellect will be the last 'Aql in the process of emanation,
and from which no heavenly body comes.

23. First: The "Becoming" of the Celestial System

B. The Cosmology of the Celestial (Heavenly) Bodies:
All heavenly bodies by their nature move in circles. Since the circle is the perfect geometrical figure, the circular motion is more suitable to the heavenly bodies.[147] The most excellent of the celestial bodies is the First Heaven and all others follow according to rank and order until the Sphere of the Moon is reached.[148]

It is clear from the diagram above that the celestial bodies consist of nine different ranks of spherical body.

The first contains one body which moves in one circular direction. Its motion is very fast.

The second (The Fixed Stars) is also one body but contains number of bodies which have a common motion, and all of them together within the second have two motions in which they all participate.

The third and the rest of the celestial bodies till the Ninth each contain one body, each one having its own particular motion.

Although all of them move in circles, their motion differs in certain respects. For example, the motion of the sphere of the Moon is faster than that of Saturn.

The celestial bodies are the first to be affected by contraries, because of their mutual relations. Thus things come into existence as we will see in the following section. These contrarieties according to al-Farabi are the most unimportant contrarieties. Contrariety is itself a deficiency of existence. Thus the celestial bodies are affected by this type of deficiency.

24. Second: The "Becoming" of the Sublunary System:
Five types of coming into existence take place according to different categories:[149]

---

[147] Al-Farabi (1985): p. 104.
[148] Al-Farabi (1985): p. 114.
[149] Al-Farabi (1985): p. 134.

1- All the celestial bodies have a common nature. From the very common nature of them prime matter follows necessarily. This prime matter (al-Maddah al-'Ula) is common to everything below the celestial bodies.

2- The difference of the substances of the celestial bodies[150] and the existence of many bodies, which differ in their substances follow necessarily.

3- The existence of contrary forms follows necessarily from the contrariety of the relations of the celestial bodies to another.

4- From the alternating contrary relations in the celestial bodies and their succession, it follows necessarily the alternating of the contrary forms which the prime matter receives in succession.

5- The mixture and blending of things, which have contrary forms, follows from the occurrence of contrary and mutually incompatible relations of a number of celestial bodies to one particular thing at the same moment.

It follows by necessity that from the types of these different mixtures many species of bodies arise, and from those of their relations, things arise according to that type of relation. If the relation repeats itself and comes back, the things arise with the type of existence that repeats itself and comes back. If it happens once, the thing will arise once.

First Material things that arise are the four elements (Fire, Air, Water, and Earth), then bodies which are of their nature. For example: vapors such as clouds and winds and other things which arise in the air. In these elements and physical bodies powers arise too:[151]

---

[150] The Sphere of the fixed stars is different in substance from that of the Moon.

[151] Compare these powers with John Locke's account of active and passive power, in his *"An Essay Concerning Human Understanding"*, Book II, Chapter XXI.

- Power by which they move themselves, as an internal force.
- Power by which they act upon one another (like an active power).
- Power by which they receive one another's actions (more like a
  passive power).

From the existence of these elements other bodies follow necessarily, and from the mixture of these elements many contrary bodies arise. These bodies mix either exclusively with one another, or with one another and with the elements, so that there will be a second mixture, and powers, and so on and so forth.

The Minerals arise as the result of a mixture, which is nearer to the elements and is less complex.
The plants arise as the result of a more complex mixture.
The animals, which lack speech and thought arises as the result of a mixture which is more complex than that of plants.
Human alone arises as the result of the last and highest mixture.

All the above existent things are those natural material things, which exist below the celestial bodies, that we can call the sublunary bodies.

25. Levels of Corporeal Existence
Existence of the corporeal material things in the sublunary area are six grades or levels:
First: celestial bodies.
Second: human bodies
Third: bodies of lower animals
Fourth: plants
Fifth: minerals
Sixth: elementary bodies (the four elements: fire, air, water, and earth)

26. Levels of Spiritual, Incorporeal Existence
The first level of existence is Allah (God).
The second level of existence (which is a second grade of being) is the nine intellects of the Spheres.

The third level of existence is the Active Intellect (al-'Aql al-Fa''al), which is also called the Holy Spirit (Rooh al-Qudus). This intellect is active in humanity, and does unite the heaven with the sublunary world. The above three levels are pure spiritual, pure incorporeal, non-material, and the very essence of which is transcendent entity that has neither substratum nor a relation to what is material.
The fourth level of existence is the Soul.
The fifth level of existence is the Form.
The sixth level of existence is the Matter.

The Soul, Form, and Matter are also incorporeal. They can enter into certain kind of relation with material bodies.

27. Two Versions of al-Farabi's Theory of Emanation
Al-Farabi presented more than one way to talk about the emanation. In his *Treatises On Zeno* and *al-Siyasat al-Madaniyya,* the process of emanation is different from that in the *Perfect State.* In the latter each intellect thinks itself and intelligizes the First only, while in the *Treatise on Zeno* the same process continues from the beginning to include the third. The fourth intellect as well as the fifth to the tenth intellect intelligize the first, second, and third intellect.[152]

The emanation in the third and forth intellects are dualistic. Intellect and heavenly body accept the second intellect that has trinity: "It is not surprising that the second intellect intelligized what pertains to its Creator and His essence and what three things should come from it, while other intellects intelligized things and three things do not come from them."[153] The following is a comparison between two of his books. Numbering is added for the sake of clarification.

---

[152] Al-Farabi (1964): p. 34.
[153] Al-Farabi (1349 A.H.): p. 7.

Two Versions of al-Farabi's Theory of Emanation
(Nadariyyat al-Faidh)[154]

Al-Madina al-Fadilah *(On The Perfect State)*	*Risalat Zenon al-Kabir*
The World above the Moon	**The relationship of things to Him**
"**1.** From the First emanates the existence of the Second.	"**1.**[T]he First Intellect intelligized Himself, as a result, from Him came an intellect that has a possibility of existence from its own essence and a necessary existence from an Other. And it [this intellect] is the second in this way [of emanation].
2. This Second is, again, an utterly incorporeal substance, and is not in matter. It thinks of (intelligizes) its own essence and thinks the First. What it thinks of its own essence is no more than its essence. As a result of its thinking of the First, a third existent follows necessarily from it; and as a result of its substantification in its specific essence, the existence of the First Heaven follows necessarily.	**2.** The Second [intellect] intelligized the First [Intellect] and intellegized its own essence; by intelligizing the First an emanation [of another intellect] necessarily came from Him, and by intelligizing Himself there comes from Him a form related to matter and the soul of a heavenly sphere.... The first existent, designated as B, intelligized its essence, as we have said, and the essence of his

---

[154] The text on the *Perfect State* is from al-Farabi (1985), pages: 101, 103, and 105. While *Risalat Zenon al-Kabir* is from the Arabic text al-Farabi (1349 A.H.), pages: 6-8, translation is based on revision of that of J. Kenny. My reading of the Arabic text might be different from that of Kenny.

Creator, and there result from it an intellect from its understanding the First Creator, and the soul of the sphere [came to exist] by its intelligizing its own essence. Its own essence is not one, but has an aspect that comes from without, namely, its existence which comes from the First, the Blessed and Most High. So this intellect intelligized it's Creator as one and real, and thought its own essence and its ordination for existence.

3. The existence of the Third, again, is not in matter, its substance is intellect, and it thinks its own essence and thinks the First.

As a result of its substantification in its specific essence, the existence of the sphere of the fixed stars follows necessarily, and as a result of its thinking of the First, a fourth existence follows necessarily.

3. The third intellect, designated as C, intelligized the Most High First Creator and its own essence, and there result from it an intellect and the soul of the sphere of the fixed stars as well as the body of this sphere.

It is not surprising that the second intellect intelligized what pertains to its Creator and His essence. Three things should come from it, while other intellects intelligized things and three things do not come from them. But it is surprising that someone should not know how these things come forth by an intellectual process that involves cause and effect...

4. This [the fourth], again, is not in matter. It thinks its own essence and intelligizes the First. As a result of its substantification in its

4. The fourth intellect, designated as D, intelligized the first, second and third intellects and there comes from it an intellect

specific essence, the existence of the sphere of Saturn follows necessarily, and as a result of its thinking the First, a fifth existence follows necessarily.

5. The existence of the Fifth, again, is not in matter. It thinks its own essence and thinks the First.....[the exact same process of emanation goes on to the sixth, seventh, eight, ninth, and tenth]

The existence of this [the tenth], again, is not in matter. It thus thinks its own essence, and it thinks the First. As a result of its substantification the existence of the sphere of the Moon follows necessarily, and as a result of it thinking the First, an eleventh existence follows necessarily.

6. The existence of the Eleventh, again, is not in matter. It thinks its own essence, and it thinks the First. But with it, that kind of existence which is in no need of matter and substratum whatsoever comes to an end-namely those 'separate' (transcendent) entities which are in their substances intellects and intelligible. And with the sphere of the Moon the heavenly bodies come to an end-namely those bodies which by their nature move in circles.

designated as E, and a soul designated as F, which the sphere of Saturn, and the body of that sphere.

5.This process [of emanation] goes on until it reaches the active intellect,

6. Which [the active intellect] is called "the giver of forms". It [the active intellect] intelligizes constantly the First and constantly thinks whatever under the First. Forms come necessary from it [the active intellect], but the forms, and the souls of the spheres help it in preparing causes for the reception of forms from it, just as a doctor does not give health, but prepares causes for the reception of health.

The Influence of al-Farabi on St. Thomas Aquinas

Al-Farabi had influenced many philosophers; Muslims, Christian, and Jewish. Some smaller Muslim philosophers and thinkers presented their ideas in the frame of Farabian system with clear influence such as al-'Amiri, al-Sijistani, and to some extent al-Tawhidi.

Al-Farabi's philosophy had more influence on Jewish and Christian philosophers than that on Muslims, with the exception of Ibn Sina. His influence on St. Thomas Aquinas is beyoned doubt. Robert Hamond in his book (1947) *The Philosophy of Alfarabi And Its Influence On Medieval Thought,* compared the language and the philosophy of St. Thomas Aquinas with that of al-Farabi. He put the text of both side by side in order to show how Aquinas was litraly following al-Farabi. The following is a short sample:

Topic	Al-Farabi 872-950	St. Thomas Aquinas 1225-1274
Proof of Motion (for Proof of God's Existence)	In this world, there are things that are moved. Now, every object which is moved receives its motion from a mover. If the mover itself is moved, there must be another moving it, and so on. But it is impossible to go on to infinity in the series of movers and things moved. Therefore, there must be an immovable mover, and this is God.	In the world some things are in motion. Now, whatever is in motion is put into motion by another... If that by which it is put in motion be put in motion, then this also must be put in motion by another, and so on. But this cannot go on to infinity. Therefore, it is necessary to arrive at a first mover, put in motion by no other, and everyone understands this to be God.

Infinity of God	The uncaused being is infinite. For, if He were not, He would be limited, and therefore, caused, since the limit of a thing is its cause. But God is uncaused. Hence, it follows that He is infinite.	Being itself, considered absolutely, is infinite... Hence if we take a thing with a finite being, this being must be limited by some other thing, which is in some way the cause of that being. God cannot be caused because He is necessary of Himself. He has infinite being, and He is infinite.
God is Intelligent	A thing is intelligent because it exists without matter. God is absolutely immaterial. Therefore, He is intelligent.	A thing is intelligent from the fact of its being without matter. It has been shown that God is absolutely immaterial. Therefore, He is intelligent.
God is Life	... God, whose intellect is His essence, must have life in the most perfect degree.	Wherefore that being whose act of understanding is its very nature, must have life in the most perfect degree.
Proof of Efficient Cause (for Proof of God's Existence)	In contemplating the changeable world, one sees that it is composed of beings which have a cause, and this cause, in turn, is the cause of another. Now, in the series of efficient causes, it is not possible to proceed to infinity... Therefore, outside the series of efficient causes, there must be an uncaused efficient cause, and this is God.	In the world of sense, we find there is an order of efficient causes. There is no case known (neither is possible) in which a thing is found to be the efficient cause of itself...Now, in efficient causes, it is not possible to go on to infinity... Therefore, it is necessary to admit a first efficient cause, to which everyone gives the name of God.

Immutability of God	God as the first cause is pure act, without the admixture of any potentiality, and for this reason He is not subject to any change.	[T]his first being must be pure act, without the admixture of any potentiality... Now, everything which is in any way changed is in some way in potentiality. Hence, it is evident that it is impossible for God to be in any way changeable.

Ibn Sina (Avicenna)
(370-428 A.H./ 980-1037 A.D.)

What is Philosophy?

The Life of The Sheikh al-Ra'is

1. Intellectual Life

Abu 'Ali al-Husain Ibn Sina (also called al-Sheikh al-Ra'is) is one of the most famous physicians and philosophers. To a lesser degree, he was a mathematician, astronomer, logician, and poet.

Ibn Sina wrote a short biography about himself. Then Abu 'Ubayed al-Juzjani, his student companion, completed it. In his biography, Ibn Sina said about his early life:

"My father was a man of Balkh; he moved from there to Bukhara in the days of Amir Nuh ibn Mansur during whose reign he worked in the administration, being entrusted with the governing of a village in one of the royal estates of Bukhara. [The village,] called Kharmaythan, was one of the most important villages in this territory. Near it is a village called Afshanah where my father married my mother and where he took up residence and lived. I was born there, as was my brother, and then we moved to Bukhara. A teacher of the Qur'an and a teacher of literature were provided for me, and when I reached the age of ten I had finished the Qur'an and many works of literature, so that people were greatly amazed at me."[155]

Ibn Sina's father was Isma'ili (a shi'ati sect believes in seven infallible Imams) and a political supporter of the Fatimyya state (that was based on the Isma'ili Shi'ati doctrin) in Egypt. The father and his older son used to discuss at home the Isma'ili opinions and issues which Ibn Sina understood but his philosophical mind found some difficulties in

---

[155] Ibn Sina (1974): p. 128.

accepting it: "I was listening to them and understanding what they were saying, but my soul would not accept it, and so they began appealing to me to do it [to accept the Isma'ili doctrines.]"[156]

The father probably noticed the talent of his son and his independent personality, thus encouraged him to learn Indian calculation and al-Jabr wal-Muqabala (algebra). However, the turning point in the intellectual life of Ibn Sina was when a teacher of philosophy came to Bukhara who changed the religious boy Ibn Sina to a philosophical youth, as Ibn Sina said:

"At that time, Abu 'Abdullah al-Natili who claimed to know philosophy, arrived in Bukhara. My father had him stay in our house and he devoted himself to educating me. Before his arrival I had devoted myself to jurisprudence with frequent visits to Isma'il the Ascetic about it. I was a skillful questioner, having become acquainted with the methods of prosecution and the procedures of rebuttal in the manner which the practitioners of it [jurisprudence] follow.

Then I began to read the *Isagoge* under al-Natili, and when he mentioned to me the definition of things of being that which is predicated of a number of things of different species in answer to the question - "What is it?" I evoked his admiration by verifying this definition in a manner unlike any he had heard of. He was extremely amazed at me; whatever problem he posed I conceptualized better than he, so he advised my father against my taking up any occupation other than learning. I continued until I had read the simple parts of logic under him; but as for its deeper intricacies, he had no knowledge of them."[157]

At this point Ibn Sina found himself at a crossroads, not only between Jurisprudence and philosophy, but also between himself and his philosophy teacher, who was no longer able to keep up with the vast mind of this young person. Ibn Sina wanted to go further in philosophy

---

[156] Ibn Sina (1974): p. 128.
[157] Ibn Sina (1974): p. 128.

and to go faster, but there was no teacher to teach him. What should he do?

Ibn Sina said:

"So I began to read the texts and study the commentaries by myself until I had mastered logic. As for Euclid, I read the first five or six figures under him; then I undertook the solution of the rest of the book in its entirety by myself. Then I moved on to the Almagest, and when I had finished its introductory sections and got to the geometrical figures, al-Natili said to me, "Take over reading and solving them by yourself, then show them to me, so that I can explain to you what is right with it and what is wrong." But the man did not attempt to deal with the text, so I deciphered it myself. He did not grasp many figures until I put it before him and made him understand it. Then al-Natili left me, going on to Gurganj."[158]

From this early age, Ibn Sina went on his own in gaining knowledge and increasing his wisdom. At this point he begins to see himself as a young thinker.

"I devoted myself to studying the texts-the original and commentaries-in the natural sciences and metaphysics, and the gates of knowledge began opening for me."[159]

Like other geniuses, Ibn Sina was intellectually a restless person. He wanted to know almost everything. Aristotelian formal logic and his philosophy were not satisfying enough. Life is richer than these empty forms and abstracted metaphysical entities. Man is mysterious, and an organic phenomenon is a challenging secret. In his Islamic belief Ibn Sina could not separate knowledge from practice or theory from application. Islamic religion urges the learners to apply their knowledge; thus, experience and practice were the burning desire inside

---

[158] Ibn Sina (1974): p. 129.
[159] Ibn Sina (1974): p. 129.

him. As a result of all these factors Ibn Sina developed a desire to learn medicine on his own.

"Next I sought to know medicine, and so I read the books written on it. Medicine is not one of the difficult sciences, and therefore I excelled in it in a very short time, to the point that distinguished physicians began to read the science of medicine under me. I cared for the sick and there opened to me some of the doors of medical treatment that are indescribable and can be learned only from practice. In addition I devoted myself to jurisprudence and used to engage in legal disputations, at that time being sixteen years old."[160]

Later on, Ibn Sina wrote a book in medicine called *al-Qanun fil Tib*, which becomes the main source of knowledge and practice in medicine till the eighteenth century in Europe.

After being deeply involved in practicing medicine, his love of philosophy led him back to logic and metaphysics and other fields of philosophy. To the brilliants, a life of reflection is always appealing. This time Ibn Sina was studying philosophy in such a systematic way that his knowledge gained from this study would constitute his future knowledge and in turn would constitute his philosophy:

"Then, for the next year and a half, I dedicated myself to learning and reading; I returned to reading logic and all the parts of philosophy. During this time I did not sleep completely through a single night nor devote myself to anything else by day. I compiled a set of files for myself, and for each proof that I examined, I entered into the files its syllogistic premises, their classification, and what might follow from them. I pondered over the conditions of its premises, until this problem was verified for me. And because of those problems which used to baffle me, not being able to solve the middle term of the syllogism, I used to visit the mosque frequently and worship, praying humbly to the All-Creating until He opened the mystery of it to me and made the difficult seem easy. At night I would return home, set out a lamp before

---

[160] Ibn Sina (1974): p. 129.

me, and devote myself to reading and writing. Whenever sleep overcame me or I became conscious of weakening, I would turn aside to drink a cup of wine, so that my strength would return to me. Then I would return to reading. And whenever sleep seized I would see those problems in my dream; and many questions became clear to me in my sleep. I continued in this until all of the sciences were deeply rooted within me and I understood them as far as is humanly possible. Everything which I knew at that time is just as I know it now; I have not added anything to it to this day."[161]

From this passage we can conclude that Ibn Sina devoted himself to philosophy at the age of seventeen. Also from this age, Ibn Sina started to give philosophy, as rational wisdom, superiority over the Islamic revealed law. According to the Islamic Divine Law, the legislation of alcohol is very clear: alcohol is prohibited in order to preserve the intellect as one of the five necessities that are essential in our existence. Although people are equal in regard to the Divine Law, Ibn Sina made himself a special case based on reasoning. Ibn Sina felt increased physical strength when consuming alcohol. Therefore according to his logic, drinking was not for personal pleasure or harming anyone. He was only drinking to achieve a great goal which was to be able to study philosophy more and more. In Islam, no matter how great and noble the end is, it does not justify the means.

It also seems that Ibn Sina's religious belief was not settled deeply in his heart. He had difficulty in spirituality or in fields other than empirical and mathematical. He reflected less maturity in religion. As a result he stopped following the Qur'anic values at an early age. His dislike of religion in general was probably based on his dislike of the Isma'ili's doctrines from his early age, as mentioned above. His devotion was to philosophy, not to God. His taste of religion was rational and lived to the end of his life praying and drinking alcohol.[162]

---

[161] Ibn Sina (1974): p. 129.

[162] Abu 'Ubayd said: "After we prayed the evening prayer, he set out candles and ordered wine to be brought. He asked his brother and me to sit down and asked us to have some wine."

With his hard work in philosophy he achieved great results. In this regard, Ibn Sina said:

"Thus I mastered the logical, natural, and mathematical sciences and I had now reached the science of metaphysics."[163]

His attitude toward spirituality and revealed wisdom manifested itself in, and affected negatively his study of metaphysics. Ibn Sina read Aristotle's book on *Metaphysics* forty times, memorizing it, without being able to comprehend it:

"I read the Metaphysics [of Aristotle] but I could not comprehend its contents, and its author's object remained obscure to me, even when I had gone back and read it forty times and had got to the point where I had memorized it. In spite of this I could not understand it or its object, and I despaired of myself and said, "This is a book which there is no way of understanding." But one day in the afternoon when I was at the bookseller's quarter a salesman approached with a book in his hand which he was calling out for sale. He offered it to me, but I refused it with disgust, believing that there was no merit in this science. But he said to me, "Buy it, because its owner needs the money and so it is cheap. I will sell it to you for three Durhams. 'So I bought it and it was Abu Nasr al-Farabi's book on the objects of the Metaphysics.' I returned home and was quick to read it, and in no time the objects of that book became clear to me because I had got to the point of having memorized it by heart. I rejoiced at this and the next day gave much in alms to the poor in gratitude to God, who is exalted."[164]

This passage is important because it reflects his relationship to al-Farabi and tells how much Ibn Sina owes to al-Farabi in understanding philosophy. Although Ibn Sina studied Aristotle and Plato, his real model and influential teacher was al-Farabi. As we will see, Ibn Sina's philosophy was indispensable footnotes on al-Farabi.

---

[163] Ibn Sina (1974): p. 129.
[164] Ibn Sina (1974): p. 130.

Ibn Sina continued his search for knowledge till the age of eighteen when he started authoring books on philosophy:

"It happened that the Sultan of that time in Bukhara, Nuh ibn Mansur, had an illness which baffled the doctors. Since my name had become well known among them as a result of my zeal for learning and reading, they brought me to his attention and asked him to summon me. Thus I presented myself and joined with them in treating him, and so became enrolled in his service. One day I asked him to permit me to go into their library, to get to know it and to read its books. He gave me permission and I was admitted to a building which had many rooms; in each room there were chests of books piled one on top of the other. In one of the rooms were books on the Arabic language and poetry, in another, on jurisprudence, and likewise in each room [were books on] a single science. So I looked through the catalogue of books by the ancients and asked for whichever one I needed. I saw books whose names had not reached very many people and which I had not seen before that time, or have I seen it since. I read these books and mastered what was useful in them and discovered the status of each man in his science.

So when I had reached the age of eighteen I was finished with all of these sciences; at that time I had a better memory for learning, but today my knowledge is more mature; otherwise it is the same; nothing new has come to me since."[165]

2. His Writings
Ibn Sina authored about one hundred books and treatises. These books cover different subjects in philosophy, medicine, astronomy, and logic. The most famous are:
- *Al-Qanun fil-Tibb*
- *Al-Shifa' (The Healing)*
- *Risalat Hayy Ibn Yaqdhan*[166]

---

[165] Ibn Sina (1974): pp. 130-131.
[166] This Risalah (treatise), which reflects the creativity of Ibn Sina, will inspire the Spanish Muslim philosopher Ibn Tufail, who wrote a great philosophical book under the same title.

- *Al-Isharat wal Tanbihat*
- *Al-Najat*
- *Al-Hikmah al-Mashriqyyah*
- *Risalah fi Ithbat al-Nubowwat*
- *Kitab al-Siyasah*
- *Risalah Adhawyyah fi Amr al-Ma'ad*

3. The Task of Philosophy is the Study of Being as Such

Philosophy according to Ibn Sina is studying being qua being. In this sense, it is similar to the Aristotelian and Farabian task. Philosophy also has a practical task to perfect the soul to be able to connect itself to the active mind and achieve happiness.

Ibn Sina (Avicenna)
(370-428 A.H. / 980-1037 A.D.)

Metaphysics

4. Essence and Existence.
The "Possible" and the "Necessary"

Existents or beings are of two kinds: the first can be conceived essentially (as an essence) without a necessity to conceive it as an existent being, because its essence is different from its existence. For example when conceiving a triangle: its conception does not require its existence and does not necessitate its existence outside the mind. Another example is designing a house: to have a design of a house in the mind does not necessitate its existence in reality; therefore, it needs a cause (builder) to make it exist. It is possible for this cause to determine its existence or to determine keeping it as a concept or a design and not a real thing, so it can determine its non-existence. This being which is possible to be and not to be is called the "possible".

The second is impossible to be conceived without conceiving it with existence, such as God; His essence and existence cannot be separated. Thus, this being does not need a cause to give Him existence because it is always in existence. To conceive of the necessary as a non-existent is impossible.

The possible must have a cause to actualize it, and the existence of this possible will be the effect. A thing cannot be the cause of itself, and the series of causes and effects cannot regress to infinity. Therefore there must be an ultimate cause for the possible which is God (the necessary being).

In his book *al-Shifa' (The Healing)*[167] Ibn Sina discussed this issue saying:

---

[167] Translated by Arthur Hyman for his volume: *Philosophy in the Middle Ages*, ed. by Arthur Hyman and James J. Walsh, Hackett Publishing Company,

"Things which are included in existence can be divided in the mind into two [kinds]. One of these is that which, when it is considered in itself, does not have its existence by necessity. And it is clear that its existence is also not impossible, for if its existence were impossible, it would not be included in existence. This thing is in the domain of possibility. The other of these is that which, when it is considered in itself, has its existence by necessity."[168]

Ibn Sina mentioned some characteristics of this necessary being as not relative, not changeable, not multiple, not sharing in respect to the existence which is peculiar to the necessary being. Ibn Sina also tried to offer logical arguments to prove them. About these characteristics he said: The necessary existent does not have a cause, while the possible does have a cause. The necessary existent is necessary in respect to existence in all of its aspects. It is not possible for this necessary by itself to be co-equal with another existence, so that each of them is equal with the other in respect to the necessity of existence; thus both cannot necessarily accompany each other. It is also not possible for that necessary being to be composed of a multitude at all. It is not possible for the true nature of the necessary being to be shared with something else in any way whatsoever.[169]

5. The Necessary does not have a Cause.

If that whose existence is necessary were to have a cause for its existence, then its existence would be through that cause. But everything whose existence is through some other thing does not have existence by necessity. However anything which does not have existence by necessity (when it is considered in itself, apart from the other) is not necessary in respect to existence through itself.

Therefore, that whose existence is necessary does not have a cause.

Indianapolis, 1973. pp. 241-255. References will be to these pages and to Ibn Sina's book *al-Najat* (1985), the Arabic edition.
Hyman translated this portion from Ibn Sina, *al-Shifa'*, al-Ilahiyyat, ed. G. C. Anawati and Sa'id Zayed, Cairo: Organization Generale des Imprimeries Gouvernementales, 1960.
[168] Also compare with *al-Najat*, Ibn Sina (1985): p. 261.
[169] See Ibn Sina (1985): pp. 262-263

6. The "Possible" cannot be the Cause of its Existence

When the possible is considered in respect to itself, it has both its existence and non-existence from a cause.

If it exists, then existence (as distinguished from non-existence) has come to it, and

If it does not exist, then the possible is in a state of non-existence (as distinguished from existence).

Now each of these two attributes (existence and non-existence) must come to it:

    A. either from something else,
    B. or not from something else.

A. If its existence comes from something else, then that other is the cause.

B. However, it is contradictory to be possible and not coming from something else because it is evident that everything, which does not exist at first and then exists, is determined by something other than itself.

Also, because either the essence of the possible is sufficient for this determination (for its existence or nonexistence) or the essence is not sufficient for it.

Now if the essence is sufficient for one of the two attributes (existence and non-existence), then that thing is something that's essence is necessary through itself (necessary being).

However, it was assumed that it is not necessary.

Therefore this is a contradiction, and its essence cannot be sufficient.

If the existence of its essence is not sufficient for its existence but something else bestows its existence upon it, then its existence proceeds from the existence of some other thing different from it and this is necessarily its cause.

Therefore the possible has a cause (which makes one of these two attributes necessary for it, not through itself, but through a necessary existent cause.)[170].

Ibn Sina also considered the argument on the regression of causes and effects to be impossible.

The necessary cause is required from the beginning. Otherwise, the effect is brought by another thing through which its existence is established instead of non-existence, and if that is brought by another cause, then the series of causes and effects would go on to infinity.

If it would go to infinity, then it would not be. (Ibn Sina meant that its existence would not be determined because the chain of infinity would not come to an end.) This is absurd because the regression to infinity is impossible and that through which it is determined (the cause) would not yet exist.

However, it was assumed that the cause exists.

Therefore, it is clear that everything whose existence is possible will not exist unless it is necessary in relation to its cause.

7. The Impossibility of Two Co-Equal Existents to be Both Necessary

This argument is long and complicated. I will clarify it after quoting the original text of ibn Sina. Ibn Sina thinks that if the two existents are both co-equally necessary, then one of them is not the cause of the other. Ibn Sina proves that both cannot be co-equal in regard to the necessity of their existence. As a result of that, he wants to prove that if the two co-equals exist, then they must have a cause other than themselves that determines their existence. His argument proceeds in the following way.

---

[170] Compare also Ibn Sina (1985): p. 262.

"It is not possible that that whose existence is necessary co-equals with another whose existence is necessary, so that the first exists with the second and the second exists with the first, and [so that] one of them is not the cause of the other, but both are co-equals in regard to the necessity of [their] existence. For, if one considers the essence of one of them in itself apart from the other, it must be [1] that it is either necessary through itself or [11] that it is not necessary through itself. Now, if [1] it is necessary through itself, it must be that [since the two are co-equal] [1a] it also possesses necessity when it is considered together with the second [that is, it is necessary through itself and necessary through another]. Thus something would exist whose existence is necessary through itself and whose existence is necessary because of another. But this is absurd, as has previously been shown. Or [1b] it is the case that [when that whose existence is necessary through itself is considered together with that which is co-equal with it] it possesses no necessity in respect to the other [that is, it is necessary through itself, possible through another]. In that case, it would not be necessary that its existence would follow from the existence of the other. But it would be necessary for it that its existence does not have a relation to the other, so that it can only exist when the other exists. [Thus one could exist without the other which is against the assumption that they are co-equal.]

Now should it be the case [II] that [the first] is not necessary through itself, it would follow [IIa] that, considered in respect to itself, it would be something whose existence is possible, while, considered in respect to the other, it would be something whose existence is necessary. Then it must be [IIai] that the second is like the first [that is, it is possible in respect to itself, necessary in respect to another], or [IIa2] the second is not [like the first]. Now, [IIa1] if the second is like the first [that is, it is possible in respect to itself, necessary in respect to another], it again must be that necessity of existence comes to the first from the second either [IIaia] insofar as the second is in the category of something whose existence is possible, or [IIaib] insofar as it is in the category of something whose existence is necessary. Now [IIaib] if necessity of existence comes to the first from the second, while the second is in the category of something whose existence is necessary-yet not necessary through itself or through some third thing which precedes it (as was stated previously)-but necessary through that which proceeds from it [that is, the second must necessarily come from the first], the necessary existence of the first would [then] be a condition in which there is contained a necessary existence which comes after the necessity of its own existence. In that case necessary existence would not come to [the first principle] at all [from the second, since it already possesses it].

But [Ilaia] if necessary existence comes to the first from the second, while the second is in the category of something [whose existence is] possible, then necessary existence comes to the first from the essence of the second, while the second is in the category of something possible. And it would be the case that the essence of the second, which is in the category of something possible, would impart to the first necessary existence, without there having been imparted to the second the category of the possible from the first, but [the first would have imparted to the second the category of] the necessary. As a result, the cause of the first would be the possible existence of the second, while the first would not be the cause for the possible existence of the second. Thus the two would not be co-equal; I have in mind, that which is its cause essentially and that which is caused essentially."[171]

Structuring Ibn Sina's Argument(s):
In this lengthy argument about the type of the existence of the two co-equals, Ibn Sina seems to argue in this way:

If we consider the essence of one of them in itself apart from the other, then it must be:

A. it is either necessary through itself, or
B. it is not necessary through itself.

A. If it is necessary through itself, then it must be that (since the two are co-equal):

---

[171] Ibn Sina (1973): pp. 234-244, in Hyman (1973).

A1. It also possesses necessity when it is considered together with the second (i.e., it is necessary through itself and necessary through another).

Thus, something would exist whose existence is necessary through itself and whose existence is necessary because of another.

However, this is absurd, as has previously been shown. Or

A2. It possesses no necessity in respect to the other (i.e., it is necessary through itself, possible through another). In that case, it would not be necessary that its existence would follow from the existence of the other.
But it would be necessary for it that its existence does not have a relation to the other, so that it can only exist when the other exists.

Thus, one could exist without the other which is against the assumption that they are co-equal.

B. It is not necessary through itself, and would follow:
B1. When it is considered in respect to itself, it would be something whose existence is possible. While considered in respect to the other, it would be something whose existence is necessary. Then it must be:
B.1.1. The second is like the first, i.e., it is possible in respect to itself, necessary in respect to another, or

B.1.2. The second is not like the first. Now, B1.1 if the second is like the first (i.e., it is possible in respect to itself, necessary in respect to another), it again must be that necessity of existence comes to the first from the second either:

B.1.2a. insofar as the second is in the category of something whose existence is possible, or

B.1.2b. insofar as it is in the category of something whose existence is necessary.

Now B.1.2b. if necessity of existence comes to the first from the second, while the second is in the category of something whose existence is necessary--yet not necessary through itself or through some third thing which precedes it (as was stated previously), but necessary through that which proceeds from it (i.e., the second must necessarily come from the first), the necessary existence of the first would then be a condition in which there is contained a necessary existence which comes after the necessity of its own existence. In that case, necessary existence would not come to the first principle at all from the second since it already possesses it.

However, B.1.2a. if necessary existence comes to the first from the second, while the second is in the category of something whose existence is possible, then necessary existence comes to the first from the essence of the second, while the second is in the category of something possible. And it would be the case that the essence of the second, which is in the category of something possible, would impart to the first necessary existence, without there having been imparted to the second the category of the possible from the first, but the first would have imparted to the second the category of the necessary.

As a result, the cause of the first would be the possible existence of the second, while the first would not be the cause for the possible existence of the second. Thus the two would not be co-equal.

8. Another Argument to Prove that the Necessary Being is One

Ibn Sina presented an argument on the oneness of God:

"That whose existence is necessary must necessarily be one essence. For if it was not, it would be a multitude each one of whose [parts] would be something whose existence is necessary.

It would follow then, that each one of these [parts] would not at all differ from another in regard to the notion which is its true nature, or that [one part] would differ from another.

Now, if one [part] would not differ from another in regard to the notion which belongs to its essence essentially (yet one [part] differs from another in that it is not the other and this is undoubtedly a difference), then one [part] will differ from another in regard to some other notion...

Now each one of these parts is differentiated from the other through this [principle], while it is not differentiated from the other through the notion itself [that is, the essence], but it is differentiated from the other through some other notion.

The things which are other than the notion [of the essence] and which are adjoined to the notion [of the essence] are the accidents and the consequences which are not essential.

Now these consequences occur to the existence of something [1] insofar as it is this [particular] existence and in this case it is necessary that the whole thing agrees in [this consequence]. But it was assumed that the whole is differentiated in respect to [the consequence]. Hence this is absurd. Or [11] [these consequences] occur to it from external causes not from its own self. In that case, if that cause does not exist, [the consequence] will not occur. Hence if that cause does not exist, the thing will not be differentiated. Further, if that cause does not exist, the essences [of the parts] will be one, or they will not be. Again, if this cause does not exist, one [part] will not be, in its peculiarity, something whose existence is necessary nor would the other [part] be, in Its peculiarity, something whose existence is necessary, [that is] something whose existence is necessary not through its [own] existence, but through accidents. Thus the necessity of existence of each one [of the parts] which is proper to it and which is peculiar to it would be provided by something other than it. But it was stated that everything whose existence is necessary through another, can not be necessary through itself; but, according to the definition of its essence, it is something whose existence is possible. Thus it would be the case that each one of these [parts], even though it is something whose existence is necessary through itself, is [also] something whose existence is possible according to the definition of its essence. This is absurd.

Let us assume then that one [part] differs from another in some inhering notion after it has agreed with it in the notion [of the essence]. Then it must be that that notion is a condition for the necessity of [the part's] existence, or that it is not. Now, if it is a condition for the necessity of [the part's] existence, it is clear that there necessarily agrees in this [notion] everything whose existence is necessary. [But this can not be, since we assumed that the parts differ in respect to this notion.] If, however, this notion is not a condition for the necessity of [the part's] existence, then necessity of existence is established without it as necessity of existence. In that case, this notion would come to it as an accident and it would be joined to it after that necessity of existence has been actualized. But we have already denied this and shown its absurdity. Therefore it is not possible that one part differs from another in the [inhering] notion."[172]

[172] Ibn Sina (1973): PP. 244-245, in Hyman (1973).

CHAPTER FIVE

Al-Ghazali
(450–505 A. H. / 1058–1111 A.D.)

What is Philosophy?

**"The aim of this account is to emphasize that one
should be most diligent in seeking the truth until
he finally comes to seeking the unseekable."**

1. Biography of the Soul

Islamic philosophy reached its peak with al-Ghazali, to the point that
we can divide Islamic philosophy, without hesitation, into two parts:
before al-Ghazali and after al-Ghazali.

With al-Ghazali, Islamic philosophy reached its deepest point of self-
realization and self-identification. Al-Ghazali was not satisfied
intellectually with the philosophy of al-Farabi and Ibn Sina. He
criticized them systematically in his most celebrated book *Tahafut al-
Falasifah (The Incoherence of The Philosophers)*; we will discuss this
book later.

Al-Ghazali's work represents not only a critical-intellectual summary
of Islamic philosophy, but also a great examination of the fields of
Islamic civilization itself: jurisprudence (fiqh), principles of
jurisprudence (usul al-fiqh), theology (kalaam), philosophy (falsafa),
and mysticism (Sufism). His soul could not settle for less than
certainty. His mind was so critical. His desire within the realm of
knowledge was infinitely divers. As a result his body, along with his
soul, suffered restlessness. He had to give up his most respected
position at the university in Baghdad because his tongue became unable
to speak. He had to take a journey for ten years searching for the truth.
Seeking the truth was his innate nature. This made him unique. 'Abdul

Ghafir Al-Farisi,[173] (historian, preacher, and friend of al-Ghazali) wrote his biography:

"Abu Hamid al-Ghazali, the Proof of Islam and the Muslims, the Imam of the Imams of Religion, whose like eyes have not seen in eloquence and elucidation, and speech and thought, and intelligence and natural ability.

In his childhood in Tus, he acquired some learning in jurisprudence from the Imam Ahmad al-Radhkani. Then he went to Nisabur where, with a group of youths from Tus, he frequented the lectures of the Imam al-Haramayn. He worked so hard and seriously that he finished his studies in a short time. He outstripped his fellows and mastered the Qur'an and became the best scholar of the men of his time and matchless among his fellows in the days of the Imam al-Haramayn. The students used to derive profit from him, and he would instruct them and guide them and work hard himself [in establishing his own independent judgments]. He finally reached the point where he began to compose works."[174]

By this time al-Ghazali mastered both: jurisprudence, according to the Shafi'e school, and the principle of jurisprudence, to the point that he was not only able to teach them, substituting his teacher, but also to author books in these fields. One of his most famous, an introduction to the principles of jurisprudence, was written at this time, called *al-Mankhul min 'Ilm al-Usul*. He also learned theology, according to the Ash'ari method, dialectic argumentation, the ethics of disagreement and discourse.

Al-Ghazali desired more knowledge and wanted to go beyond his teacher; however, he continued with his teacher until the teacher died.

---

[173] Al-Ghazali (1980): pp. 14-18.
[174] Al-Ghazali (1980): p. 14, I changed some of the translation in order to make the text easier for the reader. I based my reading on the original Arabic text of 'Abdul Ghafir al-Farisi (1968), pages: 204-214.

"Then Ghazali left Nisabur and went to the 'Askar [camp-court, political and military base] and was officially welcomed by Nizam al-Mulk. And the Master [i.e., Nizam al-Mulk] took an interest in him because of his high rank and conspicuous name and his excellence in disputation and his command of expression. And His Excellency was the stopping-place of the ulama [scholars] and the goal of the imams and the literary men. So there befell Ghazali some fine encounters from contact with the imams and meeting tough adversaries and disputing with luminaries and arguing with the distinguished, and his name became known in distant lands. He took the fullest advantage of that until circumstances led to his being appointed to go to Baghdad to take charge of the teaching in the blessed Nizamiyya School there."[175]

In Baghdad, the center of Islamic civilization, al-Ghazali will actualize his rational skills fully.

"He went off to Baghdad and his teaching and disputation delighted everyone and he met no one like himself, and after holding the Imamate of Khurasan he became the Imam of 'Iraq."[176]

In Baghdad, al-Ghazali spent most of his time disputing opponents about issues in jurisprudence, theology, philosophy, and religion. He also wrote most of his books.

"Then he looked into the science of the principles ['Ilm al-Usul, i.e., the principles of jurisprudence] and when he had already mastered it he scholarly authored some books on that science; and he smarten up the legal school [of jurisprudence: the Shafi'ite] and wrote books on it; and he patterned al-khilaf [i.e., the branch dealing with disputing differences in jurisprudential matters] and also authored new books on that. His rank and admiration in Baghdad became so great that it surpassed the admiration of the nobles and the princes and the residence of the caliph.[177]

---

[175] Also see the Arabic text 'Abdul Ghafir (1968): p. 205.
[176] See 'Abdul Ghafir (1968): p. 205.
[177] See 'Abdul Ghafir (1968): pp. 205-206.

Al-Ghazali's mind was not satisfied with this fame and indisputable progress in reason and material life (knowledge, position, money, and respect). He probably questioned himself: is that all? What is left in the realm of knowledge beyond religion, theology, and philosophy?

He actually found the answer: life is not merely material, and man is not mere intellect, human is spiritual being and should pursue "meta"-physical progress, too.
The consistency within, the inner image, the heart, what might happen after death, and transcending the existence of the soul is what al-Ghazali thought to be essential and worth devotion to further studies. His life changed. His soul was more restless now; he left his position in Baghdad and went on a journey for ten years in order to satisfy the call from within and to live in harmony and in true spirituality, as man should.

"Then, ...the matter was turned around. After studying the subtle sciences and applying himself to the books written about them, he was overwhelmed and followed the path of asceticism and godliness, and he gave up his outer superiority and cast away the rank he had attained to devote himself to the causes of piety and the provisions for the afterlife.

So he left his occupations and repaired to the House of God and performed the Pilgrimage. Then he entered Damascus and remained in that region for nearly ten years, wandering about and visiting the venerated religious shrines, and he began to compose the renowned works to which no one had preceded him, such as *Reviving of the Religious Sciences* and the books abridged there from, such as *The Forty* [Chapters] and others of the treatises which, if one reflects on them, he will know the man's place vis-à-vis the branches of learning.

"He began to battle against self and to regulate his character and to improve his qualities and to rectify his life-style. Thus the devil of frivolity and of seeking leadership and fame and of taking on bad qualities was transformed into serenity of soul and nobility of qualities, having done with [outward] forms and rites. He took on the apparel of the godly and reduced his hope and devoted his time to the guidance of men and to summoning them to what concerned them regarding the afterlife and to making the world and preoccupation with it hateful to those in via [i.e., to the afterlife], and to preparation for the departure to the everlasting abode and obedience to everyone in whom he saw a promise of or smelled the fragrance of [spiritual] succor or alertness to any glimmer of the lights of [mystical] vision until he became pliant and supple regarding that."[178]

After his journey he returned to his home devoting himself to the truth in both theory and practice.

"Then he returned to his native land where he kept fast to his house, preoccupied with meditation, tenacious of his time, a godly goal and treasure for hearts to everyone who repaired to him and visited him. That went on for some time, and [his] works appeared and [his] books circulated. ...

Then Ghazali was invited to teach in the blessed Nizamiyya School [of Nisabur]-God grant it length of days! He could not but yield to his master. By bringing forth that with which he had busied himself, he aimed at guiding the trained [educated, those with learning] and benefiting the seekers [of learning] without going back to what he had been divested of, viz. seeking honor and wrangling with his peers and condemning the headstrong.

"How often was he attacked by opposition and defamation and calumniation regarding what he did not or did and slander and vilification: but he was unaffected by it and did not busy himself with answering the slanderers nor did he manifest any distress at the calumny of the confused.

"Then we asked him how he had come to wish to leave his house and to return to what he was summoned to, viz. the business of Nisabur. In defense of that he said: According to my religion I could not conceivably hold back from the summons and the utility of benefiting

---

[178] See 'Abdul Ghafir (1968): pp. 206-207.

the seekers [of knowledge]. It was indeed imperative for me to disclose
the truth and to speak of it and to call to it-and he was truthful in that.

"Then he forsook that before being himself forsaken and returned to his
house. He set up nearby a school [Madrasa] for the seekers of
knowledge and a place of sojourn [khanqah: a kind of monastic
dwelling] for the Sufis. He apportioned his time to the tasks of those
present, such as the recital of the Qur'an and keeping company with the
men of hearts [Sufis, or, Sufi masters] and sitting down to teach, so that
not a single one of his moments or of those with him was profitless.
[This went on] until the eye of time attained him and the days
begrudged him to the men of his age. Then [God] translated him to His
gracious proximity after his endurance of the varied attacks and
opposition of his adversaries and his being led to kings.

"He passed to the mercy of God on Monday, the fourteenth of Jumada
II, in the year 505 [Dec. 18, 1111 A. D.].

He had the means of subsistence, by inheritance and by his earnings
that provided him with a sufficiency and the support of his household
and his children. He was not at ease with anyone regarding temporal
[secular] affairs; wealth had been offered to him, but he did not accept
it and shunned it and was content with the amount which would
preserve his religion [i.e., keep him independent] and with which he
would not need to address him-self to asking and receiving from
others."[179]

2. Al-Ghazali and the Search for the Ultimate Truth
Although many Western and non-Western scholars appreciate the
greatness of Imam al-Ghazali as a unique intellect in many fields, some
scholars are very critical of his ideas. In this chapter, we are trying to
reach a golden mean as much as possible in presenting his system of
thought, realizing first of all that great controversy arises only around
great people.

---

[179] See 'Abdul Ghafir (1968): pp. 206-211.

Without trying to surprise you, my dear reader, I should say from the beginning that al-Ghazali was not a philosopher, never studied philosophy in school, nor did he have any academic training in philosophy, and he had no intention to be a philosopher. However, al-Ghazali contributed to the human race the most useful, sophisticated, and practical ideas to help people live in peace, consistency, harmony, and success.

So what brought al-Ghazali to philosophy?

Probably two things:
First, his incomparable love of the truth and the desire toward attainment of knowledge. In his book *Al-Arba'een fi Usul Addeen* (*The Forty [necessary rules] in the Foundation of the Religion)*, al-Ghazali divided desires into four kinds:

1. Desire for food and survival need
2. Desire for sexual pleasure and fulfillment
3. Desire for positions of power, authority and being in control of other people
4. Desire of seeking knowledge

Al-Ghazali said that people sacrifice food for the sake of sexual pleasure, and might sacrifice sexual pleasure for the sake of running into a position, while the desire for seeking knowledge will help you get rid of the worldly desires and the arrogance of controlling people, bringing something more beneficial to you personally and to the rest of the society in turn.

Seeking knowledge is more harmonious to the essence of man as a rational being than seeking authority and controlling your fellow humans.

Seeking knowledge has both ethical and aesthetical aspects, because in seeking knowledge we seek perfection, and in perfection beauty resides.

Regarding his love of the truth, al-Ghazali commented:

"**The thirst for grasping the real meaning of things was indeed my habit and wont from my early years and in the prime of my life. It was an instinctive, natural disposition placed in my makeup by God Most High, not something due to my own choosing and contriving. As a result, the fetters of servile conformism fell away from me, and inherited beliefs lost their hold on me, when I was still quite young.**"[180]

In fact, throughout his life, al-Ghazali continued to search for knowledge and learning. Until the last year of his life, he was engaged in writing to the public what is necessary for them[181]. Until his last days, al-Ghazali was busy reading and teaching himself a better preparation for the life after death. He died with a book found open on his chest. Al-Ghazali further comments on his love of knowledge:

"**In the bloom of my youth and the prime of my life, from the time I reached puberty before I was twenty until now, when I am over fifty, I have constantly been diving daringly into the depths of this profound sea and wading into its deep water like a bold man, not like a cautious coward.**
I would penetrate far into every murky mystery, pounce upon every problem, and dash into every mazy difficulty. I would scrutinize the creed of every sect and seek to lay bare the secrets of each faction's teaching with the aim of discriminating between the proponent of truth and the advocate of error, and between the faithful follower of tradition and the heterodox innovator. I would never take leave of an interiorist without wanting to learn about his interiorism, or of a literalist without wanting to know the substance of his literalism, or of a philosopher without seeking to become acquainted with the essence of his philosophy, or of a *mutakallim* without endeavoring to discover the aim of his discussion and polemic, or of a Sufi without eagerly trying to obtain knowledge of the secret of his serenity, or of a devout worshipers without looking into the source and substance of his piety, or of an irreligious nihilist without attempting to find out his background and

---

[180] Al-Ghazali (1980): pp. 54-55.
[181] The last book al-Ghazali wrote was: *Eljam al-'Awam 'an 'Ilm al-Kalam.*

motivation in order to become aware of the reasons for his bold profession of nihilism and irreligion."[182]

The second thing that brought him to philosophy and made him a successful philosopher was his consistency with himself, his sincerity in searching for the truth and being ready to live his ideas. Al-Ghazali set some moral principles in seeking the truth.

1. We should not accept ideas because they are associated with big famous names; instead we should accept ideas because of their own validity and practicality. When we know the truth, we will be able to know people of the truth, but knowing people is not necessarily leading to the knowledge of the truth.

2. We should respect the ideas of other people, and should read them sincerely to understand and learn. We should understand their ideas the same way the authors wanted them to be understood, and we should publish in the same field, if necessary, to show our understanding and comprehension of these ideas. Then and only then we can criticize them if we disagree with them. Keeping in mind that our criticism is for the sake of better and more useful ideas, al-Ghazali said:

"I knew for sure that one cannot recognize what is unsound in any of the sciences unless he has such a grasp of the farthest reaches of that science that he is the equal of the most learned of those versed in the principles of that science; then he must even excel him and attain even greater eminence so that he becomes cognizant of the intricate profundities which have remained beyond the ken of the acknowledged master of the science. Then, and then only, will it be possible that the unsoundness he alleges will be seen as really such."[183]

---

[182] Al-Ghazali (1980): p. 54.
[183] Al-Ghazali (1980): p. 60.

3. Doubt and Certainty: Was Philosophy a Choice or Necessity to al-Ghazali?

With al-Ghazali the act of philosophizing entered a new era, under concepts different from that of Muslim philosophers and of Aristotle.

Traditionally, philosophy was understood as that endeavor of wonder that could be satisfied with different answers, different systems, and different possibilities. With al-Ghazali, philosophy was a restless act of deep reasoning that was not settled until the philosopher reached "certainty". The restless state of reasoning is not coming from the moment of astonishment, which is possible to please by systematic answers, as Aristotle thought. In fact this restlessness (which is a state of being and not mere epistemic) is coming from a continuous state of doubt as an epistemological method of seeking the truth. The intellect itself is not satisfied with just an answer, and the only answer that satisfies a person, who is in this state of doubt, is the answer that furnishes certainty and ends the state of doubting by convincing the mind that this answer presents truth immune to doubt and has intrinsic validity. When a person reaches that satisfactory answer, the state of restlessness changes to the exact opposite and to live in a state of stillness and peace. Al-Ghazali commented on the account of searching for the truth by saying:

"The aim of this account is to emphasize that one should be most diligent in seeking the truth until he finally comes to seeking the unseekable."[184]

Thus searching for the truth becomes a necessity by imposing itself on you to deal with the issue of doubt, and to recover your restlessness. Thus philosophy is not a mere dialogue between two intellects as Plato thought, but also an internal dialogue with yourself. It is a struggle that has its own existential dimension and is also an essential process of being.

---

[184] Al-Ghazali (1980): p. 58.

Al-Ghazali lived both states: the state of restlessness and the state of
stillness and peace. His life was a journey of attaining the truth. He
went through a hard state of doubt, moved from being the most
eloquent religious scholar in Baghdad, who dwelled on many subjects,
to a state of unwillingness to teach. He lost the desire to communicate
with other people, and became physically unable to talk. After studying
the work of those people known at his time as the best seekers of
knowledge, his mind went through a continuous state of searching for
certainty and doubting many types and categories of knowledge.

Let us look closely at his life, his methodological doubt, and his
journey of seeking knowledge, and then turn to his approach to
knowledge and the seekers of the truth.

Reading from al-Ghazali

DELIVERANCE FROM ERROR

Methodological Doubt and his Journey of Seeking Knowledge.[185]

"I saw that the children of Christians always grew up embracing Christianity, and the children of Jews always grew up adhering to Judaism, and the children of Muslims always grew up following the religion of Islam. I also heard the tradition related from the Apostle of God - God's blessing and peace be upon him- in which he said: "Every infant is born endowed with the fitra: [an inherent nature by which humans know the Creator] then his parents make him Jew or Christian or Magian Consequently I felt an inner urge to seek the true meaning of the original fitra, and the true meaning of the beliefs arising through slavish aping of parents and teachers. I wanted to sift out these uncritical beliefs, the beginnings of which are suggestions imposed from without since there are differences of opinion in the discernment of those that are true from those that are false.

So I began by saying to myself: "What I seek is knowledge of the true meaning of things. Of necessity, therefore, I must inquire into just what the true meaning of knowledge is." Then it became clear to me that sure and certain knowledge is that in which the thing known is made so manifest that no doubt clings to it, nor is it accompanied by the possibility of error and deception, nor can the mind even suppose such a possibility. Furthermore, safety from error must accompany the certainty to such a degree that, if someone proposed to show it to be false-for example, a man who would turn a stone into gold and a stick into a snake-his feat would not induce any doubt or denial. For if I know that ten is more than three, and then someone were to say: "No, on the contrary, three is more than ten, as is proved by my turning this stick into a snake-and if he were to do just that and I were to see him do it, I would not doubt my knowledge because of his feat. The only effect

---

[185] Al-Ghazali (1980): pp. 55-58, and 78-83.

it would have on me would be to make me wonder how he could do such a thing. But there would be no doubt at all about what I knew! I realized, then, that whatever I did not know in this way and was not certain of with this kind of certainty was unreliable and unsure knowledge, and that every knowledge unaccompanied by safety from error is not sure and certain knowledge.

... I then scrutinized all my cognitions and found myself devoid of any knowledge answering the previous description except in the case of sense-data and the self-evident truths.... therefore, I began to reflect on my sense-data to see if I could make myself doubt them. This protracted effort to induce doubt finally brought me to the point where my soul would not allow me to admit safety from error even in the case of my sense-data.....Then I said: "My reliance on sense-data has also become untenable. Perhaps, therefore, I can rely only on those rational data which belong to the category of primary truths, such as our asserting that 'Ten is more than three,' and 'One and the same thing cannot be simultaneously affirmed and denied,' and 'One and the same thing cannot be incipient and eternal, existent and nonexistent, necessary and impossible.'

Then sense-data spoke up: "What assurance have you that your reliance on rational data is not like your reliance on sense-data? Indeed, you used to have confidence in me. Then the reason-judge came along and gave me the lie. But were it not for the reason-judge, you would still accept me as true. So there may be, beyond the perception of reason, another judge. And if the latter revealed itself, it would give the lie to the judgments of reason, just as the reason-judge revealed itself and gave the lie to the judgments of sense. The mere fact of the nonappearance of that further perception does not prove the impossibility of its existence."

... It may be that this state beyond reason is that which the Sufis claim is theirs. For they allege that, in the states they experience when they concentrate inwardly and suspend sensation, they see phenomena which are not in accord with the normal data of reason. Or it may be that this state is death. For the Apostle of God- God's blessing and

peace be upon him- said: 'Men are asleep: then after they die they
awake'. So perhaps this present life is a sleep compared to the afterlife.
Consequently, when a man dies, things will appear to him differently
from the way he now sees them, and thereupon he will be told: 'But We
have removed from you your veil and today your sight is keen' (Qur'an,
50:21-22)."

When these thoughts occurred to me they penetrated my Soul, and so I
tried to deal with that objection. However, my effort was unsuccessful.
… This malady was mysterious and it lasted for nearly two months.

During that time I was a skeptic in fact, but not in utterance and
doctrine. At length God Most High cured me of that sickness. My soul
regained its health and equilibrium and once again I accepted the self-
evident data of reason and relied on them with safety and certainty. But
that was not achieved by constructing a proof or putting together an
argument. On the contrary, it was the effect of a light which God Most
High cast into my breast. And that light is the key to most knowledge.

Therefore, whoever thinks that the unveiling of truth depends on
precisely formulated proofs has indeed straitened the broad mercy of
God. When the Apostle of God-God's blessing and peace be upon him!-
was asked about "the dilation" in the Most High's utterance: "So he
whom God wishes to guide aright, He dilates his breast for submission
to Himself " (Qur'an, 6:125), he said: "It is a light which God casts into
the heart." Then someone said: "And what is the sign of it?" He replied:
"Withdrawal from the mansion of delusion and turning to the mansion
of immortality."

The aim of this account is to emphasize that one should be most
diligent in seeking the truth until he finally comes to seeking the
unseekable."

[Al-Ghazali's journey for seeking the truth
Leaving his highest position in Baghdad, and leaving Baghdad to
spend 10 years of solitude]

"...that I had learned all I could by way of theory. There remained, then, only what was attainable, not by hearing and study, but by fruit ional experience and actually engaging in the way. From the sciences which I had practiced and the methods which I had followed in my inquiry into the two kinds of knowledge, revealed and rational, I had already acquired a sure and certain faith in God Most High, in the prophetic mediation of revelation, and in the Last Day.

These three fundamentals of our Faith had become deeply rooted in my soul, not because of any specific, precisely formulated proofs, but because of reasons and circumstances and experiences too many to list in detail.

It had already become clear to me that my only hope of attaining beatitude in the afterlife lay in piety and restraining my soul from passion. The beginning of all that, I knew, was to sever my heart's attachment to the world by withdrawing from this abode of delusion and turning to the mansion of immortality and devoting myself with total ardor to God Most High. That, I knew, could be achieved only by shunning fame and fortune and fleeing from my preoccupations and attachments.

Next I attentively considered my circumstances, and I saw that I was immersed in attachments which had encompassed me from all sides.
I also considered my activities-the best of them being public and private instruction-and saw that in them I was applying myself to sciences unimportant and useless in this pilgrimage to the hereafter.

Then I reflected on my intention in my public teaching, and I saw that it was not directed purely to God, but rather was instigated and motivated by the quest for fame and widespread prestige. So I became certain that I was on the brink of a crumbling bank and already on the verge of falling into the Fire, unless I set about mending my ways.

I therefore reflected unceasingly on this for some time, while I still had freedom of choice. One day I would firmly resolve to leave Baghdad and disengage myself from those circumstances, and another day I would revoke my resolution. I would put one foot forward, and the other backward. In the morning I would have a sincere desire to seek the things of the afterlife; but by evening the hosts of passion would assail it and render it lukewarm. Mundane desires began tugging me with their chains to remain as I was, while the herald of faith was crying out: "Away! Up and away! Only a little is left of your life, and a long journey lies before you! All the theory and practice in which you are engrossed is eye service and fakery! If you do not prepare now for the afterlife, when will you do so? And if you do not sever these attachments now, then when will you sever them?"

At such thoughts the call would reassert itself and I would make an irrevocable decision to run off and escape. Then Satan would return to the attack and say: "This is a passing state: beware, then, of yielding to it! For it will quickly vanish. Once you have given in to it and given up your present renown and splendid position free from vexation and renounced your secure situation untroubled by the contention of your adversaries, your soul might again look longingly at all that-but it would not be easy to return to it!"

Thus I incessantly vacillated between the contending pull of worldly desires and the appeals of the afterlife for about six months, starting with Rajab of the year 488 (July, 1095 A.D.). In this month the matter passed from choice to compulsion. For God put a lock upon my tongue so that I was impeded from public teaching. I struggled with myself to teach for a single day, to gratify the hearts of the students who were frequenting my lectures, but my tongue would not utter a single word: I was completely unable to say anything. As a result that impediment of my speech caused a sadness in my heart accompanied by an inability to digest; food and drink became unpalatable to me so that I could neither swallow broth easily nor digest a mouthful of solid food. That led to such a weakening of my powers that the physicians lost hope of treating me and said: "This is something which has settled in his heart and crept from it into his humors; there is no way to treat it unless his heart be eased of the anxiety which has visited it."

Then, when I perceived my powerlessness, and when my capacity to make a choice had completely collapsed, I had recourse to God Most High as does a hard pressed man who has no way out of his difficulty. And I was answered by Him Who "answers the needy man when he calls on Him" (Qur'an, 27:63-62), and He made it easy for my heart to turn away from fame and fortune, family, children, and associates. I announced that I had resolved to leave for Mecca, all the while planning secretly to travel to Syria. This I did as a precaution, lest the Caliph and the group of my associates might learn of my resolve to settle in Damascus. Therefore I made clever use of subtle stratagems about leaving Baghdad, while firmly resolved never to return to it. I was much talked about by the religious leaders of the Iraqis, since none among them could allow that giving up my career had a religious motive. For they thought that my post was the highest dignity in our religion-and that was the farthest limit they had attained in learning!

Thereupon people got involved in devising explanations of my conduct. Those at some distance from Iraq thought I was acting so because I was afraid of the authorities. But those close to the authorities, who saw their attachment and devotion to me, and how I shunned them and paid no attention to what they said, were saying: 'This is something supernal: its only cause is an evil eye which has afflicted Muslims and the coterie of the learned!'

I departed from Baghdad after I had distributed what wealth I had, laying by only the amount needed for my support and the sustenance of my children. My excuse for that was that the money of Iraq was earmarked for the welfare of the people, because it was a pious bequest in favor of Muslims. Nowhere in the world have I seen a more beneficial arrangement regarding money which the scholar can use for his family."

[Al-Ghazali enters Damascus, from Damascus to Jerusalem, and then from Jerusalem to Mecca]

"Then I entered Damascus and resided there for nearly two years. My only occupation was seclusion and solitude and spiritual exercise and combat with a view to devoting myself to the purification of my soul and the cultivation of virtues and cleansing my heart for the remembrance of God Most High, in the way I had learned from the writings of the Sufis. I used to pray in seclusion for a time in the Mosque, mounting to its minaret for the whole day and shutting myself in. Then I traveled from Damascus to Jerusalem, where I would go daily into the Dome of the Rock and shut myself in. Then I was inwardly moved by an urge to perform the duty of the pilgrimage and to draw succor from the blessings of Mecca and Medina and the visit to the tomb of the Apostle of God- God's blessing and peace be upon him!- after finishing my visit to the Friend of God" -God's blessings and peace be upon him! So I traveled to the Hijaz.

[From Mecca back to Baghdad, Iraq]

Then certain concerns and the appeals of my children drew me to my native land; so I came back to it after being the person most unlikely to return to it. There I also chose seclusion out of a desire for solitude and the purification of my heart for the remembrance of God. But current events and important family matters and gaining the necessities for daily living had an effect on the way to realize my desire and troubled the serenity of my solitude, and the pure state of ecstasy occurred only intermittently. But nonetheless I did not cease to aspire to it. Obstacles would keep me away from it, but I would return to it.

For ten years I remained in that condition. In the course of those periods of solitude things impossible to enumerate or detail in depth were disclosed to me. This much I shall mention, that profit may be derived from it: I knew with certainty that the Sufis are those who uniquely follow the way to God Most High, their mode of life is the best of all, their way the most direct of ways, and their ethic the purest. Indeed, were one to combine the insight of the intellectuals, the wisdom of the wise, and the lore of scholars versed in the mysteries of revelation in order to change a single item of Sufi conduct and ethic and to replace it with something better, no way to do so would be found! For all their motions and quiescence, exterior and interior, are learned from the light of the niche of prophecy. And beyond the light of prophecy there is no light on earth from which illumination can be obtained.

... Ascertainment by apodictic proof leads to *knowledge*. Intimate experience of that very state is *fruit ional experience*. Favorable acceptance of it based on hearsay and experience of others is *faith*. These, then, are three degrees, or levels, of knowledge-"God raises in degrees those of you who believe and those to whom knowledge is given" (Qur'an, 58:12-11).

What became clear to me of necessity from practicing their Way was the true nature and special character of prophecy."

I will discuss his idea of prophecy under his epistemology.

4. The Categories of those Who Seek the Truth
Al-Ghazali divided the categories of those seeking the truth, in his time, into four groups:[186]

I. The Mutakallimun (Muslim scholastic theologians), who allege that they are men of independent judgment and reasoning.

2. The Batinites (group of Shi'ah), who claim to be the unique possessors of al-ta'lim and the privileged recipients of knowledge acquired from the Infallible Imam.

3. The Philosophers, who maintain that they are the men of logic and apodictic demonstration.

4. The Sufis (the mystics, or saints), who claim to be the familiars of the Divine Presence and the men of mystic vision and illumination.

---

[186] Al-Ghazali (1980): p. 58.

Al-Ghazali thought that the truth could not transcend these four categories because these are the men who are following the paths of the quest for truth. Al-Ghazali said:

"Hence, if the truth eludes them there remains no hope of ever attaining it. For there can be no desire to return to servile conformism once it has been abandoned, since a prerequisite for being a servile conformist is that one does not know himself to be Such. But when a male recognizes that, the glass of his servile conformism is shattered-an irreparable fragmentation and a mess which cannot be mended by patching and piecing together: it can only be melted by fire and newly reshaped.

I therefore lost no time in following these different ways and making a thorough study of the views of these groups. I applied myself first to the science of kalam, secondly to the way of philosophy, thirdly to the teachings of the Batinites, and fourthly to the Way of the Sufis."[187]

Al-Ghazali seriously committed himself to the study of these four groups. He began with the science of kalam (scholastic theology), which he summarized very well in the form of notes. He carefully studied the works of the most meticulous Mutakallimun, and he authored distinguished books on the subject both supporting and criticizing it.[188]

In Kalam al-Ghazali belongs to the Ash'ariyyah school, which is an opposing school of thought to that of the Mu'tazilah. However, in his *Munqidh* he was not talking about a specific school of theology. He was summarizing the aim and the limit of the science of Kalam and its method that Mutakallimun cannot go beyond it in seeking the truth. Al-Ghazali did not find this science offering a solution to his restlessness and doubt. It might be a remedy, but not to his illness;

---

[187] Al-Ghazali (1980): pp. 58-59.
[188] About his books see section 5.1 of this chapter.

"...their discussion of the subject was not thoroughgoing; therefore it did not provide an effective means of dispelling entirely the darkness due to the bewilderment about the differences dividing men (in seeking the truth). ... For healing remedies differ as the sickness differs."[189]

Thus al-Ghazali concluded his opinion about Kalam by saying;

"However, I found it (kalam) a science adequate for its own aim, but inadequate for mine. For its aim is simply to conserve the creed of the orthodox for the orthodox and to guard it from the confusion introduced by the innovators."[190]

5. Meta-Philosophy is the Task of Philosophy

The task of philosophy, according to al-Ghazali, lies beyond itself, and is achievable only when reason transcends itself. Al-Ghazali agrees with other philosophers that the goal of philosophy and rationalization is to reach the truth and know the ultimate reality. However, he thinks that part of the truth is when reason itself realizes its own cognitive capabilities and becomes aware of its limits. The insistence of the absolute power of reason to know is mere dogma that philosophers cannot see. Al-Ghazali saw clearly that the subject matter of metaphysics is beyond the limits of reason. When the philosophers insisted on seeking the unseekable by mere rationalization their philosophy turned to manifest mere conjectures that lacked the consistency found in their logic and mathematics. Al-Ghazali thought that our rational faculty is obligated to be consistent with itself and its goal of seeking the truth. Thus, when pure reason realizes its own limit, it should no longer seek the topics of metaphysics, spirituality, prophecy, and Divine on a pure rational basis. Instead it should stop here and let another level flow and illuminate the mind. By doing so, the reason transcends itself and still contributes to the search of the truth by the very realization of its limits first, and second, by presenting a domain of depth and personal experience that is unspeakable.

---

[189] Al-Ghazali (1980): p. 60.
[190] Al-Ghazali (1980): p. 59.

6. Divisions of the Philosophers

After finishing with the science of Kalam, al-Ghazali started on philosophy. Following his method: "that one cannot recognize what is unsound in any of the sciences unless he has such a grasp of the farthest reaches of that science that he is the equal of the most learned of those versed in the principles of that science; then he must even excel him and attain even greater eminence so that he becomes cognizant of the intricate profundities which have remained beyond the ken of the acknowledged master of the science. Then, and then only, will it be possible that the unsoundness he alleges will be seen as really such."[191]

Al-Ghazali also gave justification to his work by mentioning that none of his contemporary Muslim scholars devoted time to the study and criticism of philosophy, and what Mutakallimun did was not sufficient:

"I noted, however, that not a single Muslim scholar had directed his attention and endeavor to that end. What the Mutakallimun had to say in their books, where they were engaged in refuting the philosophers, was nothing but abstruse, scattered remarks, patently inconsistent and false, which could not conceivably hoodwink an ordinary intelligent person, to say nothing of one familiar with the subtleties of the philosophical sciences. I knew, of course, that undertaking to refute their doctrine before comprehending it and knowing it in depth would be a shot in the dark."[192]

Al-Ghazali studied philosophy on his own with no teacher, and he mastered philosophy within less than two years:

"So I girded myself for the task of learning that science by the mere perusal of their writings without seeking the help of a master and teacher. I devoted myself to that in the moments I had free from writing and lecturing on the legal sciences, and I was then burdened with the teaching and instruction of three hundred

---

[191] Al-Ghazali (1980): p. 60.
[192] Al-Ghazali (1980): p. 61.

students in Baghdad. As it turned out, through mere reading in those embezzled moments, God Most High gave me an insight into the farthest reaches of the philosophers' sciences in less than two years. Then, having understood their doctrine, I continued to reflect assiduously on it for nearly a year, coming back to it constantly and repeatedly reexamining its intricacies and profundities. Finally I became so familiar with the measure of its deceit and deception, and its precision and delusion, that I had no doubt about my thorough grasp of it."[193]

To prove that he mastered philosophy, al-Ghazali wrote his book *Maqased al-Falasifah (The Objectives of the Philosophers)* around 488 A.H. /1095 A.D., in which al-Ghazali presented objectively the ideas of the philosophers. This book was translated three times to the Hebrew language; the first was in the thirteenth century, and then the book was also translated to Latin and to old and Modern Spanish.[194] The book was used as a textbook in the Middle Ages, and Jewish scholars found it very appealing and thus, seven different Hebrew commentaries were done on this book.[195]

Al-Ghazali observed that philosophers fell into several categories and that their sciences included several divisions. But to all of them, despite the multiplicity of their categories, cleaves the stigma of unbelief and godlessness. He also noticed that there is a marked difference among the philosophers. He divided them into three groups:[196] Materialists, Naturalists, and Theists:

The **Materialists** were a group of the most ancient philosophers who denied the existence of the omniscient and omnipotent Creator-Ruler. They alleged that the world has existed from eternity as it is, of itself and not by reason of a Maker. These are the godless in the full sense of the term.

---

[193] Al-Ghazali (1980): p. 61.
[194] See Badawi, AbdurRahman (1961): pp. 54-60.
[195] See Badawi, AbdurRahman (1961): pp. 60-62.
[196] Al-Ghazali (1980): p. 61-62.

The **Naturalists** were men who devoted much study to the world of nature and the marvels found in animals and plants; they also were much taken up with the dissection of animal organs. In these they saw such marvels of God Most High's making and such wonders of His wisdom that they were compelled, with that in mind, to acknowledge the existence of a wise Creator cognizant of the aims and purposes of all things.

Hence, they thought that man's rational power was also dependent on the mixture of his humors and that its corruption would follow the corruption of the mixture of his humors, and so that power would cease to exist. Once it ceased to exist, they alleged that bringing back the nonexistent would be unintelligible. They adopted the view that the soul dies, never to return. Consequently, they denied the afterlife and rejected the Resurrection and the Reckoning. In their view, there would be no future reward for obedience, and no punishment for disobedience. These were also godless men because basic faith is belief in God and the Last Day-and these men denied the Last Day, even though they believed in God and His Attributes.

The **Theists,** were the later philosophers, such as Socrates, the master of Plato, and Plato, the master of Aristotle. Then Aristotle refuted Plato and Socrates and the Theists who had preceded him in such thorough fashion that he disassociated himself from them all. Yet he, too, retained remnants of their vicious unbelief and innovation which he was unsuccessful in avoiding.

Al-Ghazali thinks that they all must be taxed with unbelief, as must their partisans among the Muslim philosophers, such as al-Farabi, Ibn Sina and their likes. None, however, of the Muslim philosophers engaged so much in transmitting Aristotle's lore as did the two men just mentioned. Al-Ghazali clearly classified their philosophy in its relation to Islam. The sum of what he regards as the authentic philosophy of Aristotle, as transmitted by al-Farabi and Ibn Sina, can be reduced to three parts:

1. a part which must be branded as **unbelief;**
2. a part which must be stigmatized as **innovation;**
3. and a part which **need not be repudiated at all.**

Al-Ghazali's criticism of the philosophers will be discussed in detail under his metaphysics.

7. The Divisions of the Philosophical Sciences
Al-Ghazali divided the sciences of the philosophers into six divisions:

Mathematical (arithmetic, geometry, and astronomy),
Logical,
Physical,
Metaphysical,
Political, and
Moral.

Mathematics.
Al-Ghazali thinks that mathematical sciences entail neither denial nor affirmation of religious matters. On the contrary, they concern rigorously demonstrated facts which can in no way be denied once they are known and understood. However, al-Ghazali found two evils have been engendered from this branch:
First, the precision and the clarity of the mathematical proofs usually mislead the reader, who is going to admire their work in general and think that they are precise and successful in all branches of their philosophy, including metaphysics, which is not the case. [197] Al-Ghazali

---

[197] Al-Ghazali (1980): pp. 63-64. Al-Ghazali said: "One of these is that whoever takes up these mathematical sciences marvels at the fine precision of their details and the clarity of their proofs. Because of that, he forms a high opinion of the philosophers and assumes that all their sciences have the same lucidity and apodictic solidity as this science of mathematics. Moreover, he will have heard the talk of the town about their unbelief, their negative attitude, and their disdain for the Law. Therefore he ceases to believe out of pure conformism, asserting: "If religion were true, this would not have been unknown to these philosophers, given their precision in this science of mathematics."
Thus, when he learns through hearsay of their unbelief and rejection of religion, he concludes that it is right to reject and disavow religion. How many a man have I seen who strayed from the path of truth on this pretext and for no other reason!

noted that being skilled in one field does not necessitate proficiency in other fields, but what is more important in the criticism of al-Ghazali to this point is that he made a clear demarcation between mathematical science and metaphysical studies especially regarding the method of knowledge in each one. He said:

"What the ancients had to say about mathematical topics was apodictic, whereas their views on metaphysical questions were conjectural. But this is known only to an experienced man who has made a thorough study of the matter."[198]

Al-Ghazali Criticized the Ignorant Friend of Islam
The second evil is coming from an ignorant friend of Islam, who thinks that defending the religion can be achieved by rejecting anything related to the knowledge of the philosophers. Al-Ghazali said:

"*The second evil* ... derives from the case of an ignorant friend of Islam who supposes that our religion must be championed by the rejection of every science ascribed to the philosophers. So he rejects all their sciences, claiming that they display ignorance and folly in them all. He even denies their statements about eclipses of the sun

---

One may say to such a man: "A person skilled in one field is not necessarily skilled in every field. Thus a man skilled in jurisprudence and Kalam is not necessarily skilled in medicine, nor is a man who is ignorant of the speculative and rational sciences necessarily ignorant of the science of syntax. On the contrary, in each field there are men who have reached in it a certain degree of skill and preeminence, although they may be quite stupid and ignorant about other things.
What the ancients had to say about mathematical topics was apodictic, whereas their views on metaphysical questions were conjectural. But this is known only to an experienced man who has made a thorough study of the matter.
When such an argument is urged against one who has become an unbeliever out of mere conformism, he finds it unacceptable. Rather, caprice's sway, vain passion, and love of appearing to be clever prompt him to persist in his high opinion of the philosophers with regard to all their sciences."

[198] Al-Ghazali (1980): p. 64.

and the moon and asserts that their views are contrary to the revealed Law.

When such an assertion reaches the ears of someone who knows those things through apodictic demonstration, he does not doubt the validity of his proof, but rather believes that Islam is built on ignorance and the denial of apodictic demonstration. So he becomes all the more enamored of philosophy and envenomed against Islam.

Great indeed is the crime against religion committed by anyone who supposes that Islam is to be championed by the denial of these mathematical sciences. For the revealed Law nowhere undertakes to deny or affirm these sciences, and the latter nowhere address themselves to religious matters."[199]

Logic.

Al-Ghazali thinks that there is nothing in logic to contradict religion; moreover, logic has nothing to deal with religion by way of negation and affirmation. It seems that al-Ghazali grasped the essence of the Aristotelian logic, i.e., its formality. It is only a method of proofs and validity check and soundness of reasoning and thus, it is a necessary tool to every field of knowledge. In order to support his idea, al-Ghazali gave the example of a universal affirmative proposition that is convertible to a particular affirmative proposition:

If all A are B, then it necessarily follows that some B is A. He said:

"What has this to do with the important truths of our religion that it should call for rejection and denial? When it is rejected, the only effect of such a rejection in the minds of logicians is a low opinion of the rejecter's intelligence, and, what is worse, of his religion, which, he claims, rests on such rejection."[200]

---

[199] Al-Ghazali (1980): p. 64.

[200] Al-Ghazali (1980): p. 65. Regarding his view on logic and religion al-Ghazali said: "Nothing in the logical sciences has anything to do with religion by way of negation and affirmation. On the contrary, they are the study of the methods of proofs, of syllogisms, of the conditions governing the premises of

Al-Ghazali went further to suggest that logic is necessary to every field of knowledge and its study must precede the study of other fields. Al-Ghazali himself made logic as an introductory chapter in his book *Usul al-Fiqh (The Principles of Jurisprudence)*. Commentators, negatively, said that al-Ghazali was the first one to introduce logic into religious studies; however, in Usul al-Fiqh, religious scholars usually deal with logic and syllogism. Al-Ghazali saw logic as formal rules of reasoning that even correspond very well to the teaching of the Islamic religion to the point that in his book *al-Qistas al-Mustaqim (The Just Balance),* al-Ghazali elicits from al-Qur'an five different forms of logical arguments that he called necessary Qur'anic scales for reasoning.

However, al-Ghazali also found two defects in logic:

First, logic cannot lead to certainty in metaphysics. Second, as a result, people might be misled to rush to non-belief in God before studying the opinions of the philosophers on metaphysical issues. Al-Ghazali said:

"To be sure, the philosophers themselves are guilty of a kind of injustice in the case of this science of logic.

---

apodictic demonstration, of how these premises are to be combined, of the requisites for a sound definition, and of how the latter is to be drawn up. Knowledge is either a concept, and the way to know it is the definition, or it is an assent, and the way to know it is the apodictic demonstration. There is nothing in this which must be rejected. On the contrary, it is the sort of thing mentioned by the Mutakallimun and the partisans of reasoning" in connection with the proofs they use. The philosophers differ from them only in modes of expression and technical terms and in a greater refinement in definitions and subdivisions. Their manner of discoursing on such things is exemplified by their saying:
"If it is certain that every A is B, then it necessarily follows that some B is A"- for instance: If it is certain that every man is an animal, then it follows necessarily that some animal is a man. This they express by saying that a universal affirmative proposition is convertible to a particular affirmative proposition.

This is that in logic they bring together, for apodictic demonstration, conditions known to lead undoubtedly to sure and certain knowledge.

But when, in metaphysics, they finally come to discuss questions touching on religion, they cannot satisfy those conditions, but rather are extremely slipshod in applying them.

Moreover, logic may be studied by one who will think it a fine thing and regard it is very clear. Consequently he will think that the instances of unbelief related of the philosophers are backed up by demonstrations such as those set forth in logic. Therefore he will rush into unbelief even before reaching the metaphysical sciences. Hence this evil may also befall the student of logic."[201]

Physical Sciences

Al-Ghazali thinks that there is no contradiction between physical sciences and religion. Thus they should not be denied or rejected, except in specific points that al-Ghazali discussed in his book *Tahafut al-Falasifah (The Incoherence of The Philosophers),* in which he singled out the issue of causality as related to miracles. This subject will be discussed later.[202]

---

[201] Al-Ghazali (1980): p. 65.

[202] Al-Ghazali (1980): pp. 65-66. Al-Ghazali made a nice analogy between the study of physics and that of medicine. Where physical sciences study the body of the universe, the world of the heavens and their stars, and of the sublunary world, and its simple bodies, such as water, air, earth, and fire, and composite bodies, such as animals, plants, and minerals, and the causes of their changing and being transformed and being mixed.

The medicines study the human body and its principal and subsidiary organs and the causes of the alteration of the mixtures of its humors.

Al-Ghazali concludes:

"And just as religion does not require the repudiation of the science of medicine, so also it does not require the repudiation of the science of physics, except for certain specific questions which we have mentioned in our book *The Incoherence of the Philosophers.* Apart from these, it will be clear upon reflection that any other points on which the physicists must be opposed are subsumed in those we have alluded to.

The basic point regarding all of them is for you to know that nature is totally subject to God Most High: it does not act of itself but is used as an instrument

Al-Ilahiyyat (Metaphysics)

Al-Ghazali thinks that this is the weakest part of philosophy, in which philosophers are incoherent and their ideas are logically invalid. Al-Ghazali carefully examined their errors, and criticized twenty of their problems in his book *Tahafut al-Falasifah (The Incoherence of The Philosophers)*, in three of which he taxed them with unbelief, and in seventeen with innovation. Al-Ghazali said:

"It is in the metaphysical sciences that most of the philosophers' errors are found. Owing to the fact that they could not carry out apodictic demonstration according to the conditions they had postulated in logic, they differed a great deal about metaphysical questions. Aristotle's doctrine on these matters, as transmitted by al-Farabi and Ibn Sina, approximates the teachings of the Islamic philosophers.

But the sum of their errors comes down to twenty heads, in three of which they must be taxed with unbelief, and in seventeen with innovation. It was to refute their doctrine on these twenty questions that we composed our book *The Incoherence*. In the three questions first mentioned they were opposed to (the belief of) all Muslims, viz. in their affirming

> **1) that men's bodies will not be assembled on the Last Day, but only disembodied spirits will be rewarded and punished, and the rewards and punishments will be spiritual, not corporal. They were indeed right in affirming the spiritual rewards and punishments, for these also are certain; but they falsely denied the corporal rewards and punishments and blasphemed the revealed Law in their stated views.**
>
> **2) The second question is their declaration: "God Most High knows universals, but not particulars." This also is out-and-out unbelief. On the contrary, the truth is that "there does not escape Him the weight of an atom in the heavens or in the earth" (Qur'an, 10: 61).**

---

by its Creator. The sun, moon, stars, and the elements are subject to God's command: none of them affects any act by and of itself."

3) The third question is their maintaining the eternity of the world, past and future.

No Muslim has ever professed any of their views on these questions.

On other matters-such as the denial of the divine attributes, and their assertion that God is knowing by His essence, not by a knowledge superadded to His essence, and similar views of theirs-their doctrine is close to that of the Mu'tazilites. But there is no need to tax the Mu'tazilites with unbelief because of such views. We have already mentioned that in our book *The Clear Criterion for Distinguishing between Islam and Godlessness*, as well as what shows the error of anyone who precipitously brands as unbelief everything that clashes with his own doctrine."[203]

The issue of the past-eternity of the world will be discussed under his metaphysics.

The Political Science

Al-Ghazali mentioned such a novel idea when he talked about politics; he said most of the wisdom of the philosophers came down to them in this field from previous scriptures and previous revelation. Al-Ghazali said:

"In the political sciences all that the philosophers have to say comes down to administrative maxims concerned with secular affairs and the government of rulers. They simply took these over from the scriptures revealed to the prophets by God Most High and from the maxims handed down from the predecessors of the prophets."[204]

Moral Philosophy.

Al-Ghazali thinks that their study of ethics concentrates on the qualities of the soul and its struggle to avoid bad things in order to achieve the good.

---

[203] Al-Ghazali (1980): pp. 66-67.
[204] Al-Ghazali (1980): p. 67.

He also noticed that most of their studies in this field have been taken
from the knowledge of the mystics and mysticism, Al-Ghazali said:

"All they have to say about the moral sciences comes down to listing
the qualities and habits of the soul, and recording their generic and
specific kinds, and the way to cultivate the good ones and combat the
bad. This they simply took over from the sayings of the Sufis. These
were godly men who applied themselves assiduously to invoking
God,'" resisting passion, and following the way leading to God Most
High by shunning worldly pleasures. In the course of their spiritual
combat the good habits of the soul and its shortcomings had been
disclosed to them and also the defects that vitiate its actions. All this
they set forth plainly. Then the philosophers took over these ideas and
mixed them with their own doctrines, using the luster afforded by them
to promote the circulation of their own false teaching."[205]

8. Al-Ghazali's Analytic Philosophy
Al-Ghazali's analytic method was not restricted to the metaphysics of
the philosopher, but also to the very philosophical language itself and
its semantics. Al-Ghazali thinks that language has semantic reference to
one of the levels of truth, and each language designate specifically the
truth in its field. For example: the language of pure mathematics refers
to abstract entities, while that of applied physics must refer to entities
available to sense perception, and both of them are different from the
language of metaphysics which speaks about entities derived by
reflection such as substance. The language of the three kinds just
mentioned is different from the prophetic and Divine language. Thus,
mixing two types of language will lead to confusion about the truth.
This is what some philosophers did. But what the philosophers did by
mixing the saying of the Sufis and the prophetic teachings with their
writing, as the philosophers and especially the Brethren of Purity
('Ikhwan al-Safa) did, results in two evils, as al-Ghazali said:

"From the Islamic philosophers' mixing the prophetic utterances and
the sayings of the Sufis with their own writings two evils have sprung:

---

[205] Al-Ghazali (1980): p. 67.

one in the case of the man who accepts their ethical teaching, the other in the case of the man who rejects it.

The evil in the case of the man who rejects their ethical teaching is very serious. For some dim-witted persons suppose, since that borrowed prophetic and Sufi doctrine has been set down in the philosophers writings and mixed with their false doctrine, that this doctrine must be eschewed and never cited and even disavowed whenever anyone cites it. This is their attitude because they have heard that doctrine in the first place only from the philosophers. So their weak minds straightway judge it to be erroneous because the one who voices it is in error on other matters. ...

This is the practice of those dim-witted men who know the truth by men, and not men by the truth. The intelligent man, on the contrary, follows the advice of the Master of the Intelligent, 'Ali-God be pleased with him!-where he says: 'Do not know the truth by men, but rather, know the truth and you will know its adherents.'

The intelligent man, therefore, first knows the truth, then he considers what is actually said by someone. If it is true, he accepts it, whether the speaker be wrong or right in other matters. Indeed, such a man will often be intent on extracting what is true from the involved utterances of the erring, since he is aware that gold is usually found mixed with dirt. The money-changer suffers no harm if he puts his hand into the sack of the trickster and pulls out the genuine pure gold from among the false and counterfeit coins, so long as he can rely on his professional acumen. It is not the expert money-changer, but rather the inexperienced bumpkin who must be restrained from dealing with the trickster. Likewise, a clumsy and stupid person must be kept away from the seashore, not the proficient swimmer...

It is certainly true, since most men have an overweening opinion of their own competence and cleverness and think they are perfectly equipped intellectually to discern truth from error, that the door must be blocked to prevent the generality of men, as far as possible, from perusing the works of those addicted to error. For they will by no means be safe from the second evil which we shall presently mention, even if they do manage to escape the evil which we have just noted.

The second evil is that due to total acceptance of their ethical teaching. For one who studies their books, such as that of 'The Brethren of Purity' and others, and sees the prophetic maxims and Sufi sayings they interspersed with their own utterances, often approves of their writings and accepts them and forms a good opinion of them. Thereupon he may readily accept their errors mixed up with those borrowed truths because of a good opinion acquired about what he has seen and approved. That is a way of luring men into error.

Because of this evil the perusal of the philosophers' books must be prevented on the score of the deceit and danger they contain. Just as an unskilled swimmer must be kept away from slippery river banks, so men must be kept from perusing those books."[206]

9. Al-Ghazali's Writings
The writings of al-Ghazali are very consistent. Each book or treatise serves a very well defined goal. Al-Ghazali did not write books unless he was asked to answer a question or comment on an issue (sometimes students ask him to write a textbook), or there was a necessity such as the whole society suffering from a problem, and that problem needed to be properly addressed and suitably presented with a set of solutions.

Al-Ghazali fearlessly engaged in the searching for the truth and falsifying and showing the incoherence of some groups. As a result, some of his enemies started fighting against him by putting together some books and treatises contradicting the teachings of Islam, claiming that he wrote them, in order to ruin his reputation. Al-Ghazali was very aware of the fallacy of attacking the person; his interest was reaching the truth:

"How often was he attacked by opposition and defamation and calumniation regarding what he did not or did and slander and

---

[206] Al-Ghazali (1980): pp. 67-70.

vilification: but he was unaffected by it and did not busy himself with answering the slanderers nor did he manifest any distress at the calumny of the confused [or: the muddle-headed, or: the scheming]."[207]

However, his enemies especially the Isma'ilis such as 'Ikhwan al-Safa (The Brethren of Purity) were fighting him to the last day of his life, and even after his death, as Abdul-Ghafir al-Farisi said:

"Then [God] translated him to His gracious proximity after his endurance of the varied attacks and opposition of his adversaries and his being led to kings. And God protected him and preserved him and guarded him from being seized by vexing hands or from having his religion defiled by any slips."[208]

On the other side, people who liked al-Ghazali very much put together different chapters from his writings with their own writings, or chapters from other writers to make up a book that they thought was going to be useful to the public such as the book, *Mukashfat al-Quloob*, as we will see later. Thus we can divide the writings of al-Ghazali into two parts:

First: books that were written by him.
Second: books that were written by other people (intentionally to serve certain goals) and were falsely attributed to him.
I will discuss each of these with some details.

10. The Writings of al-Ghazali and its Sources:
The basic sources of the life and the writings of Al-Ghazali could be divided into three groups:

A- Traditional Islamic Sources: listed in a chronological order.

'Abdul Ghafer Al-Farisi,	d. 529 H.	History of Nisabur.
Abu Baker Ibn al-Arabi,	d. 543 H.	al-Qawasemwal-'Awasem
Ibn 'Asaker,	d. 571 H.	History of Damascus.
Ibnul Jawzi,	d. 597 H.	Al-Muntazam.

[207] Al-Ghazali (1980): p.16.
[208] Al-Ghazali (1980): p.18.

Yaqoot al-Hamawi,	d. 626 H.	Mu'jam al-Buldan
Ibn Al-Salah,	d. 642 H.	
Sibt ibnul Jawzi,	d. 654 H.	Mir'at al-Zaman.
Muhyden anNawawi,	d. 676 H.	al-Tabaqat.
Ibn Khellikan,	d. 681 H.	fiyat al-'Aayan.
Al-Hafidh Al-Thahabi,	d. 748 H.	Siar 'Aalam al-Nubalaa'.
Al-Yfie'i,	d. 768 H.	Mir'aat al-Janan.
Tajud Deen as Subki,	d. 771 H.	Tabaqatal-Shafe'iyyahal-Kubraa.
Ibn Katheer,	d. 774 H.	al-Bidayah wal-Nihayayh.
Muhammad al-Wasiti,	d. 776 H.	al-Tabaqat al-'Alyyah fi Manqib al-Shafe'iyyah.
Ibn al-Mulaqqan,	d. 790 H.	al-'Aqd al-Muthahhab fi Tabaqat al-Madhhab.
Ibn Qazi Shahbah,	d. 851 H.	Tabaqat al-Shafeyyah.
Al'Aaini,	d. 855 H.	'Aqd al-Juman.
Al-Jami,	d. 898 H.	Nafahat al-'Uns.
Tash Kubraa Zadah,	d. 962 H.	Meftah al-Sa'adah wa Mesbah al-Siyadah.
Salahud Deen, AsSafadi,	d. 964 H.	al-Wafi bil Wafiyyat.
Al-Manawi,	d. 1031 H.	Al-Kawakib al-Duriyyah fi Tarajem asSadah asSufiyyah
Al-'Aidarus Ba'Alawi,	d. 1038 H.	T'areef al-'Ahya' bi Fazaiel al-Ihya'
Al-Zabidi, (al-Murtaza),	d. 1205 H.	Ethaf asSadah al-Mutaqeen fi Sharh Asrar Ihya' Ulum al-Deen.

B- Modern Non-Islamic Sources: (The Orientalists)
In the modern time the Orientalists were involved in writing about Al-Ghazali and his writing, although they made serious mistakes. I have listed some of them below:
L. Masynion.
D. B. Macdonald, in First Encyclopedia of Islam, vol. III.
W.M. Watt.
Maurice Bouyges, his work was incomplete and unpublished.
Michel Allard, who completed and published Bouyges work.

C- Contemporary Islamic Sources:
This source relies heavily upon the traditional Islamic sources, although critically at times, it does consider the Non-Islamic sources. The only

distinguished and comprehensive work achieved yet is that of AbdurRahman Badawi, 1380 H/ 1961 C.E. *Mu'allafat al-Ghazali.*
However, I hope that my work presents a better scheme of Al-Ghazali's writings and a better classification of what he authored. I personally found myself occupied in a deep and thorough examination of his writings, attempting to distinguish what he wrote and what is falsely attributed to him. My work was based on these elements:

1. It is based on being deeply involved in the reading of al-Ghazali and concentrating on his syntax and semantics.
2. It is also based on the traditional Islamic source mentioned above in 10. A.
3. It is also based on the manuscripts of al-Ghazali that I have attained.
4. Finally my work utilizes the great effort of Dr. Badawi in his book *Mu'alafat al-Ghazali.*

11. The books that were written by al-Ghazali.
Below, I have listed his writings in groups categorized according to the subject matter and most of them are also chronologically set within. Some books will be listed more than one time because their subject matter serves more than one category or field of knowledge. An asterisk will label the occurrence of these books.

Al-Fiqh:
1. *Al-Baseet.*
2. *Al-Wasit.*
3. *Al-Wajiz.*
4. *Khulasat al-Mukhtasar wa Naqawat al-Mu'tasar.*
5. *Ghayat al-Ghaour fi Derayat al-Daour.*
6. *Ghaour al-Daour fi al-Mas'alah al-Sarijyyah*
7. *Al-Fatawa*
8. *Fatwa (about Yazid Ibn Mu'awiah)*
9. *Haqiqat al-Qawlain.*

Usul al-Fiqh:

1. *Al-Mankhul min Ta'liqat al-Usul,*
2. *Tahtheeb al-Usul.*
3. *Shifa' al-Ghaleel.*
4. *Asas al-Qiyas.*
5. *Al-Mustafa min 'Ilm al-Usul (The Essentials of the Islamic Legal Theory)*

'Ilm al-Khilaf wa Turuq al-Munadharah:

1. *Ma'akheth al-Khilaaf*
2. *Lubab al-Nadhar*
3. *Tahseen al-Ma'akhith.*
4. *Al-Mabadi' al-Ghayat.*
5. *Al-Muntakhal fi Elm al-Jadal.*

'Ilm al-Kalam (Theology):

1. *Al-Iqtisad fi'l-'tiqad (The Middle Path in Theology)*
2. *Faisal al-Tafriqah bayn al-Islam wa al-Zandaqah*
3. *Qawa'e al-'Aqe'd (Al-Risala al-Qudsiyya) (The Jerusalem Epistle),* part of *Ihya'.*
4. *Al-Maqsad al-Asna Sharh Asma' Allah al-Husna, (The Noblest Aim in explaining the Divine Names (and Attributes).*

Philosophy:

1. *Maqasid al Falasifa (The Intentions of the Philosophers)*
2. *Tahafut al Falasifa (The Incoherence of the Philosophers)*
3. *Al-Munqidh min al-Dalal (The Deliverer from Error)* *

(In *Al-Munqidh* al-Ghazali presented criticism of scholastic theology, philosophy, Batiniyya, & Sufism).

Logic:

1. *Mihakk al-Nazar Fi'l-mantiq (The Touchstone of Proof in Logic)*
2. *Mi'yar al-'ilm (The Standard Measure of Knowledge)*
3. *Al-Qistas al-Mustaqim (The Just Balance) (An attempt to deduce logical rules from the Qur'an and to refute the Isma'ilis.)* *

On The Qur'an:

    1. *Tafseer Yaqoot al-Ta'weel.*

    2. *Qanon al-Ta'weel. (al-Qanoon al-Kully fil Ta'weel).*

    3. *Jawaher al-Qur'an.*

Religion, Philosophy of Religion, Sufism, and Psychology:

    1. *Ihya' 'ulum al-din (The Revival of the Religious Sciences)*

    2. *Al-Imla' fi Mushkilat al-Ihya', Appendix, Iyha' 'Ulum al-Din*

    3. *Kimya' al-Sa'adah (Persian Language) Parallel to Ihya' in A rabic Language,*

    4. *Bidayat al-Hidayah (The beginning of Guidance). Very brief summary of topics in Ihya'.*

    5. *Zaad Akherat. (in Persian Language) parallel to Bidayat al-Hidayah in A rabic.*

    6. *Al-Risalah al-Wa'dhyyah.*

    7. *Risalah ela Ba'dh Ahl 'Asrehi.*

    8. *Al-Arba'een fi Usul al-Deen. (it is part of Jawaher al-Qur'an published separately since the time of Al-Ghazali).*

Ethics:

    1. *Mizan al-'amal (The Balance of Action),*

    2. *Ayyuha al-Walad*

Politics:

    1. *Al-Tibr al-Masbuk fi Nsiyat al-Muluk (The counsel of Kings)*

Non-Islamic Religion:

    1. *Al-Qaul al-Jameel fil Rad 'ala man Ghaiara al-Injeel.*

Firaq and against Ism'ili's doctrines (Batiniyyah):

    1. *Fada'ih al-Batiniyyah wa Fada'il al-Mustadhiriyyah (The Infamies of the Battinites and the Virtues of the Mustazhirites).*

    2. *Hujjat al-Haqq.*

3. Qawasem al-Batiniyyah.
4. Mufasal al-Khilaaf.
5. Al-Durj al-Marqoom bil Jadawel.
6. Al-Qistas al-Mustaqeem*

The last book al-Ghazali wrote on philosophy and religion:

1. Iljam al-`Awam `an `Ilm al-Kalam,

Al-Ghazali wrote this book about two weeks before his death.[209]

12. Books that were Falsely Attributed to al-Ghazali
For details about why and how the following books were falsely ascribed to al-Ghazali, please see my explanation in my book: *Fiqh al-Hadarah.*[210]

1.   *Sir al-`Alamin wa Kashf ma fi al-Daryn,*
2.   *Mukashafat al-Quloob al-Muqarreb ela Hadhrat 'Allam al-Gheyoob.*
3. *Al-Madnoon al-Sagheer (Al-Nafkh wal-taseyah) or Al-madnoon bhi 'ala Ahlihi*
4. *Al-Madnun bihi `ala Ghayri Ahlihi.*
5. *Al-Risalah al-Ladunyyah.*
6. *Mihaj al-'Arefeen.*
7. *Risalalt al-Tair.*
8. *Al-Kashf wa al-Tabyin fi Ghuroor al-Khalq jma`in*
9. *Al-Durrah al-Fakhirah fi Kashf `Ulum al-Akhirah.*
10. *Minhaj al-'Abidin,*
11. *Ma`arij al-Quds fi Ma`rifat al-Nafs*
12. *Mishkat al-Anwar.*

---

[209] *Iljam al-`Awam `an `Ilm al-Kalam*, ed., Muhammad al-Musta`sim Billah al-Baghdadi (Beirut: Dar al-Kitab al-`Arabi, 1985).
[210] Forthcoming in Arabic Language.

Al-Ghazali
(450-505 H. / 1058-1111 C.E.)

Theory of Knowledge
Methodological Doubt and Epistemology

13. In the following reading from al-Ghazali we are going to study the sources of knowledge, their validity, and their limitations. We will follow the steps of al-Ghazali's methodological doubt as a way of reaching the truth by relying only upon certain, clear and self-evident ideas, starting from senses, moving to reason, then to revelation, and mentioning briefly the knowledge of Sufism.

14. Al-Ghazali thinks that in order to reach the truth, we should utilize all sources of knowledge, according to him sources and degrees of knowledge must correspond to the levels of reality, thus there is no sole empiricism or rationalism, on the other hand al-Ghazali talked about a state of knowledge with which all human born, this state called "Fitra". It is a state of natural quality by which we posses immediate recognition about the Creator of this world. Al-Ghazali, as usual, derived this information purely from the Qur'an in Surat al-A'raf:

"And (remember) when your Lord brought forth from the children of Adam, from their Ions, their seed (or from Adam's Ion his offspring) and made them testify as to themselves (saying): "Am I not your Lord?"
They said: "Yes! We testify" Lest you should say on the day of Resurrection: 'Verily, we have been unaware of this.'." (*Qur'an, 7: 172*)

This Fitra guides mankind not only to the knowledge of the Creator, but also to the Oneness of this Creator:

"So set you (O Muhammad) your face toward the religion (of pure Islamic Monotheism) Hanif (worship none but Allah Alone).

Allah's Fitra (i.e. Allah's Islamic Monotheism) with which He has created mankind." *(Qur'an, 30:30)*

The recognition from fitra could be enhanced by sense experience and reasoning, however traditions of non-monotheistic beliefs might cover up this fitra preventing it from flourishing and sublime toward its Creator. From the tradition of the prophet Muhammad (pbuh) there is a narration of him saying:

"Every infant is born endowed with the fitra: then his parents make him Jew or Christian or Magian."

Al-Ghazali in this reading will follow up from fitra to senses, and from senses to reason, and from reason to prophecy and revelation, and then to Sufis experience in having relationship with the Creator.

Reading from Al-Ghazali

DELIVERANCE FROM ERROR
[On his Methodological Doubt and his Journey of Seeking Knowledge.][211]

"I saw that the children of Christians always grew up embracing Christianity, and the children of Jews always grew up adhering to Judaism, and the children of Muslims always grew up following the religion of Islam. I also heard the tradition related from the Apostle of God-God's blessing and peace be upon him!-in which he said: "Every infant is born endowed with the fitra: then his parents make him Jew or Christian or Magian Consequently I felt an inner urge to seek the true meaning of the original fitra, and the true meaning of the beliefs arising through slavish aping of parents and teachers. I wanted to sift out these uncritical beliefs, the beginnings of which are suggestions imposed from without since there are differences of opinion in the discernment of those that are true from those that are false.

So I began by saying to myself: "What I seek is knowledge of the true meaning of things. Of necessity, therefore, I must inquire into just what the true meaning of knowledge is." Then it became clear to me that sure and certain knowledge is that in which the thing known is made so manifest that no doubt clings to it, nor is it accompanied by the possibility of error and deception, nor can the mind even suppose such a possibility. Furthermore, safety from error must accompany the certainty to such a degree that, if someone proposed to show it to be false-for example, a man who would turn a stone into gold and a stick into a snake-his feat would not induce any doubt or denial. For if I know that ten is more than three, and then someone were to say: "No, on the contrary, three is more than ten, as is proved by my turning this stick into a snake-and if he were to do just that and I were to see him do it, I would not doubt my knowledge because of his feat. The only effect it would have on me would be to make me wonder how he could do such a thing. But there would be no doubt at all about what I knew!

---

[211] Al-Ghazali (1980): pp. 55-58, and 78-79.

I realized, then, that whatever I did not know in this way and was not certain of with this kind of certainty was unreliable and unsure knowledge, and that every knowledge unaccompanied by safety from error is not sure and certain knowledge.

The Avenues to Sophistry and Skepticism

I then scrutinized all my cognitions and found myself devoid of any knowledge answering the previous description except in the case of sense-data and the **self-evident truths**. So I said: "Now that despair has befallen me, the only hope I have of acquiring an insight into obscure matters is **to start from things that are perfectly clear**, namely sense-data and the **self-evident truths.[212]** Hence I must first study these thoroughly in order to reach a sure answer to these questions: Is my reliance on sense data and my safety from error in the case of self-evident truths of the same kind as that which I formerly had regarding the dicta of authority, and of the same kind as that which most men have regarding speculative matters?" Or is it a verifiable safety containing no deception or danger?"

With great earnestness, therefore, I began to reflect on my sense-data to see if I could make myself doubt them. This protracted effort to induce doubt finally brought me to the point where my soul would not allow me to admit safety from error even in the case of my sense-data. Rather it began to be open to doubt about them and to say: "Whence comes your reliance on sense-data? The strongest of the senses is the sense of sight. Now this looks at a shadow and sees it standing still and motionless and judges that motion must be denied. Then, due to experience and observation an hour later it knows that the shadow is moving, and that it did not move in a sudden spurt, but so gradually and imperceptibly that it was never completely at rest. Sight also looks at a star and sees it as something small, the size of a dinar; then geometrical proofs demonstrate that it surpasses the earth in size. In the case of this and of similar instances of sense-data the sense-judge makes its

---

212 Compare this to Descartes methodological doubt. Descartes used words such as "clear and distinct". Emphasis and footnote are mine.

judgments, but the reason-judge refutes it and repeatedly gives it the lie in an incontrovertible fashion."

Then I said: "My reliance on sense-data has also become untenable. Perhaps, therefore, I can rely only on those rational data which belong to the category of primary truths, such as our asserting that 'Ten is more than three,' and 'One and the same thing cannot be simultaneously affirmed and denied,' and 'One and the same thing cannot be incipient and eternal, existent and nonexistent, necessary and impossible.'

Then sense-data spoke up: 'What assurance have you that your reliance on rational data is not like your reliance on sense-data? Indeed, you used to have confidence in me. Then the reason-judge came along and gave me the lie. But were it not for the reason-judge, you would still accept me as true. So there may be, beyond the perception of reason, another judge. And if the latter revealed itself, it would give the lie to the judgments of reason, just as the reason-judge revealed itself and gave the lie to the judgments of sense. The mere fact of the nonappearance of that further perception does not prove the impossibility of its existence.'

For a brief space my soul hesitated about the answer to that objection, and sense-data reinforced their difficulty by an appeal to dreaming, saying: "Don't you see that when you are asleep you believe certain things and imagine certain circumstances and believe they are fixed and lasting and entertain no doubts about that being their status? Then you wake up and know that all your imaginings and beliefs were groundless and unsubstantial. So while everything you believe through sensation or intellection in your waking state may be true in relation to that state, what assurance have you that you may not suddenly experience a state which would have the same relation to your waking state as the latter has to your dreaming, and your waking state would be dreaming in relation to that new and further state?" If you found yourself in such a state, you would be sure that all your rational beliefs were unsubstantial fancies.

It may be that this state beyond reason is that which the Sufis claim is theirs. For they allege that, in the states they experience when they concentrate inwardly and suspend sensation, they see phenomena which are not in accord with the normal data of reason. Or it may be that this state is death. For the Apostle of God-God's blessing and peace be upon him!-said: 'Men are asleep: then after they die they awake So perhaps this present life is a sleep compared to the afterlife. Consequently, when a man dies, things will appear to him differently from the way he now sees them, and thereupon he will be told: 'But We have removed from you your veil and today your sight is keen' (50.21/22)."

When these thoughts occurred to me they penetrated my Soul, and so I tried to deal with that objection. However, my effort was unsuccessful, since the objection could be refuted only by proof. But the only way to put together a proof was to combine primary cognitions. So if, as in my case, these were inadmissible, it was impossible to construct the proof. This malady was mysterious and it lasted for nearly two months. During that time I was a skeptic in fact, but not in utterance and doctrine. At length God Most High cured me of that sickness. My soul regained its health and equilibrium and once again I accepted the self-evident data of reason and relied on them with safety and certainty. But that was not achieved by constructing a proof or putting together an argument. On the contrary, it was the effect of a light which God Most High cast into my breast. And that light is the key to most knowledge.

Therefore, whoever thinks that the unveiling of truth depends on precisely formulated proofs has indeed straitened the broad mercy of God. When the Apostle of God-God's blessing and peace be upon him!- was asked about "the dilation" in the Most High's utterance: 'So he whom God wishes to guide aright, He dilates his breast for submission to Himself (i.e. to embrace Islam)' (6.125), he said: 'It is a light which God casts into the heart.' Then someone said: 'And what is the sign of it?' He replied: 'Withdrawal from the mansion of delusion and turning to the mansion of immortality.'

The aim of this account is to emphasize that one should be most diligent in seeking the truth until he finally comes to seeking the unseekable. For primary truths are unseekable, because they are present in the mind; and when what is present is sought, it is lost and hides itself. But one who seeks the unseekable cannot subsequently be accused of negligence in seeking what is seekable." ....

Sources of knowledge
&
The limits of Pure Reason[213]

"The True Nature of Prophecy and the Need All Men Have for It"

"Know that man's essence, in his original condition, is created in blank simplicity without any information about the 'worlds' of God Most High. These 'worlds' are so many that only God Most High can number them, as He has said: 'No one knows the hosts of your Lord but He' (Qur'an, 74: 31). Man gets his information about the 'worlds' by means of perception. Each one of his kinds of perception is created in order that man may get to know thereby a 'world' of the existents-and by 'worlds' we mean the categories of existing things.

The first thing created in man is the sense of touch: by this he perceives certain classes of existents such as heat and cold, wetness and dryness, smoothness and roughness, etc. But touch is definitely unable to perceive colors and sounds; indeed, these are, as it were, nonexistent with respect to touch.

Next the sense of sight is created for man, by whom he perceives colors and shapes: this is the most extensive of the 'worlds' of the sensible.

Then the sense of hearing is opened, so that man hears sounds and tones.

Next the sense of taste is created for man; and so on until he passes beyond the 'world' of the sensible. Then, when he is about seven years old, discernment is created for him. This is another of the stages of

---

[213] Al-Ghazali (1980): pp. 83-88.

man's existence; in it he perceives things beyond the 'world' of the sensible, none of which are found in the 'world' of sensation.

Then man ascends to another stage, and intellect is created for him, so that he perceives the necessary, the possible, the impossible, and things not found in the previous stages.

Beyond the stage of intellect there is another stage. In this another eye is opened, by which man sees the hidden, and what will take place in the future, and other things, from which the intellect is as far removed as the power of discernment is from the perception of intelligible and the power of sensation is from things perceived by discernment. And just as one able only to discern, if presented with the things perceptible to the intellect, would reject them and consider them outlandish, so some men endowed with intellect have rejected the things perceptible to the prophetic power and considered them wildly improbable. That is the very essence of ignorance! For such a man has no supporting reason except that it is a stage he himself has not attained and for him it does not exist: so he supposes that it does not exist in itself.

Now if a man born blind did not know about colors and shapes from constant report and hearsay, and were to be told about them abruptly, he would neither understand them nor acknowledge their existence. But God Most High has brought the matter within the purview of His creatures by giving them a sample of the special character of the prophetic power: sleeping. For the sleeper perceives the unknown that will take place, either plainly, or in the guise of an image the meaning of which is disclosed by interpretation.

If a man had had no personal experience of dreaming and someone were to tell him: "There are some men who fall down unconscious as though they were dead, and their perception, hearing, and sight leave them, and they then perceive what is 'hidden,' he would deny it and give apodictic proof of its impossibility by saying: 'The sensory powers are the causes of perception. Therefore one who does not perceive such things when his powers are present and functioning a fortiori will not perceive them when his powers are suspended.'

This is a kind of analogy which is belied by factual experience and observation. Just as the intellect is one of man's stages in which he receives an 'eye' by which he 'sees' various species of intelligible from which the senses are far removed, the prophetic power is an expression signifying a stage in which man receives an 'eye' possessed of a light, and in its light the unknown and other phenomena not normally perceived by the intellect become visible.

[The Possibility of Prophecy and its Real Meaning]

Doubt about prophecy touches either its possibility, or its actual existence, or its belonging to a specific individual.

The proof of its *possibility* is its existence. And the proof of its existence is the existence in the world of knowledge which could not conceivably be obtained by the intellect alone-such as the knowledge of medicine and of astronomy. For whoever examines such knowledge knows of necessity that it can be obtained only by a divine inspiration and a special help from God Most High, and that there is no empirical way to it. Thus among astronomical phenomena there is a phenomenon which occurs only once every thousand years. How, then, could knowledge of that be obtained empirically? The same is true of the properties of medicaments.

From this proof it is clearly within the bounds of possibility that a way exists to grasp these things which the intellect does not normally grasp. This is what is meant by prophecy. Not that prophecy signifies such knowledge only. Rather, the perception of this kind of thing which is outside the things normally perceived by the intellect is one of the properties of prophecy. It also has many other properties; what we have mentioned is a drop from its sea. We have mentioned it only because you have in your own experience an example of it, viz. the things you perceive while asleep. You also have knowledge of the same sort in medicine and astronomy. These, too, belong to the category of the prophets' apologetic miracles-the blessing and peace of God be upon them! But men endowed with intellect have no way at all of attaining such knowledge by intellectual resources alone.

The properties of prophecy beyond those just mentioned can be perceived only by fruitional experience as a result of following the way of Sufism. For you have understood that only because of an example you have been given, viz. sleep; were it not for this, you would not assent to that. If, then, the prophet has a special quality of which you have no example and which you in no wise understand, how can you find it credible? Assent comes only after understanding. But the example needed occurs in the first stages of the way of Sufism. Then, through this example, one obtains a kind of fruit ional experience commensurate with the progress made plus a kind of assent to what has not been attained based on analogy with what has been attained."' So this single property we have mentioned is enough ground for you to believe in the basis of prophecy.

If it occurs to you to doubt whether a particular individual is a prophet or not, certainty will be gained only by becoming acquainted with his circumstances, either through personal observation or from impeccable tradition and hearsay. For when you are familiar with medicine and jurisprudence, you can recognize jurisprudents and physicians by observing their circumstances and also by hearing their dicta, even if you have not seen them yourself. Moreover, you are quite capable of knowing that al-Shafe'i (God's mercy be upon him) was a jurisprudent and that Galen was a physician-and that with a knowledge based on fact, not on uncritical acceptance of someone's say-so-by your learning something about jurisprudence and medicine and then per-using their writings and works: thus you will acquire a necessary knowledge of their scientific status.

Likewise, when you understand the meaning of prophecy and devote much study to the Qur'an and the traditions, you will acquire the necessary knowledge of the fact that Muhammad-God's blessing and peace be upon him!-had attained the loftiest level of prophecy. Then back that up by sampling what he said about the acts of worship and their effect on the purification of hearts. Consider, for example, how right he was-God's blessing and peace be upon him!-in his saying: 'Whoever acts according to what he knows, God will make him heir to what he does not know'; and how right he was in his saying: 'Whoever aids an unjust man, God gives the latter dominion over him'; and how right he was in his saying: 'Whoever reaches the point where all his cares are a single care, God Most High will save him from all cares in this life and the next.' When you have had that experience in a thousand, two thousand, and many thousands of instances, you will have acquired a necessary knowledge which will be indisputable.

Therefore, seek sure and certain knowledge of prophecy in this way, not from the changing of the staff into a serpent and the splitting of the moon. For if you consider that sort of thing alone, without adding the many, indeed innumerable, circumstances accompanying it, you might think it was a case of magic and deception, and that it was a 'leading astray' coming from God Most High, because 'He leads astray whom He will and rightly guides whom He will' (16.95/93), and the problems connected with apologetic miracles would confront you.

Furthermore, if your faith were based on a carefully ordered argument about the way the apologetic miracle affords proof of prophecy, your faith would be broken by an equally well-ordered argument showing how difficulty and doubt may affect that mode of proof. Therefore, let such preternatural events be one of the proofs and concomitants that make up your total reflection on the matter. As a result, you will acquire such necessary knowledge that you will be unable to cite its specific basis. It would be like the case of a man to whom many men report an unimpeachable tradition. He cannot aver that his sure and certain knowledge is derived from the statement of one specific individual. Rather, he does not know whence it comes: but it is neither outside the group testimony, nor is it due to pinpointing individuals. This, then, is the strong belief based on knowledge. Fruit ional experience, on the other hand, is comparable to actual seeing and handling: this is found only in the way of the Sufis.

This much, then, of the real meaning of prophecy is sufficient for my present purpose. Now I shall mention the reason why it is needed.

[The Heart as a faculty of Knowledge
&
Prophets as Doctors of Hearts]

For nearly ten years I assiduously cultivated seclusion and solitude. During that time several points became clear to me of necessity for reasons I cannot enumerate-at one time by fruitional experience, at another time by knowledge based on apodictic proof, and again by acceptance founded on faith. These points were: that man is formed of a body and a heart-and by the 'heart' I mean the essence of man's spirit which is the seat of the knowledge of God, not the flesh which man has in common with corpse and beast; that his body may have a health which will result in its happiness, and a malady in which lies its ruin; that his heart, likewise, may have a health and soundness-and only he will be saved 'who comes to God with a sound heart' (Qur'an, 26: 89), and it may have a malady which will lead to his everlasting perdition in the next life, as God Most High has said: 'In their hearts is a malady' (Qur'an, 2: 9-10); that ignorance of God is the heart's deadly poison, disobedience to God its incapacitating malady, knowledge of God Most High its quickening antidote, and obedience to Him by resisting passion its healing remedy; that the only way to treat the heart by removing its malady and regaining its health lies in the use of remedies, just as that is the only way to treat the body.

Remedies for the body effectively procure health because of a property in them which men endowed with intellect cannot perceive by virtue of their intellectual resources, but rather it must be the object of blind obedience to the physicians who learned it from the prophets, who, because of the special attribute of prophecy, came to know the special properties of things. In a similar fashion it became necessarily evident to me that the reason for the effectiveness of the remedies of the acts of worship, with their prescriptions and determined quantities ordained by the prophets, cannot be perceived by means of the intellectual resources of men endowed with intellect. On the contrary, they must be the object of blind obedience to the prophets who perceived those qualities by the light of prophecy, not by intellectual resources.

Moreover, just as medicaments are composed of mixtures of elements differing in kind and quantity, some of them being double others in weight and quantity, and just as the difference of their quantities is not without a profound significance pertaining to the kind of the properties, so, likewise, the acts of worship, which are the remedies of hearts, are composed of actions differing in kind and quantity, so that a prostration is the double of a bowing, and the morning prayer is half as long as the afternoon prayer. This difference is not without a profound significance which pertains to the kind of the properties knowable only by the light of the prophecy. Very stupid and ignorant would be the man who would wish to discover in them a wisdom by means of reason, or who would suppose that they had been mentioned by chance, and not because of a profound divine significance in them which requires them to be such because of the special property in them. And just as in medicaments there are basic elements which are their chief ingredients and additional substances which are their complements, each of them having a special effect on the workings of their basic elements, so, likewise, supererogatory prayers and customary practices are complements for perfecting the effects of the principal elements of the acts of worship.

In general, then, the prophets (Peace be upon them!) are the physicians for treating the maladies of hearts. By its activity reason is useful simply to acquaint us with this fact, to bear witness to prophecy by giving assent to its reality, to certify its own blindness to perceiving what the 'eye' of prophecy perceives, and to take us by our hands and turn us over to the prophets as blind men are handed over to guides and as troubled sick men are handed over to sympathetic physicians. To this point reason can proceed and advance, but it is far removed from anything beyond that except for understanding what the physician prescribes.

These, then, are the insights we gained with a necessity analogous to direct vision during the period of our solitude and seclusion."

15. Al-Ghazali's Conception of Reality

Ontological Levels of Reality	Epistemology Levels of Knowing
Religious Reality	1. Revelation 2. Prophecy 3. The Heart
Metaphysical Reality	Human Intellect (Logical reasoning)
Mathematical Reality	Human Intellect (Abstraction, logical reasoning, and demonstration)
Physical Reality	Human Senses and Intellect (Observation, experimentation, generalization, and abstraction)
Fitra (Instilled in man by God since first creation)	Internal and Intuitive Ability of knowing God

16. The Influence of Al-Ghazali on Descartes

The philosophical writings of al-Ghazali had an influence on the French philosopher Rene Descartes (1596-1650). In his book *Meditations*, Descartes discussed a method of doubt very similar to that of al-Ghazali; doubting sensory experience and proceeding to doubt ideas that come from reason. Under the influence of al-Ghazali, Descartes set requirements according to which ideas can be accepted. In his methodological doubt he emphasized that he will only accept ideas that are clear and distinct. In this short section I can only present portions of the writings of Descartes from his book *Meditations*: 1, 2, and 6.[214]

Descartes: *Meditations* (1596-1650)	Al-Ghazali: *al-Munqidh* (1058-1111)
1. Several years have now passed since I first realized how numerous were the false opinions that in my youth I had taken to be true, and thus how doubtful were all those that I had subsequently built upon them. And thus I realized that once in my life I had to raze everything to the ground and begin again from the original foundations, if I wanted to establish anything firm and lasting in the sciences. But the task seemed enormous, and I was waiting until I reached a point in my life that was so timely that no more suitable time for undertaking these plans action would come to pass.	**1.** For nearly ten years I assiduously cultivated seclusion and solitude. During that time several points became clear to me of necessity for reasons I cannot enumerate- at one time by fruitional experience, at another time by knowledge based on apodictic proof, and again by acceptance founded on faith. These points were: that man is formed of a body and a heart.

---

[214]*Meditations, In* Ariew & Watkins (2000): Vol. 1. pp.27-29 & 50-51.

2. I should withhold my assent no less carefully from opinions that are not completely certain and indubitable than I would from those that are patently false. For this reason, it will suffice for the rejection of all these opinion, if I find in each of them some reason for doubt.

3. But at least they do contain everything I clearly and distinctly understand.

First, I know that all the things that I clearly and distinctly understand can be made by God such as I understand them.

4. But now, having begun to have a better knowledge of myself and the author of my origin, I am of the opinion that I must not rashly admit everything that I seem to derive from the senses, but neither, for that

2. So I began by saying to myself: "What I seek is knowledge of the true meaning of things. Of necessity, therefore, I must inquire into just what the true meaning of knowledge is." Then it became clear to me that sure and certain knowledge is that in which the thing known is made so manifest that no doubt clings to it, nor is it accompanied by the possibility of error and deception, nor can the mind even suppose such a possibility.

3. I then scrutinized all my cognitions and found myself devoid of any knowledge answering the previous description except in the case of sense-data and the self-evident truths. So I said: "Now that despair has befallen me, the only hope I have of acquiring an insight into obscure matters is to start from things that are perfectly clear, namely sense-data and the self-evident truths.

4. With great earnestness, therefore, I began to reflect on my sense-data to see if I could make myself doubt them. This protracted effort to induce doubt finally brought me to the point where my soul would not allow

matter, should I call everything into doubt.

me to admit safety from error even in the case of my sense-data. Rather it began to be open to doubt about them and to say: "Whence comes your reliance on sense-data?

5. But perhaps even though the senses do sometimes deceive us when it is a question of a very small and distant things.

5. The strongest of the senses is the sense of sight. . .... Sight also looks at a star and sees it as something small, the size of a dinar; then geometrical proofs demonstrate that it surpasses the earth in size.

6. Still there are many other matters concerning which one simply can not doubt.

For whether I am awake or asleep two plus three makes five.

6. Then sense-data spoke up: 'What assurance have you that your reliance on rational data is not like your reliance on sense-data? Indeed, you used to have confidence in me. Then the reason-judge came along and gave me the lie. But were it not for the reason-judge, you would still accept me as true. So there may be, beyond the perception of reason, another judge. And if the latter revealed itself, it would give the lie to the judgments of reason, just as the reason-judge revealed itself and gave the lie to the judgments of sense. The mere fact of the nonappearance of that further perception does not prove the impossibility of its existence.'

7. Let us assume then, for the sake of argument that we are dreaming and that such particulars as these are not true: that we are opening our eyes moving our head and extending our hands.

Accordingly, I will suppose not a supremely good God, the source of truth, but rather an evil genius, supremely powerful and clever, who has directed his entire effort at deceiving me.

Moreover, I find myself faculties for certain special modes of thinking, namely the faculties of imagination and sensing. I can clearly and distinctly understand myself in my entirety without these faculties, but not vice versa: I cannot understand them clearly and distinctly without me, that is, without a substance endowed with understanding in which they inhere, for they include an act of understanding in their formal concept.

7. For a brief space my soul hesitated about the answer to that objection, and sense-data reinforced their difficulty by an appeal to dreaming, saying: 'Don't you see that when you are asleep you believe certain things and imagine certain circumstances and believe they are fixed and lasting and entertain no doubts about that being their status?
Then you wake up and know that all your imaginings and beliefs were groundless and unsubstantial. So while everything you believe through sensation or intellection in your waking state may be true in relation to that state, what assurance have you that you may not suddenly experience a state which would have the same relation to your waking state as the latter has to your dreaming, and your waking state would be dreaming in relation to that new and further state?' If you found yourself in such a state, you would be sure that all your rational beliefs were unsubstantial fancies.

Al-Ghazali
(450-505 H. / 1058-1111 C.E.)

Metaphysics

The Existence of God

17. The World cannot be Eternal

The first argument in al-Ghazali's book *Tahafut al-Falasifah (The Incoherence of the Philosophers)* is intended to be a refutation of the claim of the philosophers that the world is eternal, especially against al-Farabi, Ibn Sina, and Aristotle.

Al-Ghazali tried to show the inconsistency of the philosophers, their incoherence, and thus their logical contradiction in the field of metaphysics.

I will present his argument in his language and his way with some changes and modifications when it is needed for the sake of clarifications. I am presenting his argument in a form of dialogue between him and the philosophers. The dialogue goes in the following way:[215]

The First Proof

The philosophers:
"It is absolutely impossible for a temporal to proceed from an eternal."
In other words; it is impossible for our world to become and be created by God, and thus it is eternal, and eternally co-exist with God.

Al-Ghazali:
Why it is impossible?

---

[215] Al-Ghazali (1997): the discussion based on this book "The First Proof " pp. 13-36. Also another translation of his *Incoherence* is al-Ghazali (1958) by Kamali. I used this translation for comparison to present the best understanding of his text.

The Philosophers:
1. Because if we suppose the Eternal without the world proceeding from Him, then the world's existence would have been a pure possibility.

2. If thereafter the world were to come into existence, then a giver of preponderance or preference would:
>   A - either have come into existence anew, or
>   B - would not have come into existence anew.

3. But if no giver of preponderance or preference had come into existence anew (B), then the world would have then remained in a state of pure possibility.

4. But we know for sure that the world is not in pure possibility, because it does actually exist.

Therefore, the world (as a temporal world) did not proceed from the Eternal, there was no giver of preponderance.

The philosophers continue questioning the other part of the argument (A):
If a giver of preponderance did come into existence anew (A), then the question arises:
"Who originated this giver of preponderance and why did it originate now and not earlier?"
The question regarding the giver of preponderance persists.

The philosophers continue with another way regarding the eternity of the world:
If the states of the Eternal are similar, then
>   1- either nothing at all comes into existence through Him, or
>   2- else it comes into existence perpetually:

Because it is impossible to differentiate an existing divine state of refraining to act from another existing divine state of commencing.

The philosophers elaborate on the issue considering the "will":

1. "Why was the world not created before its creation?"

This cannot be ascribed to His inability to originate it earlier, or to the impossibility of an earlier creation. For this would lead the Eternal to change from impotence to power and the world to change from impossibility to possibility, both of which are impossible.

Also it cannot be said that earlier there was no purpose, a purpose thereafter coming into existence anew.

2. Rather the closest imaginative thing is to say: "He did not will it's existence before this,"

But which it follows that one must say: "Its existence occurred because He became a willer of its existence after not having been a willer," in this case the will would have been created.

3. But it's (the will) creation in Himself is impossible since He is not the receptacle of created things, and its creation not in Himself would not make Him a willer.
The difficulty persist regarding the source of its creation, whence did the source originate and why did it come into existence now and not earlier?

If a temporal event without an originator is allowed, then let the world be an originated thing without maker.
If the world is originated through God's origination of it, then why was it originated now and not earlier?
Is this because of a lack of an instrument, power, purpose, or nature, such that once these are replaced by existence, the world came to be originated now? But then the same difficulty recurs. Or is its not being created earlier due to the lack of a will?
But then the will would require another will to create it and likewise the first will and so on, regressing infinitely.

4. Thus it is now ascertained through incontrovertible argument that the proceeding of the temporal from the Eternal without a change of state of affairs in the Eternal by way of power, instrument, time, purpose, or nature is impossible.

5. Since any change of state in the Eternal is impossible.

6. Therefore, as long as the world exists and it's origination in time is impossible, it's past eternity stands necessarily established.

Al-Ghazali:
The objection to their proof is in two respects

Al-Ghazali's First Objection
With what kind of argument would you deny one who says:

The world was temporally created by an eternal will that decreed its existence at the time in which it came to be.

The preceding nonexistence continued to the point at which the world began.

The Philosophers:
Then why didn't the world come into existence earlier?

Al-Ghazali:
Its existence prior to this was not willed and for this reason did not occur. At the time in which the world was created it was willed by the eternal will to be created at that time and for this reason it was created then.
However, Al-Ghazali insists on his legitimate question:

What is there to disallow such a belief and what would render it impossible?

The philosophers:
This is impossible, and the impossibility is very clear.

Al-Ghazali:
How?

The Philosophers:
1. Because the temporal occurrence is necessitated and caused.

2. It is impossible for that which necessitates a thing to exist with all the conditions of its being necessitating, all the conditions of its principles and causes fulfilled, such that nothing at all remains awaited, and then for the necessitated effect to be delayed.

3. On the contrary, the existence of the necessitated effect, when the conditions of the necessitating cause are fulfilled, is <u>necessary</u> and its delay <u>impossible</u> in accordance with the impossibility of the existence of the necessitated effect without the necessitating cause.

Clarification:
The philosophers trying to establish and emphasize a kind of *necessary relationship* between the eternal and the existence of the world, in which the existence of one of them is an *implication* of the existence of the other with no temporal dimension.

To deny this necessity is a *logical impossibility* that must be eliminated. In other words it is impossible for the human mind to imagine that the world as temporal (created or came into existence), because its cause is eternal and perfect (the eternal existed, the will existed, its relation to what is willed existed, no willer came into existence anew, no will came into existence anew, and no relation that did not exist, came to exist for the will anew), because all these are changes and the eternal is not a receptacle of changes.

In a logical form:
1. If the eternal exists, then the world *necessarily* co-exists with him.
(Because if you say that the world came later on in time means that the eternal existed for a period of time without creating anything, and then decided to create the world.

But to say this is to say that the eternal is changing.

However, the eternal does not change.

Therefore, the world must be there eternally).

2. According to the philosophers if the world exists (and we can not deny that), it eternally co-exist with the eternal and cannot be created for the reasons given above.

3. If E, then W, $E \supset W$
   If W, then E, $W \supset E$

The Existence of **The Eternal** ----------▶ The Existence of **The World**

The Existence of **The Eternal** ◀---------- The Existence of **The World**

4. Since $E \supset W$ and $W \supset E$

          Therefore, $E \equiv W$

In logic, double conditional statements are not used together. We use equivalence $\equiv$, so the world becomes equivalent to the eternal and both the eternal and the world are eternal.
But this is nothing more than another way of expressing two implications meant to be equivalent.

However, from this approach the philosophers insisted on the issue of the impossibility and they asked further:

How then did the object of will come into existence anew and what prevented its coming into existence anew earlier?

Al-Ghazali:
Do you know the impossibility of an eternal will related to the temporal creation of something through the *necessity of reason* or its *theoretical reflection*?

Clarification:
The first kind of the statement that al-Ghazali is talking about is the one that it is self-evident, that is true always, and it's opposite is contradictory. These statements are subject of rational agreements. Such as a triangle have three angles. It is true by definition.

The second type is obtained by theoretical knowledge, by methods of deductive reasoning, that requires a middle term, and its truth is not necessary although it might be valid reasoning. Such as:

All *men* are mortal
Socrates is a *man*

Therefore, Socrates is mortal

The terms "men" and "man" is called the middle term that makes the connection between the two premises in order to imply a valid conclusion.

Al-Ghazali continues against the philosophers,
The philosopher's *impossibility* lacks logical foundations:
First, according to your language in logic, is the connection between the two terms, i.e., "the eternal will" and "temporal creation" known to you with or without a middle term?
If you claim a middle term, which is the reflective theoretical method, then you must show it. But this you have not shown.

Second, if on the other hand you claim knowing this *impossibility* through the necessity of reason, and it is so clear and self-evident, how is it, then, that those who oppose you do not share this knowledge with you?

Therefore, it is incumbent for you to set up a demonstrative proof according to the condition of logic that would show the impossibility of this. For in all of what you have stated, there is nothing but an expression of unlikelihood and the drawing of an analogy with our resolve and will. This is false because the eternal 'will' does not resemble temporal human intentions.

As regards the sheer deeming of something as unlikely, without demonstrative proof, this is not sufficient.

Clarification:

The core of al-Ghazali's objection is the issue of "impossibility". This is why he shifted the discussion from ontology to epistemology by challenging the epistemological foundation of their metaphysics. This shows that philosophers who are logicians are logically inconsistent and have difficulty in fulfilling the requirements of logic in their metaphysics.

We need to keep in mind that this is the goal that al-Ghazali intended to achieve in his book *Tahafut al-Falasifah (The Incoherence of the Philosophers).* By shaking the epistemological foundation of their argument, al-Ghazali was able to make their proof collapse.

The philosophers replied to him:

We know by the necessity of reason that a necessitating cause with all its conditions fulfilled is inconceivable without a necessitated effect and that the one who allows this is stubbornly defying the necessity of reason.

Al-Ghazali offers an argument based on the spherical motion to prove that the claim of the eternity of the world is contradictory and thus it is impossible:

With what argument would you deny your opponents in as much as they have said the following?

"The world's past eternity is impossible because it leads to affirming circular movements of the heavenly sphere whose number is infinite and whose individual units are innumerable, even though they divide into a sixth, a fourth, a half and so on.

For the sphere of the sun rotates in one year, whereas Saturn's rotates in thirty, so that the rotations of Saturn are three-tenths those of the sun.

Again, the rotations of Jupiter are a twelfth of the rotations of the sun; for it rotates once in every twelve years.

Now, just as the number of the rotations of Saturn is infinite, the number of the solar rotations, although three-tenths of the latter, is also infinite. Indeed, the rotations of the sphere of the fixed stars, which rotates once in every thirty-six thousand years, are infinite, just as the sun's movement from east to west, taking place in a day and a night, is likewise infinite."

If one then were to say:

"This is one of the things whose impossibility is known by the necessity of reason," how would your position differ from his statement?

Another argument from Al-Ghazali:
Indeed, how are you to answer if one were to say:

"Is the number of the rotations even or odd, or
both even and odd, or
neither even nor odd?"

Should you answer either that the number is both even and odd or that it is neither even nor odd? This would again be something whose falsity is known through rational necessity.

If you were to say that the number is even, then how can the infinite be in need of one? If, on the other hand, you answer that it is odd, then how would the infinite be in need of that one which would render it even?

You are then necessarily forced to uphold the statement that it is neither even nor odd.

The philosophers:
It is only the finite that is described as either even or odd, but the infinite is not so described.

Al-Ghazali:
An aggregate composed of units has as has been mentioned, a sixth and tenth which is yet not described as either even or odd. It is something whose falsity is known by necessity without theoretical reflection.

With what argument can you disentangle yourselves from this?

The philosophers:
The place of error lies in your statement that the heavenly movements consist of an "aggregate composed of units"; for these rotations are nonexistent, the past having ceased to exist, the future not yet existing; the 'aggregate' refers to existents that are present, but here there is no such existent.

Al-Ghazali argues that Mathematics has nothing to deal with the perishing moments or movements:
Number divides into the even and the odd, and it is impossible for it to lie outside this division, regardless of whether or not what is enumerated exists and endures or ceases to exist.[216]

---

[216] Al-Ghazali offers another argument based on the idea of the soul:
According to your own principles, it is not impossible that there should be existents that are here and now, individual entities varying in descriptions that are infinite. These are the souls of humans that are separated from bodies after death. These then are existents that are not characterized as even and odd.
With what argument would you deny the statement of someone who says: "The falsity of this is known through the necessity of reason in the same way you claim that the falsity of the connectedness of the eternal will with the act of temporal creation is known through the necessity of reason"? This view of souls is the one chosen by Avicenna.
The Philosophers:
The truth is Plato's view namely that the soul is pre-eternal and one which it is divided only in bodies, and that once it separates from them, returns to its origin and unites.
Al-Ghazali:
This is repugnant, and more worthy to uphold as contrary to rational necessity. For we say: "Is the soul of Zayd identical with the soul of 'Amr, or is it another?"

Al-Ghazali singling out Necessity as the core of the discussion:
The intention of all this is to show that they have not rendered their
opponents unable to uphold belief in the connectedness of the eternal
will with the act of temporal creation, except by invoking rational
necessity. Also that they are unable to disengage from those who in
turn invoke rational necessity against them in those matters opposed to
their own belief. From this they have no escape.

Summarizing the position of al-Ghazali:
We can summarize al-Ghazali's argument in general as follows:

1. If the world were eternal (although it is full of events that come into
existence), then it is possible to find in it events that has no beginning
in time, (as a result the motion of the heavenly sphere must be infinite).

2. But this is impossible, because:
      a. the events of this world come into existence and perish.
      b. Whatever has a beginning must have a cause.

3. Therefore, the implication of this hypothetical statement (If the world
were eternal) is impossible.

The previous discussion was just the first part of the first objection
against the philosophers, and it was totally centered around the

---

If it is stated that it is identical, this would be necessarily false. For each
individual is aware of his self and knows that he is not the self of another.
Moreover, if identical, then both would be equal in having the same cognitions
which are essential attributes of souls and which are included with the soul in
every relation.
If on the other hand you say that it is another, being individuated through
attachments to bodies, we say:
"The individuation of the one that has no magnitude in terms of size and
quantitative measure is known by the necessity of reason to be impossible.
How, then, wall the one become two-nay, a thousand-then revert to becoming
one? This is only intelligible in things that have magnitude and quantity, but
how can that which is not quantitative be divided?"

epistemological foundation of the *impossibility* as Al-Ghazali stated it above.

The following is the second portion of the first part of the first objection in which the philosophers are going to disagree by presenting the issue of the will.

18. Creation, Will, and Time

The philosophers:
This turns against you, because before the world's creation God was able to create by a year or by years, there being no limit to His power. It is as though He waited, not creating, and then created.

What then, of the duration of His refraining from creating; is it finite or infinite?

If you say that it is finite, then the existence of God would be of a finite beginning.

If you say that it is infinite, then a period wherein there are infinite possibilities would have elapsed.

Creation of Time and Duration

Al-Ghazali:
According to us, duration and time are both created.[217]

The philosophers:
The times are equal with respect to the possibility of the will's attachment to any of them.

---

[217] Al-Ghazali (1997): p. 20 he said: We will be clarifying the true answer to this when we dissociate ourselves from their second proof.

What, then, would have differentiated a specific time from what precedes and succeeds it when it is not impossible for any of the prior and posterior times to have been willed as the beginning of creation?

What differentiated one of the two possible from the other with respect to the will's attachment to it? We know by rational necessity that a thing is not distinguished from what is similar to it except through that which specifies. If this were allowed, then it would be permissible for the world, whose existence and nonexistence are equally possible, to originate in time, and the side of existence, similar in terms of possibility to the side of nonexistence, would thus be specified with existence without there being that which would specify it.

If you (al-Ghazali) say that the will specifies it, then the question arises about the will's act of specifying and "why" it specified one possible rather than another.

Al-Ghazali:
1. The world came to existence whence it did, having the description with which it came to exist, and in the place in which it came to exist, through will.
2. This "will" being an attribute whose function is to differentiate a thing from its similar.

3. If this were not its function, then power would be sufficient.
4. But since the relation of power to two contraries is the same and there was an inescapable need for a specifying agent that would specify one thing from its similar, it was said:

"The Eternal has, beyond power, an attribute that has as its function the specifying of one thing from its similar."

5. If asked: "Why did the will specifically relate to one of the two similar?" His question is similar to this:

"Why does knowledge entail as a requirement the encompassing of the object of knowledge as it is?" For to the latter one would reply, "This is because 'knowledge' stands as an expression for an attribute that has this as a function." Similarly:

"Will stand as an expression for an attribute whose function-nay, its essence-is to differentiate a thing from its similar."

The philosophers: two glasses of water
Affirming an attribute whose function is to differentiate a thing from its similar is incomprehensible-indeed, contradictory. For to be similar means to be indiscernible and to be discernible means that it is dissimilar.

Indeed, if in front of a thirsty person there are two glasses of water that are similar in every respect in relation to his purpose of wanting to drink, it would be impossible for him to take either. Rather, he would take that which he would deem better, lighter, closer to his right side if his habit was to move the right hand, or some such cause whether hidden or manifest. Otherwise, differentiating something from its like is in no circumstance conceivable.

Al-Ghazali:
The objection to this argument of the philosophers is in two ways:

The first, is regarding your statement that this is inconceivable: do you know this through rational necessity or through theoretical reflection?

- It is impossible for you to appeal to either of these.
- Moreover, your using our will as an example constitutes a false analogy that parallels the analogy between human and divine knowledge. God's knowledge differs from human knowledge. Why, then, should the difference between the divine and the human in the case of the will be unlikely?

Al-Ghazali continues challenging the philosophers on the issue of the "Divine Will".
With what argument would you then deny one who says that rational proof has led to the establishing of an attribute belonging to God,

exalted be He, whose function is to differentiate a thing from its similar?

Is the issue terminological?
Al-Ghazali presenting a conventional approach to language:
If the term "will" does not correspond to this attribute, then let it be given another name; for there need be no dispute about names, and we ourselves have only used it because the religious law permits its use. Otherwise "will" is conventionally used in language to designate that which has an objective fulfilling a need and there is never such an objective in the case of God. What is intended is the meaning, not the utterance.

Al-Ghazali illustrate the issue of the "will" by an example of two dates:
Even so, in our own human case, we do not concede that the choice between similar things is inconceivable.

Suppose that there are two equal dates in front of someone gazing longingly at them, unable, however, to take both together. *He will inevitably take one of them through an attribute whose function is to render a thing specific, differentiating it from its like.*

All the specifying things you have mentioned by way of goodness, proximity and ease of taking, we can suppose to be absent, the possibility of taking one of the two yet remaining. You are hence left between two alternatives.

You could:
- either say that equality in relation to the individual's purpose is utterly inconceivable, which is sheer foolishness, the supposition of this equality being possible;
- or else, that if the equality is supposed, the man yearning for the dates would ever remain undecided, looking at them but taking neither through pure will and choice that according to you are dissociated from the objective of taking a specific one. This also is impossible, its falsity known by rational necessity.

Therefore, It is inescapable for anyone engaged in theoretical reflection on the true nature of the voluntary act, whether in the realm of the observable or the unseen, *but to affirm the existence of an attribute whose function is to render one thing specifically distinct from its similar.*

The second way of objecting is:
You (the philosophers) in your own doctrine have not been able to dispense with the rendering one of two similar specifically distinct, for you hold the world to have come into being through its necessitating cause, having specific configurations similar to their opposites. Why has it been specified with certain aspects and not others, when the impossibility of differentiating one thing from its similar as you uphold does not differ, whether in the voluntary act or in that which follows by nature or by necessity?

The Philosophers:
The universal order of the world can only be in the way it has come to be. If the world were smaller or larger than what it is at present, then this order would not be complete. The same holds when speaking of the number of these spheres and stars.

These, then, are not similar, but different, except that the human faculty falls short of apprehending the modes of wisdom pertaining to their quantities and details.

The secret is not apprehended, although their differences are known. It is not unlikely that a thing is differentiated from its opposite by reason of its relation to the established order.

In the case of times, however, they are absolutely similar in relation to possibility and the established order. It is impossible to claim that if the world had been created later or earlier by one moment, the order would be inconceivable. For the similarity of temporal states is known by rational necessity.

Al-Ghazali:
Even though we are able to use a similar argument against you in terms of temporal states, since there are those who say that God created the world at the time which was best for its creation, we will not restrict ourselves to this comparable argument.

Rather, we will force on you, in terms of your own principles, *the admission of rendering specific one similar as distinct from another,* in two instances where it is not possible to suppose a difference between their similar.

- One is the difference of direction of the world's motion.
- The other in assigning the position of the pole in the ecliptic movement.

Regarding the pole:
Heaven is a sphere rotating around two poles as though both are stationary. Now, the heavenly sphere is of similar parts. For it is simple, particularly the highest heaven and the ninth has no stars at all. These two spheres, the ninth and the rest, rotate around two poles, northern and southern.
Thus, we say, *"There are no two opposite points among the points that according to you (the philosophers) are infinite but could be conceived as being the pole."*
Why is it, then, that the northern and southern points have been assigned to be the poles and to be stationary? And why does not the ecliptic line shift, moving with it the two points so that the poles would revert to the two opposite points of the ecliptic?

If, then, there is wisdom in the extent of the largeness of heaven and its shape, *what differentiated the place of the pole from another place,* singling it out to be the pole from the rest of the parts and points *when all the points are similar and all parts of the sphere are equal?*
There is no way out of this for you (the philosophers).

The Philosophers:
Perhaps the position where the point of the pole lies differs from other positions by a peculiarity that renders it suitable to be a place for the pole so as to be rendered stationary. Perhaps, then, that position for the pole has precedence over others for being stationary.

Al-Ghazali:
In this there is a declared admission of a natural inequality of the parts of the first sphere and that it is not of similar parts. This is contrary to your principle, since one of the principles on which you base your proof for the necessity for the heavens to be spherical in shape is that it is a simple nature, similar in its parts, having no inequality: The simplest of the figures is the sphere.

However, the question regarding that peculiarity remains: are the rest of the parts receptive of this peculiarity or not?

If you say, "Yes," then why did this peculiarity attach specifically to one of the similar and not the rest?

The Philosophers:
This peculiarity does not belong to any but that position, the rest of the parts not being receptive of it.

Al-Ghazali:
The rest of the parts, inasmuch as they constitute a body receptive of forms, are necessarily similar. The place is not deserving of that peculiarity by simply being a body or by simply being a heaven. For this intended meaning is shared by all parts of heaven.
It is thus the inescapable conclusion that assigning a particular place with a specific characteristic is:

- either arbitrary or else
- realized through an attribute whose very function is to render one thing more specific than its exact similar.

This is to show that just as it is legitimate for you (the philosophers) to say that the temporal states are equal in their receptivity of the world's occurrence, it is also legitimate for your opponents to say that the parts of heaven are equal in terms of the receptivity of the idea due to which precedence is given to the fixity of one position for the pole as against its replacement. From this there is no escape.

Second is the direction of the motions of the spheres, Al-Ghazali argues:
What is the cause for assigning the direction of the motions of the spheres-some from east to west, some in the opposite direction-this despite the equivalence in direction when the equivalence in direction is similar to the equivalence in times, there being no difference?

The philosophers:
If all the whole of the spheres were to rotate in one direction, then their positions would not differ and the relationships between the stars in terms of being trine, sextine, having conjunction, and the like would not come about. The whole would then be in one state, without any differentiation at all, when in fact these diverse relationships are the principles of temporal events in the world.

Al-Ghazali:
We do not object to the difference in the direction of the movement. On the contrary what we say:
The highest sphere moves from east to west and what is beneath it in the opposite direction. Everything that can be achieved through this is achievable through its opposite-namely, in that the higher would move from west to east and that which is beneath it in the opposite direction, thereby differences taking place.

Now, the directions of the motion after being circular and opposite are equivalent.
Why, then, did one direction differ from another similar direction?

The Philosophers:
The directions are opposite and contrary; how, then, are they similar?

Al-Ghazali:

This is similar to someone's saying that priority and posteriority in terms of the world's coming into existence are contraries, how can one then claim their similarity?

They claim, however, that one knows the similarity of times in relation to the possibility of existence and every beneficial end in existence whose conception is supposed. But then, one can similarly claim that one knows the equivalence in space, position, and direction with respect to the receptivity of motion and every beneficial end related to it.

If, then, they are allowed the claim of difference despite this similarity, their opponents are also allowed the claim of difference in times and configurations.

19. Al-Ghazali's Second Objection

Al-Ghazali:
You deem the occurrence of a temporal event through an eternal improbable when it is incumbent on you to acknowledge it.

1. Because in the world there are temporal events which have causes.
2. If temporal events were to depend on [other] temporal events *ad infinitum,* this would be impossible-this is not the belief of a rational person.
3. If this were possible, you would then have had no need to acknowledge [the existence of] the Maker and affirm a necessary existent who is the ground of [all] the possible [existents].
4. If, then, events have a limit with which their chain terminates.
5. Then this limit would be the Eternal.
6. It is hence inescapable in terms of your (the philosophers) principle to allow the proceeding of a temporal from an eternal.

The Philosophers:
1. We do not deem improbable the proceeding of a temporal event, whichever event this is, from an eternal; rather, we deem improbable the proceeding from an eternal of an event which is a first event.

2. Because the state of coming into existence does not differ from what precedes it with respect to the preponderance of the direction of existence, whether in terms of the presence of a temporal moment, an organ, a condition, nature, purpose, or any cause.

3. But if the event is not the first event, then it is possible [for the temporal event] to proceed from [an eternal] with the temporal occurrence of some other thing such as preparedness in the receptacle, the presence of a suitable time, or something of this sort.

Al-Ghazali:
The question regarding the occurrence of the preparedness, the presence of the [suitable] time, and whatever comes into being anew, remains.

- Either [these occurrences] regress ad *infinitum* or
- It terminates with an eternal from which a first temporal event comes about.

The Philosophers:
1. None of the materials receptive of forms, accidents, and qualities are temporally created.

2. The qualities that come into being in time are the movements of the spheres, i.e., the circular motion, and whatever descriptions relating to it by way of triadic, hexagonal, and quadratic configurations that come into existence anew. These consist of the relation of some parts of heaven and the stars to each other and some to the earth-as with the occurrences that take place by way of astral ascent, appearance in the firmament, the decline from the highest point and greatest distance from the earth by the star's being at its apogee, and its proximity by being at its perigee and inclining away from some climes by being in the north or in the south. This relation is by necessity a concomitant to the circular motion; it is hence necessitated by the circular motion. As regards the events contained in the sublunary sphere namely, the elements with respect to what occurs in them by way of generation and corruption, combination and separation, and transformation from one description to another-all these are events dependent on each other in a lengthy detailed way. In the end, the principles of their causes terminate with the circular heavenly movement, the relations of the stars to each other, and their relation to the earth.

3. The outcome of all this is that the perpetual, eternal circular motion is the basis of all temporal events. That which imparts the circular motion of the heavens is the souls of the spheres. For these are alive, having the same relation to the spheres as our souls to our bodies.

4. The [spheres'] souls are eternal. No wonder, then, that the heavenly motion necessitated by the souls is also eternal.

5. And since the states of the souls are similar, due to their being eternal, the states of the movements become similar; that is, they circulate eternally.

6. It is hence inconceivable for a temporal event to proceed from an eternal except through the mediation of an eternal circular movement that in one respect resembles the Eternal, for He is everlasting, and that in another respect resembles the temporal: for each of its parts that are supposed comes into existence after not being.

7. Hence, inasmuch as the circular movement is temporal in terms of its parts and relationships, it is the principle of temporal events; and inasmuch as it is eternal, of similar states, it proceeds from an eternal soul.

8. Thus, if there are events in the world, there must then be a circular motion.

9. But in the world there are events.

10. Therefore, the eternal circular motion is established.

Al-Ghazali:
This lengthy elaboration does you no good.

The Philosophers:
Why?

Al-Ghazali:
Because, is the circular motion, which is the foundation of all temporal events, temporally originated or eternal?

-   If eternal, how does this foundation become a principle for the first temporal event?

- If temporal, it would require another temporal event, and so on, regressing ad *infinitum*.

The Philosophers:
In one respect it resembles the eternal and in another respect the temporal. Being constant and renewed-that is, it is constant in being renewed, and it's constancy ever renewed.

Al-Ghazali:
Is it the principle of temporal events in as much as it is permanent, or in as much as it is being renewed?

- If in as much as it is permanent, how is it then that it would precede from something permanent whose states are similar to something that occurs at certain times but not others?

- If in as much as it is renewed, what is the cause of the renewal in itself? It would then require another cause and this would regress infinitely.

This is the final word in confirming the necessary absurd consequences of their position.

20. Al-Ghazali on Causality and Miracles

Scientific Method, Logical Necessity, and Miracles

Al-Ghazali was the earliest philosopher to deny the necessary connection between the cause and its effect. His theory of causality had a great impact on the course of philosophical reasoning in the west. Nicolas de Malebranche (1638-1715) reflects this impact through his philosophy of Occasionalism. David Hume (1711-1776) also reflects this impact in his discussion of causality and the problem of justifying induction.[218] This issue became a central topic in philosophy of science. B. Russell presented an analytic approach of discussing it, while Herbert Feigl and Hans Reichenbach discussed a pragmatic justification of induction.

Al-Ghazali discussed causality in his book *The Incoherence of The Philosophers (1997)*, chapter 17, pages 170-181 to which I will be referring in my discussion.

From the opening of his chapter al-Ghazali clearly said:

"The connection between what is habitually believed to be a cause and what is habitually believed to be an effect is not necessary, according to us [al-Ghazali].

But [with] any two things, where "this" is not "that" and "that" is not "this," and where neither the affirmation of the one entails the affirmation of the other nor the negation of the one entails negation of the other, it is not a necessity of the existence of the one that the other

---

[218] The influence of al-Ghazali on Hume in regard to the issue of causality is clear enough. Also Hume was acquainted with Islamic philosophy and Islamic religion, in his *A Treatise on Human Nature* (1739) Hume said: "To begin with contiguity, it has been remarked among the *Mohametans* [Muslims] as well as *Christians* that those pilgrims who have seen *Mecca* or the *Holy Land* are ever after more faithful and zealous believers than those who have not had that advantage." See R. Ariew and E. Watkins (2000): Vol. II. P. 270.

should exist, and it is not a necessity of the nonexistence of the one that
the other should not exist-for example, the quenching of thirst and
drinking, burning and contact with fire, light and the appearance of the
sun, death and decapitation, healing and the drinking of medicine, and
so on to [include] all [that is] observable among connected things in
medicine, astronomy, arts, and crafts."[219]

21. The General Formula of Causality
In order to understand what al-Ghazali saying we need to understand
first causality.

Causality is the relationship between a cause and its effect. It might
take this form:
        If a cause occurs, then its effect must follow.

We can summarize causality by this general formula:

(A) (B) [h (A) ----------▶ h (B)]

For every A and B the happening of A causes the happening of B. This
formula is general enough to be applied in different scientific fields and
we will call it the general scientific formula. In which the logical
symbols can stand for different variables. Let us understand A as
temperature and B as pressure of a gas. Thus, if you increase the
temperature, then you will cause the pressure to be increased too. This
is called Boyle's law. In which there is a causal relationship between
the temperature and the pressure.

Or let A stand for temperature and B for expansion of metal, if you
increase the temperature you cause the metal to expand. After doing
this on different kinds of metals you can easily develop a simple
scientific formula which says:

All metals expand by heating. This general formula is reached by a
method of observation and experimentation, by which we moved from

---

[219] Al-Ghazali (1997): p. 170.

studying empirically many particular cases to a general formula presented in the form of "All". This method called induction, or to be more specific it is imperfect induction.

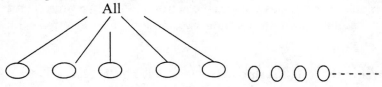

By this method scientists formed their most famous scientific laws and theories, and by this method too scientists claimed that these scientific theories are capable of predicting the future. Let us take this example, based on the general formula of causality: A stands for distance and B for gravity, then any change in the distance will cause change in the force of gravity; the longer the distance is the less gravity, and the shorter the distance the stronger the force of gravity. There is a causal relationship between the force of gravity and the reverse of the distance. This was summarized in Newton's law of gravity. Newton said: "to the same natural effects we must, as far as possible, assign the same causes."

In physics the formula of causality deals with the basic concepts of space, time, and mass. For example to find the cause of motion which is called force in physics we need to know the mass of the body, its first velocity and its second velocity, in addition to knowing the first time of motion and the second time, then the force can be calculated in this way:

$$F = M \frac{(V2 - V1)}{(T2 - T1)}$$

$F = M \times Ac$ (the second law in Newton's physics)

These equations help in knowing the motion of a body in a straight line, however, knowing the momentum ($M = M \times V$) and the place of a body will help in predicting the motion of this body in the future.

But this specific physical formula has been criticized by W. Heisenberg in his principle of uncertainty, noticing that it is applicable in macrophysics but not in microphysics where it is impossible to measure both the motion and the position of an electron at the same time. Thus, we cannot predict the future position and motion of an electron with certainty.

22. Analyzing the Relationship between Cause and Effect

Let us go back to the general formula of causality in order to pursue further analysis.

The general formula states that:

If A (the cause) happened, then (B) the effect happens too.

In this formula we find three things:

- The cause (A)
- The effect (B)
- Relationship between A and B

What kind of relationship is this?

1. It is conditional; (if ..... , then......)
2. It is transitive; (if A causes B, and B causes C, then A is the main cause of both.)
3. It is asymmetrical; (if A causes B, it is impossible for B to cause A.)
4. It is temporal; (A, as a cause, precedes B, the effect, in time.)
5. Is it a necessary relationship?

Al-Ghazali answered: "No" it is not necessary.[220]

But if the answer were no, then how can we explain the continuous connection between the cause and its effect?

---

[220] Malebranche and Hume, following al-Ghazali, would answer negatively too.

Al-Ghazali thought that the connection between cause and effect exists but has two aspects:

First, it is a habitual connection.
Second, it is not necessary.

Al-Ghazali said:

"The connection between what is habitually believed to be a cause and what is habitually believed to be an effect is not necessary, according to us. ...it is not a necessity of the existence of the one that the other should exist, and it is not a necessity of the nonexistence of the one that the other should not exist."

In order to understand what he said I think we have to understand what he meant by "habitual" and "necessity" by giving an example of fire as the cause of burning cotton:

Al-Ghazali said:

'The first position of the philosophers is to claim that the agent of the burning is the fire alone, it being an agent by nature and not by choice-hence incapable of refraining from acting according to what is in its nature after contacting a substratum receptive of it. And this is one of the things that we deny.'[221]

Al-Ghazali replies to the philosophers:

The one who enacts the burning in the cotton, causing separation in its parts, and making it ashes, is God. As for fire, which is inanimate, it has no action.

And what kind of proof do you (the philosophers) have that fire is the agent of burning?

---

[221] Al-Ghazali (1997): p. 171.

Al-Ghazali continues:

They have no proof other than observing the occurrence of burning upon contact with the fire.

Observation, however, only shows the occurrence of burning **at** the time of the contact with the fire, but does not show the occurrence of burning **by** the fire and that there is no other cause for it.[222]

It is clear that existence "**with**" a thing does not prove that it exists "**by**" it.

Al-Ghazali further explain the confusion in this issue by referring to the habit of correlating ideas by saying:

"The **continuous habit** of their occurrence repeatedly, one time after another, fixes unshakably in our minds the belief in their **occurrence according to past habit**."[223] (Emphasis mine)

According to al-Ghazali fire has no intrinsic natural qualities of burning, and cotton has no intrinsic natural qualities to be burnt. If it worked this way, then fire would always be burning out of necessity and cotton would always be burned, again out of necessity, and there would be no way to interrupt this process.

But we know that the course of natural happening some times is interrupted. Therefore, the connection between cause and effect is not necessary.

The philosopher replied that however, we know that they are always connected to each other.

To this al-Ghazali answered: the continuous connection between them that has been always observed from past experience does not justify that they are going to be necessarily connected in the future. In fact

---

[222] See al-Ghazali (1997): p. 171.
[223] Al-Ghazali (1997): p. 174.

their connection, which is undeniable, due to a cause external to them acting upon them.

Al-Ghazali said:

Their connection is due to the prior decree of God, who creates them side by side, not to its being necessary in itself, incapable of separation. On the contrary, it is within [divine] power to create a sense of fullness without eating, to quench the thirst without water, and so on to all connected things.[224]

The philosophers denied the possibility of this and claimed it to be impossible.

So for the burning of cotton, for instance, when in contact with fire, al-Ghazali allowed the possibility of the occurrence of the contact without the burning, and he allowed as possible the occurrence of the cotton's transformation into burnt ashes without contact with the fire.

Al-Ghazali denied the *necessary* connection between cause and effect based on past experience; instead he presented the issue of *possibility* of different happenings in the future. In other word, the past experience cannot justify the necessity of future happening. There are possibilities that may or may not occur.

What does al-Ghazali mean by possible and impossible?

---

[224] Compare with Nicolas Malebranche (1638-1715): as a Cartesian philosopher Malebranche dealt with dualism trying to solve the philosophical problem of the relationship between the two separate substances, i.e., mind and body. He offered the occasional approach that mind and body cannot interact but God enacts the motion of bodies only on occasion of corresponding mental processes. Thus, neither mental processes, nor bodily movements have any intrinsic natural ability to interact as cause and effect and God is the only working agent and the only real cause of all events by creating an occasion for one thing to affect another. The cause does not actually bring about its effect, but only presents an occasion on which God works to produce the effect.

He said:

"The impossible consists in affirming a thing conjointly with denying it, [or] affirming the more specific while denying the more general, or affirming two things while negating one [of them].
What does not reduce to this is not impossible, and what is not impossible is within [divine] power [possible]."[225]

Causality is none of these three categories of impossibilities; therefore, the future relationship between the cause and its effect does not necessarily resemble the relationship that occurred in the past. Causality is not tautological and our knowledge about it is not a priori; causality belongs to the empirical experience. In the realm of empiricism there is no necessity that past experience will justifies the future happenings.

Al-Ghazali's discussion of Necessity and Possibility is related to two kinds of propositions: the analytic and synthetic.

The analytic proposition is true by definition and its negation is self-contradictory. Since its truth is obtained before experience it is prior to experience and is called a priori. Thus it is necessarily true. For example, one can say: "all triangles have three angles" and "all bachelors are unmarried." To then say a triangle has six angles is self-contradictory, similar to saying that a bachelor is married. You need no experience to prove the truth of such statements because they are true by definition. In this sense, a priori proposition is tautological adding no new information; meaning the predicate "has three angles" or "unmarried" gives no new information about the subject "triangle" or "bachelor," it only repeats what was already in the subject.

Thus, there is a necessity here but the proposition is analytic, it is about nothing but itself, while causality is not analytic and it is about a thing happening in the external world.

---

[225] Al-Ghazali (1997): p. 179.

The synthetic statements are derived from experience, and the opposite of which is not contradictory, they cannot be true by necessity, their truth-value can be determined through observation. Knowledge of cause and effect belongs to this type and thus has no necessity to be always the same.

Al-Ghazali said:

As for God's moving the hand of a dead man, setting him up in the form of a living person who is seated and writes so that through the movement of his hand ordered writing follows, [this] in itself is not impossible as long as we turn over [the enactment of] temporal events to the will of a choosing being.
It is only disavowed because of the continuous habit of its opposite occurring.[226]

23. Al-Ghazali on Miracles
Al-Ghazali's attempt to establish that there is no necessary connection between cause and effect was intended to prove that miracles are possible and God can intervene in the natural setting of causes and effects, producing results that did not exist in past human experience. This intervening is called miracles. If the connection between the causes and effects is necessary and is due to their intrinsic powers, then breaking this connection would be impossible by God, and miracles would be impossible too. Our knowledge in regard to the connection between causes and effects is entirely coming through past experience and through induction, and we cannot be certain that the future will resemble the past, and there is no certainty in inductive reasoning, also there is no logical impossibility that the future could be different from the past.

24. Induction and the Uniformity of Nature
Induction is possible because it is based on the connection between causes and effects, the latter is possible only because nature is uniform, and thus future prediction and knowledge can be based on past

---

[226] Al-Ghazali (1997): p. 180.

experience. But how do we know that nature is uniform? Is our knowledge about it a priori or a posteriori? Can we prove that nature is uniform by deductive valid argument or by inductive strong argument?

Some philosophers such as John Stewart Mill thought that the uniformity of nature can be established on the basis of empirical inductive knowledge, but this begs the question, because induction presupposes uniformity of nature in the first place, in order to make any generalization in the form of a scientific law.

Thus induction presupposes causality and causality presupposes the uniformity of nature.

25. David Hume (1711-1776) on Justifying Induction
According to Hume knowledge cannot go beyond experience, but his conception of experience is restricted and limited to sense perception. How much of knowledge, then, we can get from sensory experience about the principle of causality, and how we justify the necessary connection between cause and effect in order to justify future knowledge based on past experience.

Hume thought that there was no evidence for cause and effect relationships more than our perception of a constant correlation between two observable effects. In other words, Hume thought, as al-Ghazali mentioned before, that observation is the ultimate reference of this justification. But observation, as al-Ghazali pointed out before, is not sufficient to prove the necessary connection between cause and effect.

Hume divided human inquiry into two kinds of propositions:
First, Relations of Ideas, such as $3 \times 5 = \frac{1}{2}$ of 30 expresses a relation between these numbers and has dependence on the knowledge of the external world, the opposite of which is contradictory.
Second, Matters of Fact, such as the sun will not rise tomorrow. This proposition implies no contradiction with its opposite that the sun will rise tomorrow. It depends on observation.

But the assurance that the sun will rise tomorrow is only based on past experience and on "the record of our memory" and all reasoning concerning propositions that are related to matters of facts seem to be founded on the relationship of cause and effect.

This relationship of cause and effect alone can go beyond sensory experience and the record of our memory to predict an occurrence such as the sun rising tomorrow. If you ask what kind of assurance that we have for such a prediction, the answer would be that we have it in the record of our past experience.

Hume emphasizes that this is not a priori knowledge, meaning it is not necessary for the cause to produce the effect, it is only related to induction and observation of the past but through which we can not predict the future with certainty.

26. The Pragmatic Justification of Induction

In order to establish that the future will necessarily resemble the past, then we have to establish that there is a necessary connection between the cause and its effect. But this is only based on induction; therefore, we have to justify induction as a valid basis for scientific knowledge.

Induction can be justified by either deductive valid argument or inductive strong argument. However, deductive valid argument is impossible here because its conclusion can make no factual claims that were not already included in the premises, but knowledge of the future is not a factual claim. Therefore, deductive argument cannot justify induction.[227] Then could we justify induction by an inductively strong argument?

If we do so, then we beg the question, because to assume something to be true that is needed to be proven to be true is a fallacy. The main question was how to justify induction in the first place, then how can we use something unjustified to justify itself?

---

[227] Or simply because every thing in the conclusion of a deductive valid argument must be already in the premises, but the future is not included yet.

Herbert Feigl and Hans Reichenbach tried to offer a pragmatic justification of induction. According to Reichenbach:

If any scientific method were guaranteed to be successful, then it would seem rational to accept induction as being successful.

"Suppose that you were forcibly taken into a locked room and told that whether or not you will be allowed to live depends on whether you win or lose a wager. The object of the wager is a box with red, blue, yellow and orange lights on it. You know nothing about the construction of the box but are told that either all of the lights, some of them, or none of them will come on. You are to bet on one of the colors. If the colored light you choose comes on, you live; if not, you die. But before you make your choice you are also told that neither the blue, nor the yellow, nor the orange light can come on without the red light also coming on. If this is the only information you have, then, you will surely bet on red. For although you have no guarantee that your bet on red will be successful (after all, all the lights might remain dark) you know that if any bet will be successful, a bet on red will be successful. Reichenbach claims that scientific inductive logic is in the same privileged position vis-a-vis other systems of inductive logic as is the red light vis-a-vis the other lights."[228]

Reichenbach presented his attempt of rational justification of induction on the basis of uniformity of nature.

1. Either nature is uniform or it is not.
2. If nature is uniform, scientific induction will be successful.
3. If nature is not uniform, then no method will be successful.

    ----

4. Therefore, if any method of induction will be successful, then scientific induction will be successful.

---

[228] Skyrms, Brian (2000): p. 46. Also see H. Reichenbach (1938) *Experience and Prediction.*

This argument is deductively valid. Its first and second premises are both known to be true. How does Reichenbach then support his third premise as true?

Reichenbach said: " Suppose that in a completely chaotic universe, some method, call it method X, were successful. Then there is still at least one outstanding uniformity in nature: the uniformity of method X's success. And scientific induction would discover that uniformity. That is, if method X is successful on the whole, if it gives us true predictions most of the time, then sooner or later the statement "Method X has been reliable in the past" will be true, and the following argument would be judged inductively strong by scientific inductive logic:

Method X has been reliable in the past.

Method X will be reliable in the future.

Thus, if method X is successful, scientific induction will also be successful."[229]

This argument tends to establish reliability or workability, however it begs the question: how to justify that it will be *necessarily* reliable in the future.

---

[229] Skyrms, Brian (2000): pp. 46-47.

CHAPTER SIX

Philosophy in Spain

Ibn Baja, Ibn Tufail, Ibn Rushd

1. Two Philosophical Characteristics

Philosophy in Spain has two major aspects, if not difficulties, one of them related to its social task and the other to the Islamic religion:

First: The lack of social dimension:
After the work of al-Ghazali in criticizing philosophers whose ideas are not Islamic in essence and contradict the Islamic creed, the philosophers lost their impact on the social life of Muslims. The best manifestation of this decline of the social role of philosophy is philosophy in Spain. The philosophy of Ibn Baja and Ibn Tufail, concentrates on the attainment of the happiness of the intellectual person (the philosopher) alone more than any concern about the rest of the society as in Ibn Baja's book *Tadbeer al-Mutawahhed (the conduct of the Solitary)*, or even to talk about a philosopher living in a vacuum, alone with no society as in Ibn Tufail's *Hayy Ibn Yaqdhan*.

Second: The inability to establish a consistent and successful relationship between reason and revelation:
Islamic philosophy in Spain, after al-Ghazali's work, couldn't avoid dealing with the issue of the relationship between reason and revelation ('Aql and Naql) or pure reason and Divine Law. Actually this issue became the central problem of the philosophers' work, it does deal with the very justification of their existence as philosophers in the first place. Ibn Tufail discussed thoroughly the journey of reason in the struggle of Hayy in establishing a steady relationship with a society lives according to the revelation. Ibn Rushed devoted a book to discussing this issue called; *Fasl al-Maqal*.

2. Historical note:

One prince of the Umayyad caliphate named Abdul-Rahman al-Dakhil was able to survive after the 'Abbasid caliphate took over in 749. Al-Dakhil managed to escape and go from Syria to North Africa and then to Spain where he established a small state or Emara.

With al-Hakam II who reigned from 961-976, Cordoba became comparable to Baghdad as a major world center of learning.

In Spain in this era of Islamic philosophy flourished in a unique intellectually diverse society (Muslims, Christians, and Jews) protected by the Islamic divine law and Muslim government. In this cultural environment the Jewish philosopher Maimonides wrote his famous book: *Guide for the Perplexed* in the Arabic Language.

From this area Europe received the most beneficial ideas in sciences and philosophy, especially in twelfth century that helped to progress Europe toward Renaissance in the fourteenth century and toward modernity in the seventeenth century.

The most famous Muslim philosophers in the West (Spain) were Ibn Baja, Ibn Tufail, and Ibn Rushd who we are going to study in the following chapters.

CHAPTER SIX

6. Ibn Baja (Avempace)
(a. 500-533 A.H. / 1106-1138 A.D.)

1. Intellectual Life

Abu Bakr Muhammad bin Yahya known as Ibn Baja, also known as Ibn al-Sayigh, was born in Saragossa around 500 A.H. / 1106 A.D., after the fall of Saragossa to the Christian in 513/1118, he moved to live in Seville and then Granada where he practiced as a physician. Later he moved to Fez in Morocco, worked in politics as a Minster (Wazir) and died in Fez 533 A.H. /1138 A.D. Some historian said that he died poisoned by his enemies after he was accused of atheism.

What we know about his life is very little. Ibn Abi 'Usaibi'a said that Ibn Baja was the most famous in philosophy and science, a distinguished physician, with great knowledge in Arabic and literature, and expert in music. Ibn Baja himself played 'Ud (Lute).

The intellectual environment in Spain was more emphasizing sciences such as mathematics, physics, astronomy, medicine, etc, than philosophy and metaphysics. Ibn Tufail commented on this intellectual state in Spain as follow:

"You should certainly not assume that the extant philosophical writings of Aristotle and Farabi, or Ibn Sina's *The Healing*, are sufficient by themselves, or that any Andalusian [Spanish] has written about it in a satisfactory manner.
Before logic and metaphysics developed here, scholars occupied themselves exclusively with mathematics, in which they reached an advanced level but failed to take matters further. Their successors made some progress in logic and demonstrated an intellectual curiosity in our subject but, nonetheless, were not led to perfect truth. One of them wrote these lines:

The sciences of men are of only two kinds and anything more is impossible to find:

A true, which to try and obtain is futility, and a false which, when mastered, has no utility."[230]

The emphasis on science and not on metaphysics might be due to the following reasons:

First, the new establishment of the Islamic state which was in need of practical ideas and applied science.
Second, which I think is stronger, is the rejection of the futile metaphysics by al-Ghazali, and in turn by the majority of Muslims. Strengthening our thesis, that the second was more influential, is what Ibn Tufail himself said in his book *Hayy Ibn Yaqdhan*, responding to a request regarding theoretical wisdom or philosophy:

"On the other hand, you may wish me to introduce you to this subject through the methods of systematic reasoning. Now that (and may God bless you with closeness unto Him) is something, which it is possible to speak of and to put down in writing but it is rarer than the philosopher's stone, especially in this land of ours. Curiously, only a very few individuals have managed to convey anything at all about it and, even then, only symbolically. The Islamic establishment has given explicit warning and forbidden any involvement."[231]

However, Ibn Baja decided to take sciences to their ultimate questioning and their ultimate rational philosophical horizon in as much as he could, even though it contradicted his Islamic belief. In this sense Ibn Baja was the first philosopher in Spain.

His student Ibn al-Imam said that there was no one who succeeded al-Farabi who was as successful in philosophy as Ibn Baja. The most unique aspect about Ibn Baja's philosophy mentioned by Ibn al-Imam himself, is his deep and sound understanding of Aristotle.[232] This point is worthy of notice in that most of the philosophers in the east

---

[230] Ibn Tufail (1999): pp. 6-7.
[231] Ibn Tufail (1999): P. 6.
[232] See Ibn Abi 'Usaibia' (1882): p. 63.

especially al-Farabi and Ibn Sina understood Aristotle, to a reasonable extent, through Neo-Platonism. While in Spain Muslim philosophers tried to go to Aristotle directly, and thus they captured a good understanding of his philosophy, this approach manifested itself very well in the works of Ibn Rushd who is considered as a major reference in understanding Aristotle until our time.

Ibn Tufail thinks that none of Ibn Baja's contemporaries are equal to him. Ibn Tufail also commented on Ibn Baja when he spoke about: "thinkers who came closer to the truth. Among these, Abu Bakr ibn Sa'igh [Ibn Baja] had the subtlest mind, the soundest reasoning and the most genuine perception. However, was preoccupied with mundane matters and died before the hidden treasures of his wisdom could be disseminated. Most of his extant works, example, *On the Soul* and *The Organization of the Solitary Life*, as well his writings on logic and physics, are incomplete. Those which are complete are merely summaries, as he himself acknowledges. He admits he was able to give expression to his theme in *The Treatise on the Conjunction of the Intellect with Man* only with difficulty and after much effort His style leaves something to be desired, in places and, had time permitted, he might have been inclined to revise."[233]

2. Ibn Baja's Writings

Ibn Baja authored many books on different fields of knowledge such as: physics, geometry, meteorology, medicine, plants, biology, logic, ethics, politics, soul, intellect, and metaphysics. He probably left more than 30 books and treaties as Ibn Abi 'Usaibi'a listed. Most of his famous work translated to Hebrew and Latin. Moses bin Joshua of Narbonne (Musa al-Narbuni) translated Ibn Baja's *Conduct of the Solitary*[234] into Hebrew as an abridged edition to make it available to Jewish scholars. The most important of Ibn Baja's writings, as related to philosophy, are:

---

[233] Ibn Tufail (1999): p. 7.
[234] His translation listed with his commentary on Ibn Tufail's Hayy Ibn Yaqdhan.

1. *Tadbir al-Mutawahhid (Biography of a Solitary Man or Governance of the Solitary)*. Ibn Baja mentioned this book in Risalat al-Ittisal.[235]

2. *Kitab al-Nafs (On the Soul)*. Mentioned in Risalat al-Ittisal.[236]

3. *Risalat Ittisal al-'Aql bil Insan (The Treatise on the Conjunction of the Intellect with Man)*.

4. *Al-Wuquf 'ala al-'Aql al-Fa'al (Knowing The Active Intellect)*.

5. *Al-Wahda wal-Wahid (The Unity and The One)*.

6. *Fil-Mutaharrek (On The Moved)*.

7. *Risalat al-Wada' (A Farwell Letter)*.

3. The Task of Philosophy
Intellect and rationalization was the core theme of Ibn Baja's philosophy. The maximization of the rationality of man is not merely epistemological, but is also intended to have a metaphysical dimension, in which the human connects itself to the active mind, at the end of this process man will attain the highest level of happiness.

4. Theory of Knowledge
Reason is the only reliable source of knowledge. More than that reason is the source of attaining happiness and a good life, morally speaking.
Ibn Baja intentionally emphasized reason as the only reliable source of knowledge in order to criticize any other source of knowledge and happiness such as that of the Sufis, and to reduce the level of sensible knowledge to the natural scientists and the majority (Jumhor) who have no idea about philosophy.
Since the rationality of man cannot be fully attained without connection with the active mind or the agent intellect (the last intellect in charge of the sublunary system) therefore, connection or conjunction (ittisal) of the human mind with the active intellect becomes the main goal of

---

[235] Ibn Baja (1991): p. 159, the Arabic text.
[236] Ibn Baja (1991): p. 162, the Arabic text.

philosophization. To this subject Ibn Baja devoted his effort and his treatise on Ittisal or connection.

Ibn Baja first emphasized that this active intellect is one and is a form without matter.

The human mind cannot achieve the connection with the active intellect and the intelligibles immediately. Man developed from vegetative state of embryo to a state similar to that of an animal by motion and desires, and lastly to a state of rational reflection.

Although the human mind seems to be connected to many material things, but this is only an apparent multiplicity coming from the mind being related to many different material subjects. The human mind is also one in number. By connection with the active intellect the human mind in potentiality becomes mind in actuality through knowing the intelligibles, which Ibn Baja calls al-Suwar al-Ruhaniyya (spiritual forms), by having this knowledge the mind in actuality becomes the main active power of man and the main source of rationality.

In his treatise *al-Wuquf ala al-'Aql al-Fa'al (Knowing the Active Intellect)* Ibn Baja, following al-Farabi, gave some reasons to prove the necessary existence of a form (Surah) not in a body at all, also to prove the existence of a body that does not perish, and to prove the existence of a body that is not generated.[237]

It is not clear what Ibn Baja meant by Surah (form) that is not in a body, whether he meant "form" as a metaphysical principle or "form" in the pure intellectual sense as an idea in the human mind, or spiritual form as he emphasized in his other treatise on Ittisal (conjunction)?

---

[237] Ibn Baja (1991): p. 107. I think that his Arabic language is not strong enough and it is not accurate in the philosophical sense, take for example, what he said here (p.107):

"وجود صورة لافي جسم أصلا ... وأما وجود جسم في لامادة أصلا" "existence of a form which is not in a body ... And in regard to the existence of a body which is not in matter." It is contradictory in the Arabic language to say: Jism (body) not in Madda (matter), because the Arabic word Jism (body) is always a reference to a material or physical magnitude, i.e., with extension and dimensions, to the point that Arab people use the word Jasuma as 'Aduma means become a magnitude or dimensional. See al-Razai (1989): p. 92. The word Jism.

It seems from the first proof that he was discussing the existence of things as elements in the physical sense; while from the fourth proof, at the end, he discussed forms as intellectual perceptions or intelligibles. The followings are his four arguments:

1. The first argument: a form which is not in a body exists because the generated and perishable bodies depends on, and is ruled by the heavenly bodies. The heavenly bodies, which are circular in motion, are neither generated nor perishable. Therefore, "it necessarily follows that there is a form that can not be in matter at all."[238]

Clarification:
What Ibn Baja saying is similar to the saying that the earth, for example, is a corruptible body which rotates around the sun, but rotation is a circular motion, in which the earth follows the motion style of the heavenly bodies, since circular motion according to Ibn Baja is eternal, neither generated because it has no beginning, nor perishable because it has no end, therefore, there is a form that is not in matter at all but it is the very cause of the existence of the earthly motion. With the first argument Ibn Baja injected another one as follow:

Generated and perishable bodies were made of elements or Istaqsat (the four basic elements). These elements are perishable if they were considered in parts and portions, but if we consider these elements in their entirety they are not generated. "The elements taken in their entirety are not generated, but they are generated in portions,"[239] when their portions make different perishable bodies.

Philosophical Implication that Contradicts the Qur'an
What Ibn Baja just said about the elements that are not generated (see the original Arabic text in the footnote) clearly implies that matter is eternal. It does not come into existence as whole or in its entirety (bekulleha), it is not generatable. These elements are the principles of material existence, all bodies (al-mawjudat al-haulaniyya) exist or were generated because of having portions of these elements, thus bodies

---

[238] Ibn Baja (1991): p. 107.
[239] Ibn Baja (1991): p. 107. "فالإسطقسات غير كائنة بكلها كائنة بأجزائها"

come into existence and cease existence by the combination and dis-combination of these parts. The elements themselves are the eternal principles of these bodies and the cause of their existence.

Ibn Baja seems to take the eternity of matter as de facto, he did not even bother with offering an argument to prove that these elements are not generated. Ibn Baja neglected the philosophical inquiry regarding this issue, avoiding the dealing with the Islamic philosophical heritage on the issue of generation and essence, which was one of the top and first concerns of Muslim philosophers. The first philosopher in Islam, al-Kindi, studied the issue thoroughly, by raising the question whether it is possible for a body to generate its own essence.[240]

Ibn Baja contradicts the teaching of the Islamic religion; that God creates matter, and God is the only Creator who created bodies from nothing.

2. The second argument: that which is acted upon has a conjunction with the universal form but not with the specific agent that causes the act. For example, grass comes to be on fire. Its fire only resembles the fire that acted upon it as a universal meaning, without taking anything from the characteristics of the specific fire of the agent, which is particular, it takes the form of the fire only.

3. The third argument: by the imaginative faculty animals seek what is general and universal such as food and water, but not specific or particular food, because their desire is toward nourishment only.
4. The fourth argument: the intellect in actuality understands particular subjects only when these subjects are predicated. The predicate is universal. The particular, as an object, is usually perceived by a faculty other than itself (sensation), and it (the body) is not perception either. Only after the particular is perceived it becomes available to the faculty of imagination, by which we have a perception (image) of the body. The perceiving faculty of imagination is different from the object itself.

---

[240] See al-Kindi's metaphysics.

The case is different in regard to the intellect. The intellect perceives and it perceives its perception by a single faculty. Therefore, it is neither a body nor a power or faculty in the material body. It is thus, a form that is not in matter.

The four arguments mentioned above shows the influence of al-Farabi and Aristotle on Ibn Baja.

5. The main question is: if this mind is one, then how could we explain the multiplicity of individuals who vary in knowledge?

Ibn Baja seems to answer by emphasizing that the intellect is one, but people are multiple in two senses: either by their matter, in which the intellect spreads in a way similar to that of the magnetic power in many metals. Second, they multiply and differ in regard to their relation and connection with the intelligibles, thus they vary in understanding and in comprehension.

6. Levels of Knowledge and Levels of People

The human mind by acquiring knowledge becomes an "acquired intellect" that is perfected by certain knowledge. While by intelligizing the forms this mind becomes in act continuously.

Ibn-Baja used the knowledge of the intelligibles or forms (al-Suwar al-Ruhaniyya) as a criterion of ranking the level of people. He listed them in three ranks:

1. **The majority of people (al-Jumhor)** deal only with sensible or material knowledge, and from these particulars only they can proceed to the universal form. Their comprehension of the intelligibles is for a practical sake of application in professions.

2. **The theoretical reasoner (al-Nuddhar)** and the natural scientists who deal with the knowledge of forms but only as abstracted from sensible matter. But they cannot reach full abstraction. The form still conceived by means of particulars.

These groups of people will not be able rationally to connect themselves or their mind to the agent intellect. The Sufis according to him will not be able to use this rational conjunction too.

3. **The level of the happy (al-Su'ada'):** Those who can see the reality of things as such without any need for any kind of a mediator. The philosophers only can perceive these intelligibles as such. This state is similar to a state of simultaneously seeing the light and the lightened objects. It is a level in which the human mind in actuality and the active mind become a connected and one. Reaching this goal is the ultimate level of attaining happiness. Ibn Baja thought that Aristotle achieved this level.

7. Prophecy and Philosophy

From the three levels above it is clear that Ibn Baja ranked the human intellect superior to revelation. He gave the intellect an absolute value. The only way to reach the truth is by rationalization, or by philosophy, not through revelation. As a result the only one who knows the truth is the philosopher not the prophet. Thus the Creator of man (with His divine knowledge) has no need to reveal to people what He created, philosophers can inform people about it. The knowledge of the prophets is inferior and less in degree than that of the philosophers, because prophets are divinely inspired while philosophers actualized their intellect to know truth.

This not only contradicts the Islamic belief, it also has some internal inconsistencies and difficulties:

First: How do the philosophers reach this level of connection and perception of forms without matter? Is not it by gradually gaining knowledge and by going from the level of particulars to the more abstract and more universal? If the answer is yes, then, philosophers were practicing the way of Jumhor and Nuddar on a theoretical (no application) basis. Was not Aristotle himself a student of Plato, who remained Platonic in regard to pure form in his Metaphysics? Is not it possible that philosophers make mistakes in their knowledge about these forms? Is not it possible that philosophers contradict each other about knowledge of these forms?

Second: Ibn Baja used special terminology in talking about the state of the philosophers. He used the word *"yaroun"* *"they see"*. Seeing is a personal experience that cannot be communicated to others objectively, especially as Ibn Baja is talking about seeing intelligibles or spiritual forms. How can a philosopher convey his experience to others? It is either the philosophers holding themselves superior to the rest of society, and keeping their knowledge to themselves, thus falling into a self canceling stand-point regarding the question of why they seek knowledge of the truth in the first place.

Or their experience with spiritual forms is un-conveyable; in this case their knowledge of the truth is impossible to be communicated with people. If this is the conclusion, then Ibn Baja loses his case with Sufis whom he criticized. Ibn Baja's position in this issue seems at least to be indefensible and incomplete.

8. Proving the Existence of the Soul
The soul is one entity, one unit, simple and uncompounded. It is imperishable as an intellect of the human species. But it is perishable as an individual soul[241]. Because the individual soul is within the form of the body, when the body perishes the soul perishes too, because a form cannot exist in natural beings without matter or hyle. The soul is "the entelechy of a natural organic body."[242] Ibn Baja thinks that the knowledge of the soul precedes all sciences; physical and mathematical. Every science depends upon the science of the soul.[243]

The existence of the soul according to Ibn Baja is self-evident. He said: "[T]he soul is one of the things whose existence is evident; and to ask for an explanation of its existence is like asking for a proof for the existence of nature. Such a question can only be asked by someone who does not know the difference between self-evident knowledge and the knowledge through something else."[244] However, Ibn Baja thinks that some of the known self-evident things, such as the soul, can become more coherent in knowledge through consideration of all that of which

---

[241] As an implication of this point the resurrection will not be for the bodies, but for the soul only. This point already criticized by al-Ghazali because it contradicts the Islamic belief.
[242] Ibn Baja (1956): p. 25.
[243] Ibn Baja (1956): p.18.
[244] Ibn Baja (1956): pp.23-24.

soul is predicated. Ibn Baja thinks this is why Aristotle studied the souls of all animals.

In spite of the self-evident existence of the soul, Ibn Baja gave some argument to prove the existence of the soul and its immortality:

The Natural Proof

Motions are of two kinds voluntary and involuntary. One is from within, the other from outside, the motion that contradicts the natural setting of physical bodies such as moving up instead of moving down, in the case of the motion of a flying bird. This motion is opposite to nature according to Ibn Baja, and this cannot be achieved unless there is "something" internal other than the body that operates as a power. This thing is called the soul (al-Nafs). This force of motion is not natural like that of nature; instead it is a psychological (nafsi) motion (haraka nafsaniyya). Ibn Baja said:

"Natural bodies move to their natural places only when they are in places not natural to them, for, then, there exists in them a capacity according to nature and therefore they have their movements to their places. They only change their directions by accident. For their not being in their natural places is only due to an obstacle that prevents them, but when the obstacle is removed, they move to their natural places. Hence, it has been assumed that the mover in natural bodies is the same as the moved. But this is not so. For in so far as the stone is in potentiality is below and moves inasmuch as it has weight, the thing moved in it is its potentiality of moving downwards, and the mover is the weight. Hence, it moves with one kind of movement that is natural for it.

There is nothing in the thing moved in opposition to the mover, for the thing moved is only its potentiality. This is not the case with those bodies that possess souls. For the thing moved possesses a form for the sake of which it performs a certain action, and either the mover moves them in opposition to their natural action, or moves them according to their nature, e.g. raising the hand and jumping, for through it the body is moved and this is a motion upwards, and therefore the soul moves through an instrument, i.e. the natural warmth or something like it."[245]

This argument is very similar to that of Ibn Sina. However, It was necessary for both of them to discuss the will here, because we are only moving hands up because we will that.

The Psychological Proof
There are certain psychological aspects in man such as: feelings, emotions, laughing, crying, and embarrassment. In addition there are aspects of reasoning such as: making generalization and dealing with abstract concepts. Humans are also able to make moral and aesthetics judgments. All these activities prove that they belong to a power in man other than the body. It is the soul.[246] This argument is also similar to that of Ibn Sina.

The Continuity Proof
Ibn Baja mentioned this argument in *Risalat al-Ittisal*. The loss of human organs such as hands, legs, and teeth, although it alters the body and reduces its organs, however, the person continues to be the same being. We continue considering the person as one[247]. This means that the moving power of the body is not physical, rather it non-physical, it is something else we call the soul. Although the physical body changes, the soul does not.[248]

9. The Immortality of the soul
Ibn Baja's theory of the soul is related to his theory of the connection between form and matter. In natural bodies matter and form are

---

[245] Ibn Baja (1956): pp. 16-17.

[246] Ibn Baja (1973): p. 147 in his treatise *"Fil Fahs 'an al-Quwwa al-Nuzu'iyya,"* and p. 138, *"Fil Mutaharrek."*

[247] Ibn Baja (1973): p. 139.

[248] Might be useful here to refer again to Ibn Sina's argument: Man in a Vacuum: If we imagine a person hanging in space in a state in which he loses sensation about his organs he will still feel something about himself. That he is he. This identification achieved only by the existence of the soul.

connected. It is impossible in nature and natural bodies to have the physical form exist after the death of the body. Thus the individual soul, which is inside the form of the physical body, is mortal. However, the soul of the species is immortal, in fact it is eternal. The human mind or the intellect of the species man is similar to that of the active mind, thus its relation to the active mind is possible. Philosophers are qualified for this connection with the active mind. This point as I mentioned before contradicts the Islamic belief because it implies that resurrection is for the soul only, and not the body.

10. A problem
The last point creates an issue because the mind of a philosopher is nothing more than an individual intellect and it is a perishable according to Ibn Baja, unless he thinks that philosophers are the presentation of the species, or he thinks that human intellect can move from mortality to immortality which is contradictory too.

Ibn Baja (Avempace)

Biography of a Solitary Man

11. Introduction

Ibn Baja (Avempace) in this philosophical story *Tadbeer al-Mutawaheid* (*Biography of a Solitary Man* or *The Governance of the Solitary*) continues on the heritage of Islamic political philosophy of perfect and imperfect states. A theme presented as utopia by Plato and others, but it was discussed in its Islamic perspective by al-Farabi in his *al-Madina al-Fadila (The Perfect State).* Muslim philosophers discussed the conception of what the state ought to be in order to be perfect and achieve happiness of its citizens. Ibn Rushd (Averroes) noticed that Ibn Baja was the first to establish a way for the 'Governance of the Solitary' in Spain.

Ibn Baja's book has a central theme, which is the life of the philosopher who lives in solitude in an imperfect city and struggles to achieve happiness. This theme is closely related, in Ibn Baja's philosophy, to the connection between the human mind and the active intellect and also related to the type of the form the solitary is seeking, whether in spiritual or corporeal form. The discussion of the latter almost overweighed the main theme of the progression of the life in solitude. Ibn Tufail and Ibn Rushd both noticed the inconsistency of the book. Ibn Rushd said:

"[B]ut this book is incomplete, and besides, it is not always easy to understand its meaning. . . . He is the only one to treat this subject, and none of his predecessors surpassed him in this respect."

This translation is based on the original Arabic text of *Tadbeer al-Mutawahhed*, edited by Majid Fakhry and published in Lebanon 1991. This translation presents a summery of the main theme of the text.[249]

---

[249] The work of translating, summarizing, and publishing this text started since the middle ages, Moses Narbuni offered a Hebrew paraphrase of the text

12. The Text of Ibn Baja (Avempace)

Biography of a Solitary Man

Tadbeer al-Mutawahhed
(Governance of The Solitary)

[PART I: The Meaning of tadbeer or governance]
"In the language of the Arab the utterance "tadbeer" [management, conducting, governance] designates many senses, which were enumerated by the experts of that language.

And its most famous references, in general, are used to signify, the ordering [arranging] of actions toward an intended end. For this reason, they do not utter it on someone who performs a single action with the intention to achieve an end. Whoever believes that that action is a single action, he does not call it "tadbeer" [governance]. Whereas whoever believes that it is many actions and considers it as act of an order, he then calls that order "tadbeer". For this reason, they say that the God is the "Mudabber" [The designer] of the world.

This [tadbeer or governance] might be in potentiality and might be in actuality. But the reference of the word tadbeer in signifying what is potential is more frequently used and well known.
And it is evident that if tadbeer [governance] of certain affairs was done potentially, then, indeed, it was by means of idea [reasoning]; because this [potential order] is related to reasoning, and cannot exist unless

---

around 1349. Asin Palacios published *Tadbir al-Mutawahhid*, Madrid, Granada, 1946. There is the publication of D. M. Dunlop: "Ibn Bajjah's *Tadbiru'l-Mutawahid* (Rule of the Solitary)," journal of the Royal Asiatic Society of Great Britain and Ireland (1945), pp. 63-73 (corresponding to Asin Palathius Selection 2). Dunlop published only the first two chapters of the book. For more details see Lerner, R. and Mahdi, M. (eds.): *Meedieval Political Philosophy*.

from it alone. Therefore, it cannot exist accept for man.[250] And the utterance of the word al-mudabber [the governor] on [any one other than man] is merely analogical. Tadbeer then, is said to be in priority and posteriori.[251]

Tadbeer (order) may also designate the bringing out of this [potential] order into being in the way it will be, this is more frequent in human action and more apparent, but it is the least in the actions of the irrational animal.

If tadbeer is being applied in this manner, then it could be used in a general and a restricted sense. If it is used in a general sense, it designates all human actions of whatever kind. This is applied to the crafts and to the faculties, except that it is more frequent and common to apply it to the faculties. Therefore it is said to the ordering of military affairs and hardly ever to the arts of shoemaking and weaving. When it is said in this manner, again it might be used in a general and a restricted sense.

And if it is used in a general sense, it designates all actions that are covered by the arts called "faculties." I have summarized it in [my work(s) on] political science.

If it is used in a restrictive sense, then, it designates the tadbeer (governance) of cities.

Some of what is meant by tadbeer (order) precedes some others by nobleness and perfection. The most noble of these, which are called tadbeer, are the governance of cities and the management of the household.

---

[250] Since this act requires setting things according to an end, thus it requires: intentions, ideas, will to decide on them, and power, to achieve them. These attributes exist in man.

[251] He meant that the act of tadbeer or order that occur potentially on the level of ideas comes prior to that action of tadbeer that comes later in actuality as posterior. For example: arranging the order how to put furniture in your house before buying them is happening first on the level of ideas and comes prior to that arrangement of the furniture when you buy them and actually put them inside the house, the last act is posteriori.

But the household is seldom called tadbeer (order), to the extent that the expression "tadbeer (order) of the household" is used in a metaphorical and restricted sense.

As for the tadbeer (arrangement) of war and so forth, they form parts of these two kinds [of tadbeer: cities and household]...

When tadbeer (governance) is said in an unqualified sense, as we have explained it above, it designate the governance of cities, and when it is said in a restricted sense [the household], it is divided into right and wrong governance. It might be thought that governance might be free of these two opposite [qualifications], but if it is examined and followed by investigation it will appear that they adhere to it necessarily. Investigating that is easy on anyone has a minimal understanding of political philosophy.

Thus, the two types designated by the name tadbeer (governance) can properly be divided into the right and the wrong [governance.]

As far as the governance of cities, Plato has explained it in the political philosophy [The Republic]. He explained the meaning of the right governance of cities and the source of its wrongness....

And as in regard to the management (governance) of the household, the household as household is a part of a city. ...

Some authors have exaggerated the studying of the tadbeer (governance) of these imperfect households, which is the diseased one. And of those [authors], whose books on the management of the household have reached us, their arguments are rhetorical.

It is clear from the position we stated that except for the virtuous household, the households are diseased; they are all corrupt; and they do not exist by nature but only by convention. ...

Let us, then, turn aside and leave the study of it [imperfect households] to those who devote themselves to the investigation of such matters as exist at particular times.

Moreover, the perfection of the household is not something intentioned for its own sake, but either for the sake of perfecting the city or the natural end of man. The treatment of the latter clearly forms part of man's tadbeer (governance) of himself [ethics]. ...

[No need for a doctor or a judge]
Since the virtuous city is differentiated by the absence of the art of medicine and of that of law. Because love binds them [citizens] all, and there is no quarrel among themselves at all. Therefore, if one of its [the city] part is deprived of love and quarrelsomeness breaks out, then, the need arises for the laying down of justice and the need arises necessarily for someone to dispense it, which is the judge.

Moreover, because all the actions of the virtuous city are right, this being the distinctive characteristic that adheres to it, its citizens do not devour harmful foods. Therefore, they do not need to know about the treatment for the suffocation caused by mushrooms and the like, nor do they need to know about the remedy for wine [alcoholic people], for nothing there [in this city] is not properly ordered.

Also if they [the citizens of this city] give up exercise, this gives rise to several diseases; and it is evident that it [the virtuous city] is not subject to such diseases.

I hope that it may not even need any treatments more than that which is for dislocation and the like. And, in general, for such diseases whose specific causes are external and that the healthy body cannot, by its own effort, ward off. For it has been observed that serious wounds of many healthy people heal by themselves, and there are other kinds of evidence for this.

It is, then, from the characteristic of the perfect city that there is neither a doctor nor a judge in it. And from the general inherent of the four simple cities that they are in need of a doctor and a judge. And the more removed a city is from the perfect one, the more it is in need of these two and the more dignified the rank of these two types of men in it.

It is evident that in the virtuous-perfect city, every man is given the highest merit he is fit to pursue. And all of its thoughts are true, and there is no false opinion in it, and its actions alone are absolutely virtuous. Any other action if it is virtuous, then, it is so only in relation to some existent vice. ...

Therefore, in the perfect city, there are no arguments dealing with those who hold an opinion other than that of its citizens, or perform an action other than their action. While, this is possible to happen in the four [imperfect] cities....

As for the ones who discovered a right action or learned it in a true way and that does not exist in the city, then, for this class there is no common name to designate it.

While for the ones who come up with a true opinion that does not exist in the city or the contradictory of which is held in the city, then, they are called Weeds (Nawabit). The more their opinions were greater in number and the more crucial in opposition, the more appropriate the title is on them.

And this name is said on them in particular, although it might be applied, in general, to anyone who holds an opinion other than the opinion of the citizens of the city, regardless of whether his opinion is true or false.

This name has been reassign to these men from the weeds that spring up of themselves among plants. Let us, then, identify the use of this name to the ones who hold true opinions.

It is evident that among the characteristics of the perfect city is that it is free of Weeds, whether this name is said in the specific sense, because it is free of false opinions, or in the general sense, because their presence means that the city is already diseased and decayed and has ceased to be perfect.

However, in the four [imperfect] cities the weeds have been found, and their existence is the cause that leads to the rise of the perfect city, as explained elsewhere.

Since all the ways of life [in the cities] that exist in this time and have existed before, based on the great majority of the reports reaching us about them, accept of what Abu Nasr [al-Farabi] narrates about the early Persians' way of life, are mixtures of the five ways of life. But the majority of what we find in them is mixtures of the four [imperfect] ways of life. Summarizing that is a matter that we will leave. Also we had not devoted time for the investigation of the ways of life that exist in this time.

Yet the three types of them possible to exist and they do exist, those are:

> The Weeds (al-Nawabit),
> The judges, and
> The doctors.

As if the happy [al-Su'ada' which is the fourth type], if it were possible for them to exist in these cities, will possess only the happiness of an isolated individual [al-mufrad].

The most proper tadbeer [governance] is the governance of an isolated individual, whether the isolated individual was one or more than one, so long as a nation or a city has not adopted their opinion. These individuals are the ones meant by the Sufis when they speak of the "aliens" (Ghuraba'); because although they are in their homelands and among their companions and neighbors, they are strangers [alienated] in their opinions, having traveled in their minds to other stations that are like homelands to them, and so forth of the Sufis sayings.

[The purpose of the book]

We intend in this book to discuss the governance of this solitary man. It is evident that he suffers from something that is unnatural. Thus, we will state how he should manage himself so that he may achieve the best existence proper to him, just as the doctor states how the isolated man in these cities should manage himself in order to be healthy: either by preserving his health, as Galen wrote in his book Preservation of Health, or by recovering it once it is lost, according to what is described in the art of medicine.

This book is also addressed to the isolated Weed individual, which is:

(a) How he is to achieve happiness if he does not possess it, or how to remove from himself the conditions that prevent his achieving happiness or achieving the portion he can achieve of it, which in turn depends either on how far his insight takes him or on what is established deeply in him.

(b) And the preservation of it [his happiness] is similar to the preservation of health, it is impossible in the three ways of life and those mixed of them. What Galen and others prescribe in this situation is similar to alchemy and astrology.

What we are discoursing here is the medicine of the soul, and that [which they prescribe] is the medicine of the body. And the government is the medicine of social relations.

It is evident that the latter two arts disappear completely in the perfect city and are, therefore, not to be considered among the sciences.

Similarly, the subject we are discussing would disappear when the city were perfect, and so would the utility of this subject, just as would the science of medicine, the art of judication, and every other art developed according to the need of the imperfect governance. And just as the true opinions contained in medicine belong to the natural sciences, and those contained in the art of judication to the art of politics, similarly those contained in this subject revert to natural sciences and the art of politics.

[PART II: The Human Actions]
...The human actions, which belong to man, are what is performed by his own choice. Thus, everything man does by free choice is human action, and every human action is an action by free decision. By free choice I mean the will that comes to be from [pure] rationality. ....

[PART III: The Spiritual Forms]
The spiritual forms are different kinds:
First type: the form of the heavenly bodies. The second type: the active intellect and the acquired intellect (al-'Aql al-Mustafad). The third is the material intelligibles, and the fourth: the meanings that exist in the faculties of the soul, which exist in the common sense and in the faculty of imagination and in the power of remembrance.

The first type is not material at all. While the third type has connection to the matter (hyle). It is called material (hayulaniyya) because it is material intelligibles and because it is spiritual in its essence, since its existence is in matter.
Whereas the second type in this regard is not material at all, since there is no necessity for matter at anytime. It refers to the material because it is the completion of them, it is the acquired intellect, or as an agent to it. It is the active intellect.
The fourth type is in the middle of the material intelligibles and the spiritual forms. ...

[The goal of the solitary individual]
As for the ends that the solitary individual intends for himself are three: an end for his corporeal form, or for his particular spiritual form, or an end for his universal spiritual form, [intelligizing of the intelligible ideas].
The ends of the solitary individual when he is a part of a perfect city (Imamiyya) have been summarized in political science. As regards the ends he establishes for himself in a city, in so far as he is a part of a city, among his action in it is what is suitable to the solitary individual to perform, thus, he pursues one of these [ends]. And as regard of him being in the virtuous city, the general account of the city has been summarized in the political science.
One has to use reflection, investigation, inference, and, in general, idea [reasoning] being used in achieving each one of them [ends]; for if he did not use reasoning, that activity then, is animalistic, not partaking of the human in any way beyond the fact that its object is a body that has a human form.
Whereas the one whose end was an animalistic end, whether it is achieved through human reasoning or not, the purpose of his humanity

and of that of the beast, are one. And there is no difference at this point whether this man possesses a human form that conceals a beast, or he is a solitary beast.

It is obvious that who posses this animalistic act do not form a city nor they can, at all, form a part of a city.

This [reasoning] indeed exists only to the solitary individual and his ends, as we have stated them.

Therefore, the end of the animalistic is one of these three [ends]. But, this [animalistic end] cannot be the universal spiritual form; for this pertains to the intellect, which achieves it through inquiry. It is evident, then, that it must be the two: the particular [spiritual] forms, and the corporeal.

Some of the people, as we stated previously, are merely concerned with their corporeal form-, they are the base. And others occupy themselves only with their [particular] spiritual form; they are the high-minded and the noble. Just as the basest among [the men concerned with their] corporeal form would be the one who disregards his spiritual form for the sake of the corporeal and does not pay any attention to the former, so the one who possesses highest degree of nobility would be the one who disregards his corporeal form and does not pay any attention to it. However, the one who completely disregards his corporeal form reduces his longevity. As that [the basest of men] deviates from nature, this [the one of highest nobility] like him he does not exist. But there are men who destroy their corporeal form in obedience to the demands of their spiritual form. ...

And among the noble and the magnanimous men a lower type, which forms the majority. This is the man who disregards his corporeal form for the sake of the spiritual, but does not destroy the former, either because his spiritual form does not compel him to do so, or in spite of its compelling him to that [to destroy his corporeal form] he decides in favor of keeping it.

This is similar to what Hatem al-Ta'i did when he slaughtered his horse and sat hungry, not eating any of it himself or feeding any of it to his family, while his young children were convulsing with hunger. ...For this type, as the act of al-Ta'i and his like, there is no position for not acknowledging that the action is noble and high-minded, and that this nature is [responsible for it is] honorable, sublime, and spiritual. It occupies the most sublime position, next only to that occupied by wisdom; and it must necessarily be one of the qualities of the philosophic nature, for without it the philosophic nature would be corporeal, and the philosopher would be fictitious [fake].

In order to achieve its highest perfection, the philosophic nature must, then, act this action [noble and high-minded].

Therefore, whoever prefers his corporeal existence to anything pertaining to his spiritual existence will not be able to achieve the final end. Hence no single corporeal man is happy and every happy man is completely spiritual.

But just as the spiritual man must perform certain corporeal acts-but not for their own sake and perform spiritual acts for their own sake, similarly, the philosopher must perform numerous spiritual acts, but not for their own sake, and perform all the intellectual acts for their own sake.

By the corporeal acts man exists, and by the spiritual acts he is more noble, and by the intellectual acts he is divine and virtuous. The man of wisdom is therefore necessarily a man who is virtuous and divine. He only takes up the best of every kind of activity and he shares with every class of men the best states that characterize them. But he stands alone as the one who performs the most excellent and the noblest of actions. When he achieves the final end, that is, when he intelligizes the simple essential intellects, which are mentioned in the Metaphysics, On the Soul, and Sense and the Sensible, he then becomes one of these intellects.

It would be right to call him simply divine. He will be free from the mortal sensible qualities as well as from the high spiritual qualities: it will be fitting to describe him as a pure divinity.

The solitary individual can obtain all these qualities in the absence of the perfect city. By virtue of his two lower ranks [the corporeal and the spiritual] he will not be a part, the end, the agent, or the preserver of this perfect city. By virtue of this third rank he may not be a part of this perfect city, but he nevertheless will be the end aimed at in this city. Of course, he cannot be the preserver or the agent of the perfect city while a solitary man. ... The solitary individual, as it is clear from his situation, that he must not associate with those whose end is corporeal nor with those whose end is the spirituality that is adulterated with corporeality. Rather, he must associate with those who pursue the sciences. But those who pursue the sciences are few in some ways of life [cities] and many in others, there even being ways of life in which they do not exist at all, therefore, it is competent upon the solitary in some of the ways of life to isolate himself from people completely so far as he can, and not socials with them except in indispensable matters and to the extent to which it is indispensable for him to do so; or emigrate to the ways of life in which the sciences are pursued, if such are to be found.

This does not contradict what was stated in political science and what was explained in natural science. It was explained there that man is social by nature, and it was explained in political science that all isolation is evil. But it is only evil as such; while accidentally it is good, which happens with reference to many things pertaining to nature. An example of that, is bread and meat are by nature beneficial and nourishing, while opium and colocynth are mortal poisons. But the body may possess certain unnatural states in which the [latter] two are beneficial and must be employed, and the natural nourishment is harmful and must be avoided.

However, such states are necessarily diseases and deviations from the natural order. Hence these [the drugs] are beneficial in exceptional cases and by accident, while nourishments are mostly beneficial as such. These states are to the body as the ways of life are to the soul. Just as health is believed to be one in opposition to these multiple [diseased] states, and health alone is the natural state of the body while the multiplicity [of diseased states] are deviations from nature, similarly the leading way of life is the natural state of the soul and is one in opposition to the rest of the ways of life, which are many, and these many [ways of life] are not natural to the soul." **[The End of Ibn Baja's Text]**

13. Dimensions of the Solitary Being (al-Mutawahhed)

The actions of man are different from those of animals because they are actions toward an end, which Ibn Baja called Tadbeer or governance. Setting goals is an activity of reasoning, thus, it manifests the ability of man to rationalize and it also manifests the exercise of free will. Only these actions based on free will are the ones that are the subject of moral evaluation and can be virtuous or not. Also, moral responsibility is only based on this liberty or freedom. The best of tadbeer or governance is that of a man who seeks pure intellectual goals free from any animalistic or corporeal pleasure. This is the ultimate goal in achieving happiness in the intellectual sense. It is clear that this is the happiness of the philosophers or the wise. This level of happiness is achieved through the abstraction of intellectual forms and at the conjunction of the human intellect with active intellect. By this conjunction the human intellect becomes an acquired one in perceiving knowledge and it is free from the connection with the soul. It is this rationality, and not intuition or Sufi experience, that is the ultimate source of happiness. But this state is very rare and seldom available to those of daily life, and the philosopher who achieves it might be alone and in solitude.

14. The Procedures of the Solitary for Ultimate Happiness

The concept of happiness in Ibn Baja's philosophy is related to his conception of the soul. The soul is nonmaterial and immortal. Thus it actualizes itself as such away from the corporeal and the material things.

The solitary being must follow these steps to achieve the ultimate goal of happiness:

1. The solitary individual must give priority for the spiritual forms over the corporeal one, because among the materialists there is no single happy individual. However, the solitary individual should not make the spiritual forms as the very end itself, it is only a level toward the ultimate happiness.
2. The solitary individual should go beyond the goal of the spiritual forms to the intellectual one, and should not socialize

with the pure materialist or those who mix their spiritual form
with the corporeal one.

3. The solitary individual must socialize with those who seek the
   intellectual forms; those of knowledge, philosophy, and
   sciences. But those are very rare and might not exist at all.

4. The solitary individual must isolate himself from the society
   and do not socialize with the society except in some
   indispensable situations.

15. Defining the Solitary Being (al-Mutawahhed)
This Solitary individual, socially speaking, can be living within a
society but he is alone, he is an alien to the rest of people. He is
Mutawahhed, but this term in Ibn Baja's philosophy has three possible
meanings, all of them are required to understand his philosophy:

First: the existential meaning, the solitary individual is Mutawahhed as
an -unified existential being- in the sense that he combines the multiple
parts of the human soul and its goals into one which is the intellectual
form, that transcends other faculties of the soul.

Second: the Meta-epistemological, the solitary individual is
Mutawahhed in the sense of being –united or conjuncted-, as an
intellect, with the active intellect.

Third: the social, the solitary individual is Mutawahhed in the sense of
being –alien- and different from the rest. He socially speaking with
them, but he is alone and in solitude, he isolate himself because they do
not understand him, they pull him down to corporeal goals and material
pleasures, to drown him in a none sense utterance and futile
disputations, while he wants sublime and the nobility of the high
minded, a state in which pleasure overflows.

16. Is the Social Nature of Man Contradicts Solitude?
This life of the solitary being present him with a critical socio-political
states which is to be alone, while the very nature of man, as Ibn Baja
admits, is that he is social by the very human nature. So how can Ibn
Baja give a consistent account to this issue?

In fact Ibn Baja answered this question implicitly when he mentioned that he agreed with the philosophers such as Aristotle and al-Farabi that man is social in nature and life of solitude is evil in all aspects since it is contradictory to the very nature of man as a social being. However, Ibn Baja justified the life of the solitary individual as an accidental possibility although it is not essential.

As a physician Ibn Baja said that in the normal situation bread and meat are good nutrition as such, and some poisons are harmful as such, however, in case of illness what was essentially useful, such as meat, becomes accidentally harmful, and what was essentially harmful, such as poison, might become accidentally useful and used as medication for recovery in restoring the normal state of health.

The solitary individual might treat himself with isolation in order to reach his goal. But the illness, according to Ibn Baja, does not belong to the solitary individual, instead it is the society itself that suffers the illness that forces the solitary individual to isolate himself from the society, even though his social nature cries for association instead of isolation, since the socialization becomes accidentally harmful to him. The solitary being by his very nature tends toward socialization but in a society that achieves the ultimate ends of man.

We understand that this solitary being cannot flourish alone; every human needs the rest of the society. Ibn Baja also emphasizes the necessity of the socio-political state not as an end in itself but only as a means to the ultimate goal of man in his process of perfection, this is why Ibn Baja thinks that the solitary individual can flourish only in a perfect city while imperfect cities increase his struggle. But what how many kinds of cities are there according to Ibn Baja? And which one is the best?

17. Different Kinds of Cities

1. The perfect or virtuous city
In this city the solitary individuals live together. The city has no physicians and psychologists because the solitary individuals live according to the highest level of harmony of the soul, and they live according to a necessary and healthy diet.

This city also has no jurisdiction system or courts, because the solitary individual live according to high stander of moral codes with love and peace, thus they do not have conflicts and enmity or hatred against each other.

Since the citizens of this city are virtuous and follow path of truth, there is no lie or falsehood in this city.
Also the division of labor in this city is set to the best that matches the skills, knowledge, and qualification of each person.

2. The city of dignity (Madinat al-Karamah)
The citizens of this city cooperate in order to live in dependence, fame, and dignity. This might correspond to one level of the faculties of the soul, but it does not sublime to the ultimate goal of man as such.

3. The city of conquer (Madinat al-Taghallub)
The citizens of this city aim at conquering other nations. Thus, their happiness can be achieved in this goal.

4. The city of the crowd (al-Madinah al-Jama'iya)
The citizens of this city follow the dictate of their own desire, with no order. They are equal to each other and none of them is better than the rest. Their happiness is achieved by fulfilling the materialistic needs.

CHAPTER SEVEN

Ibn Tufail
(a. 510-581 A.H./ 1116-1185 A.D.)

Hayy Ibn Yaqdhan[252]

1. His Life
Abu Bakr Muhammad Ibn Tufail was born in Spain, northeast of
Granada in a small town called Wadi Ash (in the modern Spanish is
called Guadix). His education was in the field of natural sciences and
Islamic religion. His main profession was medicine. Ibn Tufail
practiced as a physician in Granada, Ceuta, and Tangier. He was then
appointed as a court physician of al-Mowahhid sultan of Morocco and
Andalusia for almost 20 years; from 1163-1182.

Physicians and astronomer are probably the most entitled to reflect
upon the issue of design and telos. Ibn Tufail's observation from
biology and anatomy and the consistency of human body led him to
more philosophical reflections about the design of the universe, as we
will see in his philosophy.

Ibn Tufail was the second most important Muslim philosopher in Spain
after Ibn Baja. He did not author in philosophy as much as other
Muslim philosophers did due to the fact that his time was dedicated to
his profession as a doctor. However, his only extent work in
philosophy; *Hayy Ibn Yaqdhan (Alive The Son of Awake)* was enough
to establish him as an eminent philosopher East and West.

Hayy Ibn Yaqdhan as a philosophical story reflects the philosophical
system of Ibn Tufail in a holistic way:

---

[252] Author's translation, based on the Arabic text published by Farooq Sa'ad
(1980). The paragraph's numbering and subtitles added by the translator.

- His epistemology in its relation to biology, anatomy, mathematics, and astronomy.
- His metaphysics in relation to logic, natural philosophy, and religion.
- His Religion in its relation to reason and revelation.
- His social and political philosophy, in relation to pure mind, religion, isolation and socialization.

2. The Story Hayy Ibn Yaqdhan in Europe

Ibn Tufail's book *Hayy Ibn Yaqdhan* was translated from Arabic into many languages and Ibn Tufail was known to the Latin world as Abubacer. The first translation was made to Hebrew language by Moses Narboni who gave a summary of the book in which he found in it a good resemblance for his own philosophical growth.

Another translation made to Latin language at 1671 by Edward Pocock. In 1674 George Keith made an English translation. Another translation made by George Ashwell. The story also translated to modern Spanish and modern English language. A famous translation into English also made in 1708 by Simon Ockley a professor of Arabic at Cambridge University. A.S. Fulton, who wrote an introduction to Ockley's translation, made good and through commentary on the history of the translation of Hayy Ibn Yaqdhan and its popularity in the West:

"Ibn Tufail's popularity outside the Muhammadan [Muslim] world, particularly in the seventeenth and eighteenth centuries, may be judged from the following list of the texts, translations and adaptations of his story which have appeared in Europe.

The Arabic text was first published, together with a scrupulously literal Latin translation, under the title *Philosophus Autodidactus,* by Edward Pocock junior (son of the great English pioneer in Oriental studies), at Oxford, in 1671, and reprinted there in 1700.

Pocock's Latin was rendered anonymously into Dutch in 1672, a second edition appearing in 1701, in which the translator's name figures as " S.D.B." George Keith, the Quaker, in 1674 (for propaganda purposes), and George Ashwell, in 1686, published English translations, each of them from Pocock's Latin.

In 1708 Simon Ockley's version, made direct from the Arabic, was published in London, reprinted there in 1711, and again in Dublin in 1731. (From 1711 till his death in 1720 Ockley was Professor of Arabic at Cambridge.)

Two German versions were produced in the eighteenth century, one made from Pocock's Latin by J. Georg Pritius in 1726, and the other, an accurate rendering of the original Arabic by J. G. Eichhorn, in 1783. An anonymous Crusoe story was printed in London in 1761, entitled *The Life and Surprising Adventures* of *Don Antonio de Trezzanio,* much of which is either " conveyed " or paraphrased from Ockley's version of *HayyIbnYaqzan. The Awakening of the Soul* (Wisdom of the East Series, London, 1804), by Paul Bronnle, is a translation from the Arabic of the most interesting parts of the romance.

A translation in Spanish of the complete story, more exact than any of its predecessors, was published by F. Pons Boigues at Saragossa in 1900, with an introduction by M. MenCndezy Pelayo.

But by far the most important advance since the days of Pocock was made by Prof. L. Gauthier, whose excellent critical edition of the text accompanied by a careful French rendering appeared in 1900 at Algiers.

Pocock's Latin version has all the merits and defects of a slavish adherence to the letter of the Arabic. Ockley's tendency is very much to the other extreme. His keen relish of the spirit of the original and his aversion from pedantry reveal themselves repeatedly in renderings of singular neatness. On the other hand he often takes liberties with his original which are quite unwarranted. In the present edition an attempt has been made to correct such lapses, without offering any unnecessary violence to Ockley's work. A number of emendations have been made at the dictation of Gauthier's Arabic text, which is our best authority and much superior to the text upon which Ockley depended.

Ibn Tufail wrote a short introduction to his romance, in which he discusses briefly some of the views held by the leading Muslim exponents of mystic philosophy before his time, namely, al-Farabi, Avicenna, al-Ghazali and Avempace. This is omitted from Ashwell's translation and from the 1731 edition of Ockley's version. We also have omitted it since it contains nothing of general interest.

In Ockley's first edition (1708) the bookseller commends the work to the reader in these words, which it may not be inappropriate to repeat:

And though' we do not pretend to any Discoveries in this Book, especially at this time of Day, when all parts of Learning are cultivated with so much Exactness; yet we hope that it will not be altogether unacceptable to the curious Reader, to know what the state of Learning was among the Arabs, five hundred Years since. And if what we shall here communicate, shall seem little in respect of the Discoveries of this discerning Age; yet we are confident that any European who shall compare the Learning in this book, with what was published by any of his own Countrymen at that time, will find himself obliged in Conscience to give our Author fair Quarter."[253]

Two recent retranslations also made in 1999: one by Jim Colville and another translation by Lenn Evan Goodman.

Our translation is based on the Arabic text published by Farooq Sa'ad (1980) and on a revision of Ockley's translation (1708) and of Colville (1999). The translation presents a summary of the main theme of the text. It is an attempt to offer a complete translation based on the new Arabic text (1980), in this portion the paragraph's numbering and subtitles added by the translator.

---

[253] Ockley, S. (1929): pp. 35-37.

Ibn Tufail

The Story of

Hayy Ibn Yaqdhan

"[The Island in which a human being was born without parents]
Our virtuous ancestors, may God be pleased with them, mentioned that an island lying off the coast of India, on the equator, in which a human being comes into existence without mother and father.

[Ibn Tufail's natural explanation]
Because this island enjoys the most temperate climate on Earth and is perfectly receptive to the highest sunlight ... Some affirmed the conclusion of the story that Hayy Ibn Yaqdhan was one of a number of individuals who came into being on that island without mother or father. And some of them denied that account and narrated a different version, which we shall tell you.

[An alternative version of the becoming of Hayy Ibn Yaqdhan.]
They say: that facing this island there was a large neighboring island, rich and prosperous, well populated with abundant resources, which was governed by a king among them who was very arrogant and with vigilant care. This king had a sister of exquisite beauty whom he kept restrained from husbands, because he could not find for her an equivalent match. However, he had a relative called Yaqdhan who married her secretly, according to their rite at their time that legalizes this marriage as permissible. Then from this husband she conceived and gave birth to a son. And then being terrified that her secret should ever become known, she placed the child inside a chest and secured the lid, after she had nursed him enough. At nightfall, she took the baby to the seashore, with her servants and trustworthy friends, and with a heart equally inflamed by extreme love and care of him, she bade farewell to him:

"O Allah, You created this child when he was nothing to be spoken of, and You sustained him in the dark recesses of my womb, until he perfectly formed. In fear of the cruelty of this stubborn and tyrant king, I surrender him to Your subtleness and mercy. O Most merciful (Allah) be with him always and never leave him."

Then she cast the chest into the sea. During that very night, the motion of the waves of water by the force of strong tide carried the chest to the coast of the other island, mentioned above. At that time of year, the tide reaches a height to which it would not return for another year. The water lodged the chest into a pleasant thicket, set with trees, fertile soil, where it was sheltered from the wind and rain and veiled from the sun, whose rays shone obliquely when it rose and when it set. Then the tide ebbed, and the chest was left there. As the wind rising blew a heap of sand filling the inlet of that thicket, thus water could not reach it. The nails of the chest and its boards were loosened when the waves throw it in that thicket.

When the baby became very hungry, he wept and cried for help, and struggled trying to move. A gazelle whose foal had been carried off by an eagle heard the sound of his voice and, thinking it was the crying of her foal, then she followed the sound until she came to the chest. Hearing the cries coming from inside, she searched with her hooves until a top board broke off. Immediately, the gazelle felt a maternal love for him and affectionately treated him, and she gave him her udder and fed him her own tasty milk. The gazelle remained nursing him continuously and raising him, looking after him and protecting him from harm."

[Ibn Tufail commenting on this alternative]
This is the account of his origin according to those who deny the [idea of] spontaneous generation. And we will describe here [in this book] how he grew up and progressed through his stages until achieving the sublime fulfillment.[254]

---

[254] The version which claims that Hayy was born from the earth describes how, beneath the island, deep within the earth, there was a great mass of clay that had been in a state of ferment over the course of many years. Hot vapors mixed with cold and moist vapors fused with dry to produce a homogenous balance of forces. In some parts, the mixture of vapors developed a greater

balance and disposition to form humors than in others. The most perfect
balance was in the center, where the vapors most fully resembled the humors
of man. As the clay churned, bubbles were formed by its extreme viscosity. In
the center, a tiny bubble formed that split into two, separated by a fine
membrane and each part filled with a gentle, ethereal substance of the most
suitable balance. At that point, the spirit that proceeds from the command of
the Lord attached itself and so firmly did it bind, it would have been hard for
either sense or reason to separate the two. This spirit emanates eternally from
God - His are the power and the glory - and could be likened to the sunlight
shining constantly on Earth.

[The becoming of Hayy as a spontaneous generation]
When the spirit attached itself to the chamber, the account continues, all
faculties became subject to it, made absolutely obedient by the Will of God.
Alongside this chamber, another bubble forined that divided into three, each
part separated from the others by delicate membranes but connected by
pathways and filled with an ethereal substance similar to that which filled the
first, only more delicate. In these three hollow spaces divided from one, a set
of subject faculties was located, charged with the protection and preservation
of their hosts and the transmission of any impression, however subtle, to the
primary spirit attached to the first chamber.
Beside these two chambers, a third bubble formed, filled with an ethereal
substance similar to, but coarser than, the first two. A set of subject faculties
was located there and likewise charged with its protection and preservation.
These three chambers were the first to be created from the great fermenting
mass of clay, in the manner we have outlined.

[The becoming of the heart, brain and liver]
Each had need of the others. The first needed the service and utility of the
other two, while they needed the first, as the governed need a governor and the
led require a leader. To subsequently created organs, however, the latter two
stood in the relation of governor to governed, with the second being more
suited to this than the third.
When the spirit attached to the first chamber, its temperature rose and it took
on a conical, flame-like shape. The coarse substance surrounding it took on a
similar shape and became solid tissue, around which a protective membrane
formed. This entire organ is known as the heart. Because of the exhaustion of
vapors following its temperature rise, the heart could not have long survived
without something to supply nutrition and compensate for its continuous
action. It also required the ability to sense what it may be in harmony and
conflict with, in order to attract and repel accordingly. By virtue of their
faculties, whose source is the heart itself, the other two organs supplied these

[The life of Hayy on the Island, the two versions of the story coincide]
Then from this point on, this version [of the story] coincides with the
first one in regard to his upbringing. Both said: That the gazelle that
cared for him lived in a fertile land of plenty and her rich, abundant
milk provided excellent nourishment. She remained with him [all
times], leaving him only when it was necessary to graze. The baby
became so attached to the gazelle that, if she stayed away too long, he
would cry loudly, then she would come rushing back.

[Hayy passes two years of age]
So the child grew up and nourished on the gazelle's milk until two years
had passed, and he gradually began to walk and grow teeth. He
followed the gazelle everywhere.

[The child Hayy began observation, sense experience, and comparison]
Thus the child lived among the deer, imitating their calls with his voice
until it was scarcely possible to differentiate them. Similarly, he was
also imitated all birdsong and the sounds of other animals accurately.
The wild animals were as used to him as he was to them; so they were
not afraid of him nor he was. And as the images of experiences

---

needs - the brain providing feeling and the liver supplying nutrition. In turn,
the brain and liver required the heart to supply them with heat and their
specific faculties, of which it is the source. As a result, a network of
connections and pathways developed, some wider than others, as dictated by
necessity. These are the arteries and veins.
[The becoming of the fetus]
This version of the story goes on to describe the process of formation and
development of the organs in great detail, in the same way that natural
scientists describe the development of the embryo in the womb until, with
development complete and all the organs formed, the fetus is ready to descend.
[To conclude the description of the spontaneous generation of Hayy]
To conclude the description, we are again referred to the great mass of
fermenting clay and how its condition was such as to furnish everything
required for human creation, including the membranes surrounding the fetus.
When development was complete, the membranes split - as in normal labor -
and what was left of the clay dried up and cracked. With its source of nutrition
gone, the infant became hungry and cried for attention. It was then that the
bereaved gazelle came to the rescue. See Colville (1999).

impressed themselves upon his soul, after their absence from his observations [the things themselves are no longer objects of his immediate sensory experience], he formed a liking for some and a dislike of others.

However, he was observing all the animals noticing that they were covered with fur or hair or feathers. He saw how swiftly they could run, how strong they were, and how they had natural weapons for defense against any attack, such as, horns, antlers, fangs, hooves and talons.

Then [in comparison with animals] he was looking back at himself realizing how naked, unarmed, weak in running, and limited in attack he was. This was disturbing him making him unhappy.

[Hayy reaching the age of seven]

He was nearly seven years old when his concerned had been focused on these matters and become distressed by his shortcomings and despairing of any change, he took from the broad tree leaves and put them some in front and some behind. Then fastened them around his waist with a sort of belt made from esparto grass and palm fiber.

From trimmed branches of trees he made sticks; balancing its shafts and sharpening its points. He used it [the sticks] to chase away any animals that threatened him. He could now attack weaker ones and at least put up a good fight against the stronger. This gave him some sense of self-respect.

[Hayy passing seven years old and improving his artifacts]

He came to realize that his hands gave him many advantages over those of them [the animals]. By them he was able to cover his nakedness [with leaves] and to make sticks by which to defend himself. So he no longer needed a tail and natural weapons [that animals have].

The gazelle who had nursed him and raised him grew too old and weak, he was leading her to the fertile meadows and gather ripe fruits to feed her.

[Hayy's Mother (the gazelle) is dying]

Weakness and emaciation were still taking over her until at last death caught up with her and all her movements and responses ceased. When the boy saw her like that, he became overwhelmed with sadness and his soul seemed to burst in grief.

[Hayy searching for the cause of death]
When he had examined her external organs and found no visible
damage, and at the same time, he noticed that her inactivity was total
and not confined to any one limb. It then occurred to him that the
problem from which she suffered must be in an organ hidden from sight
within the body. That organ must be indispensable to the functioning of
the external limbs and when it had become sick, the harm was general
[the rest of the body]. If he could find this organ and remove whatever
had affected it, the resulting benefit would spread throughout the body
and the bodily functions would resume.

[Hayy cut open the gazelle's chest and examine the inside]
So he decided to cut open her breast and examine what was inside.
Using sharp pieces of stone and dry splinters of cane similar to
knives."[255]

"In addition to his past accumulated sense experience, the death of the
gazelle forced him to a new level of experience, not only sadness, but
also, and more importantly, the reasoning about life and death, what
causes them, and the very meaning of life itself. He observed the dead
body thoroughly, and concluded that the sick organ that cause the death
had to be inside the gazelle's chest, he decided to search it, locate and
examine it, hoping to discover the disorder and remove it. So he cut
open her breast and examines the inside. He made an incision between
the ribs, and cutting through the flesh, came to the diaphragms; which
he finding very tough, assured himself that such a covering must needs
belong to that organ which he looked for, and that if he could once get
through that, he should find it.

The first part he met with was the Lungs, which he at first sight
mistook for that which he searched for, and turned them about this way
and that way to see if he could find in them the seat of the disease. He
first happened upon that lobe which lay next the side which he had

---

[255] This is the end of my translation. The following part is a brief summary of
the story based on both translations of Ockley (1708) and Colville (1999),
however, some of the summary is my own wording based on the Arabic text.

opened and when he perceived that it did lean sideways, he was satisfied that it was not the organ he looked for, because he was fully persuaded that that must needs be in the midst of the Body, as well in regard of Latitude as Longitude. He proceeded in his search, till at last he found the Heart, which when he saw closed with a very strong cover, and fastened with stout ligaments, and covered by the lungs on that side which he had opened, he began to say to himself: " If this organ be so on the other side as it is on this which I have opened, then 'tis certainly in the midst, and without doubt the " same I look for; especially considering the "conveniency of the situation, the comeliness and regularity of its figure, the firmness of " the flesh, and besides, its being guarded with "such a membrane as I have not observed in any other part.'' Upon this he searches the other side, and finding the same membrane on the inside of the ribs, and the lungs in the same posture which he had observed on that side which he had opened first, he concluded this organ to be the part which he looked for.

Then when he had laid the heart bare, and perceived that it was solid on every side, he began to examine it, to see if he could find any apparent hurt in it; but finding none, he squeezed it with his hand, and perceived that it was hollow.

He began then to think that what he looked for might possibly be contained in that Cavity. When he came to open it, he found in it two cavities, one on the right side, the other on the left. That on the right side was full of clotted blood, that on the left quite empty. "Then (says he) without all doubt, one of those two cavities must needs be the receptacle of what I look for; as for that on this right side there's nothing in it but congealed blood, which was not so, be sure, till the whole body was in that condition in which it now is" (for he had observed that all blood congeals when it flows from the Body). This blood does not differ in the least from any other; and I find it common to all the organs. What I look for cannot by any means be such a matter as this; for that which I seek is something which is peculiar to this place, which I find it could not subsist without, so much as the twinkling of an eye. And this is that which I looked for at first. As for this blood, how often have I lost a great deal of it in my skirmishes with the wild beasts, and yet it never did me any considerable harm, nor rendered me incapable of performing any action of life, and therefore what I look for is not in this cavity. Now as for the cavity on the left side, I find it is altogether empty and I have no reason in the world to think that it was made in vain, because I find every organ appointed for such and such particular functions. How then can this ventricle of the heart, which I see is of so excellent a frame, serve for no use at all? I cannot think but that the same thing which I am in search of once dwelt here, but has now deserted his habitation and left it empty, and that the absence of that thing has occasioned this privation of sense and cessation of motion which happened to the body.

Now when he perceived that the Being which had inhabited there before had left its house before it fell to ruined, and forsaken it when as yet it continued whole and entire, he concluded that it was highly probable that it would never return to it any more, after its being so cut and mangled.

Upon this the whole body seemed to him a very inconsiderable thing, and worth nothing in respect of that Being he believed once inhabited, and now had left it. Therefore he applied himself wholly to the consideration of that Being. What it was and how it subsisted? What joined it to this Body? Whither it went, and by what passage, when it left the body? What was the cause of its departure; whether it were forced to leave its mansion, or left the body of its own accord? And in case it went away voluntarily, what it was that rendered the body so disagreeable to it, as to make it forsake it? And whilst he was perplexed with such variety of thoughts, he laid aside all concern for the carcass, and banished it from his mind; for now he perceived that his mother, which had nursed him so tenderly and had suckled him, was that *something* which was departed; and from it proceeded all her actions, and not from this inactive body; but that all this body was to it only as an instrument, like his cudgel which he had made for himself, with which he used to fight with the wild beasts. So that now, all his regard to the body was removed, and transferred to that by which the body is governed, and by whose power it moves. Nor had he any other desire but to make enquiry after that.

In the mean time the body of the gazelle began to decay and emit noisome vapors, which still increased his aversion to it, so that he did not care to see it. It was not long after that he chanced to see two Ravens engaged so furiously, that one of them struck down the other stark dead; and when he had done, he began to scrape with his claws till he had dug a pit, in which he buried the carcass of his adversary. The boy observing this, said to himself:

'How well has this Raven done in burying the body of his companion, although' he did ill in killing him. How much greater reason was there for me to have been forward in performing this to my mother?' Upon this he dug a pit, and lays the body of his mother into it and buries her.

By discovering the fire, Hayy thought that fire is similar to that thing that depart the body, so he start examining animals to verify his idea, he captured a wild animal and cut into it as he had done with the gazelle, until he reached the heart. He noticed that the left chamber is filled with a vapor that looked like mist. He poked his finger inside and found it was almost hot enough to burn him. The animal died on the spot. Hay convinced that this warm vapor is the life-giving, and when it departs the body, the animal dies. Hayy then involved more in anatomy to explore that vapor; where does it come from? Why does its heat not dissipate?

Likewise he perceived that this animal spirit was *One,* whose action when it made use of the Eye, was *Sight;* when of the Ear, *Hearing;* when of the Nose, *Smelling;* when of the Tongue, *Tasting;* and when of the Skin and Flesh, *Feeling.* When it employed any Limb, then its operation was *Motion;* and when it made use of the Liver, *Nutrition* and *Concoction.* And that though' there were members fitted to every one of these uses, yet none of them could perform their respective offices without having correspondence with that spirit by means of passages called nerves; and that if at any time it chanced that these passages were either broken off or obstructed, the action of the corresponding member would cease. Now these nerves derive this spirit from the cavities of the brain, which has it from the heart (and contains abundance of spirit, because it is divided into a great many partitions) and by what means so ever any Limb is deprived of this spirit, its action ceases and 'tis like a cast off tool, not fit for use. And if this spirit departed wholly from the body, or is consumed or dissolved by any means whatsoever, then the whole body is deprived of motion and reduced to that state which is death.

Thus far had his observations brought him about the end of the third seventh year of his age, i.e., when he was one and twenty years old. In which time he had made abundance of pretty contrivances.

He made himself both clothes and shoes of the Skins of such wild beasts as he had dissected. He learned the making of threads. He learned the art of building from the observations he made upon the swallows nests. He had built himself a storehouse and a pantry, to lay up the remainder of his provision in, and made a door to it of canes bound together, to prevent any of the beasts getting in during his absence.

He made all these discoveries whilst he was employed in the study of anatomy, and the searching out of the properties peculiar to each part, and the difference between them; and all this before the end of that time I speak of the Age of 21 years. By this age Hayy reached a level of insight to affirm that the spirit is more essential than the physical body, and it is the cause of its life and death.

He then moved from anatomy to natural philosophy, by observing nature, plants and animals, he realized that they go through the process of generation and corruption. He was confused for while about the issue of unity and multiplicity regarding member of species.

Thus he continued, considering nothing but the nature of bodies, and by this means he perceived that whereas at first sight, *Things* had appeared to him innumerable and not to be comprehended; *Now,* he discovered the whole mass and bulk of creatures were in reality only *One.*

In like manner he considered other bodies, both animate and inanimate, and found their essence was composed of corporeity, and some one thing or more superadded to it. And thus he attained a notion of the *forms* of bodies, according to their differences. These were the first things he found out, belonging to the spiritual world; for these *Forms* are not the objects of sense, but are apprehended by intellectual speculation. Now among other things of this kind which he discovered, it appeared to him that the *animal spirit* which is lodged in the heart (as we have mentioned before) must necessarily have some attribute superadded to its *corporeity,* which rendered it capable of those wonderful actions, different sensations and ways of apprehending things, and various sorts of motions; and that this attribute must be its *form,* by which it is distinguished from other bodies, which is the same that the philosophers call the animal soul. And so in plants, that which was in them the same that natural heat was in beasts, must have something proper to it, which was its *Form,* which the philosophers call the vegetative soul. And that there was also in inanimate things *(*all bodies, besides plants and animals, which are in this sublunary world) something peculiar to them, by the power of which every one of them performed such actions as were proper to it, namely, various sorts of motion and different kinds of sensible qualities; and that thing was the *form* of every one of them, and this is the same which the philosophers call *nature.*

And when by this Contemplation it appeared to him plainly that the true essence of that *animal spirit* on which he had been so intent, was compounded of corporeity and some other attribute superadded to that corporeity, and that it had its corporeity in common with other bodies; but that this other. Attribute which was superadded was peculiar to it self: immediately he despised and rejected the notion of corporeity, and applied himself wholly to that other superadded attribute (which is the same that we call the *soul)* the nature of which he earnestly desired to know. Therefore he fixed all his thoughts upon it, and began his contemplation with considering all bodies, not as bodies, but as endued with *forms,* from whence necessarily flow these properties by which they are distinguished one from another.

Thus Hayy start to reason that the reality of the animal consists of two things: the concept of corporeity and a concept additional to corporeity and that is called "the soul". This second concept is what hay was eager to know.

However, his sense could not represent to him any body existent in nature, which had this only property, and was void of all other forms: for he saw that every one of them had some other notion superadded to the said Extension.

Now he knew that every, thing that was produced anew must have some producer. And from this contemplation, there arose in his mind a sort of impression of the nature of that form, though' his notion of him as yet was general and indistinct. Then he paused on the examining of these forms which he knew before, one by one, and found that they were produced anew, and that they must of necessity be beholden to some *Efficient Cause.*

Then he considered the essences of forms, and found that they were nothing else, but only a disposition of body to produce such or such actions. For instance, water, when very much heated is disposed to rise upwards, and that disposition is its form. For there is nothing present in all this, but a body; and some things which are observed to arise from it, which were not in it before (such as qualities and motions) and an *Efficient* Cause which produces them. And the fitness of a body for one motion rather than another is its *disposition* and form.

The same he concluded of all other forms, and it appeared to him that those actions which emanated from them were not in reality owing to them, but to the *Efficient Cause* which produced in them those actions which are attributed to them. Which notion of his is exactly the same with what the Apostle of God says (may God bless him and grant him Peace): "I am his Hearing in which he hears, and his Seeing by which he Sees."

Now, when he had attained thus far, so as to have a general and indistinct notion of this *Agent,* he had a most earnest desire to know it distinctly. And because he had not as yet with- drawn himself from the sensible world, he began to look for this *Agent* among sensible things; nor did he as yet know whether it was one Agent or many. Therefore he enquired strictly into all such bodies as he had about him, i.e., those which he had been employed about all along, and he found that they were all liable to *generation* and *corruption* and if there were any which did not suffer a total corruption, yet they were liable to a partial one, as *water* and *earth,* the parts of which, he observed, were consumed by fire. Likewise among all the rest of the bodies which he was conversant with, he could find none which were not produced anew and therefore dependent upon some Agent.

Upon which account he laid them all aside, and transferred his thoughts to the consideration of the heavenly bodies. And thus far he reached in his contemplations when he was eight and twenty years old.

At the age of 28 Hayy was, to some extent, able to transcend sensory perception and reach the beginning of pure intellectual world. What he was interested in could not be grasped by sensory perception, he starts to reason about possibility and necessity; for everything that is possible to be brought about, there must necessarily be something which brings it about. By this way of reasoning Hayy formed a general, and yet vague, idea about the Efficient Cause of the existent things.

By having general idea of an efficient cause, Hayy desired for more precise knowledge, he wanted to transcend the natural physical world and its level of sensory perception, Hayy started observing the celestial bodies, major question imposed itself on Hay:

Is the mass of the cosmos extends to **infinity** in all directions, or it is finite?

By pure reasoning Hay came to the conclusion that a body of infinite size is impossible practically, in other words it is an absurdity. He convinced himself by some arguments and proofs, one of them was:

"Imagine two lines beginning from where it is known to be finite and extending infinitely with and through the mass of the cosmos.

Then imagine a long section cut from one of these lines at its finite end. Take the remainder and place the end which was cut beside the beginning of the intact line so that the two lines lie in parallel.

Now consider these two lines as they extend into supposed infinity.

Either we find that both lines extend forever into infinity with neither being shorter than the other, in which case the line from which the section was removed is equal to the line which remained intact, and that is impossible.

Or we find that the line from which the section was removed does not extend infinitely with the intact line but stops short, in which case it is finite.

If the finite section that was initially removed is then replaced, the whole, likewise, becomes finite although it is neither shorter nor longer than the other, intact, line but is, in fact, the same.

It therefore follows that both lines are finite.

The body on which these lines were supposed is also finite and, because we can suppose lines like these on any body, all bodies are finite. The supposition that a body can be infinite is, therefore, absurd."[256] Thus, the cosmos is finite.

He then observed the spherical shape of it, and its orbital motion. Hayy questioned: Is the universe as a whole, something that was originated in time and came into being from non-being, or it was something that was never preceded by non-being but has always existed? Is the universe eternal? Or it was created?

He was not certain about the answer, and could not reach a definite conclusion one way or the other. Some contradictions arose if he assumed belief in the origination of the universe. He raised more questions against creation:

"If the universe was originated, it must have an originator. Why has this originator brought the universe into being now and not at some time in the past? How could it have been brought into being as a result of some external force acting upon the originator, if there was nothing else in existence? And if it was brought into being by some spontaneous change occurring in the originator, what could have caused the change?"[257]

---

[256] Ibn Tufail (1999): pp. 33-34.
[257] Ibn Tufail (1999): p. 35.

Hayy spends several years on this issue with mind full of contradictory and opposing arguments. He switched to another approach to evaluate these arguments by considering the implications of each one of them.

If the universe came into being after non-being, then it necessarily followed that it could not have come into being by itself but must have been brought into being by an agent.
It is impossible for this agent to be just another body, otherwise it would be originated, and if this second originator was also a body, there would have to be a third originator then a fourth and so on, ad infinitum, which is absurd.
Therefore, the universe must have a non-corporeal agent.

If this agent is non-corporeal, then it cannot be perceived by the senses. It will also be impossible to perceive it with the imagination, because imagination based on sense data that are no longer present.
This agent (as non-corporeal) must be free from the principal attribute of corporeity and all other corporeal attributes. This agent of the universe must have perfect knowledge.

Now on the other hand to suppose that the universe to be eternal, it followed that its motion must be pre-eternal and infinite in respect of beginning, for every moving must be a mover, This moving force must be the first cause. Hayy concluded from both arguments the necessity of the existence of the First Cause that nothing could exist without Him. He is the cause of every thing.

"The whole universe, then, and everything within - the earth, sky, planets and stars and everything between and above and beneath them - is His work and His creation and consequent to Him in essence, although not subsequent in respect of time."[258]

Although both eternally co-exist, but the universe is consequent to God, imagine yourself holding a pen in your hand then moving your hand, the object will move in keeping with the movement of your hand. Its

---

[258] Ibn Tufail (1999): P. 38.

motion will be consequent, in essence, upon the motion of your hand but not subsequent to it in time, since the two motions began together.

The universe is the Creator's effect and creation, out of time. His command is such that if He wants a thing to be, all that He need to say is "Be! and it is."

Hayy is now reaching the age of 35, he is now more involved in the recognition of the power of the Creator, he starts meditating on how "He gave each animal species its creation and its guidance." Without His guidance, no animal could use as He intended the limbs He gave it, which would instead be burdensome. He realized then that The Creator is the Most Generous and Compassionate.

Hayy reflects differently on the beauty and goodness of things as they emanated from the existence and the work of the Creator, may He be praised! Hayy dived into the understanding of the Creator's essence as much greater and more perfect, more complete and more beautiful, more lovely and more lasting, far beyond compare.
With this level of understanding his heart become so attached to the Agent that he thought of nothing but Him. As a result Hay lost interest in the study of things. He became more interested to understand how to know Him more and with what faculty he can perceive Him further. Of course senses and imaginations are not suitable since they deal with corporeal things, on the other hand the reason stuck with equivalence of the strength of logical arguments, as what turned out in discussing the issue of eternity.

Hayy knows that he had become aware of this Being with his self and that the knowledge he had of Him was firm and fast. It therefore appeared that the self, was something non-corporeal. He also concluded that the perfection of his self and its happiness lay exclusively in bearing actual and constant witness to the Necessarily Existent Being. He then began to find out how to make this actual and constant witness in such a way that he would not turn aside or be distracted. Continuous meditation was the key word; Hayy observed the planets and stars and observed their ordered and harmonious movements. What kind of activities he need to perform to be closer to the Necessary Existence, should he seek identification with the dumb animals, or with the celestial bodies, or identification with the Necessarily Existent Being?

"The first was necessary inasmuch as he had an oppressive body, with individual limbs and organs, distinct functions and various instincts.

The second was necessary because he possessed the animal spirit, located in the heart as the principal part of the body and source of its faculties.

The third was necessary by virtue of his being who he is, i.e. the self which knows of the Necessarily Existent Being."[259]

Hayy realized that the third kind is his goal but it cannot be achieved without self-discipline and practicing both the second and the first.

Thus he started a kind of Sufi program on diet and exercise, eating the most readily available food, and spending more time on meditation, then he developed a great sense of compassion and commitment toward plants and animals to relief them from any danger. He gave attention to himself keeping himself clean at all times, washing as often as possible.

He perfumed himself as he could with plant fragrances and aromatic oils and kept his clothes clean and scented, until he quite sparkled with cleanliness, fragrance, smart grooming and good looks.

He also starts certain exercises by various kinds of orbital movement (imitating the motion of the celestial bodies), he walked around the island's coast-line, turned circles on the shore, but sometimes, Hayy spun around on the spot until he dropped down in a faint.[260]

---

[259] Ibn Tufail (1999): p. 46.
[260] Today a Sufi sect called Malawiyyah practices such spiritual exercise by spinning while they are in the process of remembrance of God (Thikr). There is nothing in the teaching of the Islamic religion to suggest such a way of worship. Many Muslim scholars disprove such practice.

Hayy went to the third identification and starts concentrating his thoughts upon the Necessarily Existent Being and detached himself from senses experience.

How can he accomplish this? Hayy followed four things; he closed his eyes and second blocked his ears, and third Hay made a great effort not to let his imagination distract him and fourth he did his best to think only of the Necessarily Existent Being alone and associated with nothing. To confuse the senses and imagination Hayy starts the procedure of spinning around faster and faster, until his sensory perceptions gradually disappeared, his imagination and other faculties weakened and the working of his self as a result intensified.

What are the attributes of the Necessarily Existent Being? He asked in order to meditate and identify himself with. Some of these attributes are positive, such as knowledge, power and wisdom, and some are negative, like freedom from corporeity. Hayy succeeded purifying himself by pure heart he witnessed the Truth, every thing disappeared from his mind. His own self, too, disappeared with them. Everything faded away and vanished like dust in the wind. Only the One Reality, the Eternally Existent Being, remained. He asks: "To whom belongs dominion now? To God, the One, the Almighty." He drowned in that state and there witnessed what no eye has seen, no ear has heard and no heart of man has ever felt. How can this be described? It is impossible. Language is very restrictive. Hayy continued with this experience until he reached the age of fifty, when he returned to the physical world after his journey, and when he rejoined the world of the senses afterwards, he was able to engage and disengage himself at will. He stayed there constantly, until he met Asal.

One of the two versions of Hayy Ibn Yaqdhan's origin mentioned the existence of a neighboring island and to that island a true faith based upon the teachings of one of the ancient prophets (may God bless them), had come. Two sons of that island, young men of good-will and honor by the names of Asal and Salaman, encountered this faith and embraced it wholeheartedly. Together, they committed themselves to following its teachings and upholding its duties and rituals.

Asal was interested in esoteric interpretation and spiritual meaning, while his friend Salaman was concerned with literal meaning and had little time for interpretation, contemplation, and independent judgment. Nevertheless, each applied himself to doing good works, examining conscience and controlling desire. Certain passages of scripture encouraged retreat from the world and solitary meditation, indicating that therein lay salvation and success, while others advocated social engagement and commitment. His contemplative nature, desire for understanding, and eagerness for insight into deeper meaning, led Asal to advocate the pursuit of solitude and he drew support from verses recommending this. The solitary life, he believed, was the path to the achievement of his aim. Salaman, averse to contemplation and personal choice, urged commitment to society and similarly referred to appropriate passages of scripture for support. Commitment, he believed, was what kept the whisperings of negative thoughts at bay and protected against the temptations of demons.

Their difference of opinion led to the two parting company. Asal knew of the neighboring island (the one where Hayy Ibn Yaqdhan was living), its resources, abundance and temperate climate and that solitude was there for whomever so sought it. Deciding to withdraw from society and spend the rest of his life there, he collected what money he had, spent some on the hire of a boat and divided the rest among the poor. He bade farewell to his friend Salaman and set off across the sea. The ship's crew ferried him to the island, set him ashore and sailed away.
Asal stayed on the island to worship and glorify God and contemplate His names and sublime attributes. There was nothing to disturb his mind or cloud his meditation. As need arose, he picked fruit or hunted to satisfy his hunger and, for a time, remained in perfect happiness and communion with his Lord. Daily, he witnessed His goodness, benevolence and grace towards him in easing his quest and sustenance. This gladdened his heart and confirmed his certainty.

Hayy Ibn Yaqdhan, meanwhile, was totally absorbed at the stations of sublimity. He only left his cave once a week to search for the food he needed. Consequently, Asal did not come across him at first and,

although he wandered the length and breadth of the island, he saw no
sign of anyone. This increased his sense of communion and joy, since it
was the pursuit of solitude that had led him to renounce society. One
day, however, it happened that Asal was in the area when Hayy
emerged to look for food and they caught sight of one another.

Certain that here was a solitary ascetic, come to the island to withdraw
from society as he had himself had done, Asal was afraid to intrude and
make Hayy's acquaintance lest he disturb his state of mind and frustrate
the fulfillment of his aim. For his part, Hayy had no idea who or what
Asal was, never having set eyes on any animal like him before. He was
wearing a kind of loose black tunic made of hair and wool that Hayy
thought was his skin. He stood staring at him for a long time,
astonished.
Afraid of disturbing him, Asal retreated. Natural inquisitiveness,
however, made Hayy follow but, seeing how anxious the other was to
avoid him, he kept his distance and himself, out of sight. Believing that
Hayy had left the area, Asal began to pray, recite scripture, invoke
God's names and prostrate himself in humility in order to calm his
mind. Unnoticed to Asal, however, Hayy had crept up close enough to
see and hear him in his devotions. He listened to the lovely, rhythmical
sound of his voice intoning scripture and watched him humble himself
in prayer, something which he had never known any other animal do.
He studied his shape and appearance and realized they were the same as
his own; and it was obvious that the tunic he wore was not his natural
skin but something made, like his. Appreciating that Asal's prayer,
humility and devotion was something good, he became convinced he
was an essence that is conscious of the Truth. He wanted to find out
what he was up to and what the reason was for his prayer and devotion.
He drew closer until, suddenly, Asal became aware of his presence and
fled. Hayy gave chase and, with his natural strength and cunning,
caught up with Asal and pinned him firmly to the ground.

Asal stared at this man dressed in furs, whose hair had grown so long
that most of it reached the ground. He realized that Hayy's speed and
physical strength were much greater than his own and tried to appease
and placate him in a language that Hayy could not understand - he

knew only that it betrayed all the signs of fear. Hayy tried to calm Asal
with sounds he had learned from the animals and by patting his head.
He stroked his cheeks and smiled at him until, eventually, Asal
regained composure and realized that Hayy meant him no harm.

Asal's devotion to scriptural interpretation had led him to learn many
languages fluently and he began to ask Hayy questions in every
language he knew in an effort to make himself understood but to no
avail. Hayy was puzzled by what he heard but had no idea what it
meant, except that it seemed to be friendly. Each thought the other so
very strange.

When he discovered that Hayy could not speak, Asal stopped worrying
about his faith and resolved to teach him language and instruct him in
religious knowledge and practice. Thus would his reward from God be
greater. Slowly at first, Asal taught him to speak by pointing at an
object and pronouncing its name, repeating it and then having Hayy say
the word while pointing at the thing. In this way, he gradually built up
his vocabulary until, within a relatively short time, he could speak.

Asal asked Hayy about himself and how he had come to the island.
Hayy replied that he knew nothing about his origin and parents, apart
from the gazelle who had raised him. He described everything he could
about himself and how he had advanced in knowledge and understanding until finally reaching the level of union. He described the
truths and the essences, transcendent of the material world, which are
conscious of the Divine Essence. He described the Divine Essence,
with His attributes of goodness and as much as he could of the rapture
of those who had united and the torment of those excluded, he had
witnessed when he attained union.

As he listened, Asal had no doubt that everything in scripture about
God, His angels, revelation, the prophets, the last day and heaven and
hell was an allegory of the things which Hayy Ibn Yaqdhan had
actually witnessed. The perception of his heart was opened, the fire of
his mind was lit and he grasped the conformity between rational
understanding and received wisdom. The different paths of scriptural
interpretation were reconciled and all the difficulties he had
encountered with scripture were resolved. What had before been

ambiguous and obscure now became clear and he became a man of understanding. He looked at Hayy Ibn Yaqdhan with reverence and respect realizing him to be one of those close to God who have no fear neither do they grieve. He undertook to serve and to follow him and be guided by him over any apparent contradictions in the teachings of his faith.

Asal told Hayy all about himself and, in answer to his questions, described conditions on his island, the level of knowledge, how the people had lived before the arrival of religion and the way that they lived now. He told him how scripture described the divine world, heaven, hell, resurrection, judgment and the true path. Hayy understood it all and saw nothing to contradict what he witnessed at the sublime station. He realized that whoever had so described and communicated it, had done so truthfully and was sincere in his claim to be a messenger of God's word. So he declared his belief and testified to the message.

Hayy asked what scripture said about religious duties and the practices of worship. Asal told him about prayer, taxation, the pilgrimage, fasting and other similar, external aspects of the faith. Hayy accepted and undertook to perform these, in line with his belief in the prophet's authenticity. There were, however, two points which surprised him and the wisdom of which eluded him.

First of all, why did this apostle use allegory in most of his descriptions of the divine world and avoid direct disclosure?
He had similar misgivings about punishment and reward in the hereafter.

Secondly, why did he circumscribe religious obligations and the duties of worship yet make the acquisition of wealth and excessive consumption permissible? The result is that people occupy themselves in futile ways and turn their backs on truth. He, of course, thought that no one need to eat anything unless it was to keep body and soul together and the concept of money had no meaning for him. He found the regulations of religious law about money, such as the various aspects of taxation, buying and selling, interest and fines all very strange and long-winded.

"If people really understood," he said, "they would avoid these futile things, dispense with them entirely and devote themselves to the truth. No one needs to be so obsessed with money and property that it has to be begged for, that hands be cut off for stealing or that lives be lost in robbery."

But he had made the mistake of assuming that people are thoughtful, perceptive and resolute. He had no idea of their lack of knowledge, inadequacy, lack of judgment and weak character.

Hayy developed a deep compassion for humanity and desire to be the cause of mankind's salvation. He became determined to go and explain the truth, in order to enlighten them. He discussed this with Asal and wondered if he could see any way of reaching his island. Asal told him about the people's lack of character and how they had turned from God's will without realizing. However, as Hayy remained so attached to his idea, Asal offered encouragement, cherishing the hope that, through him, God might guide an aspiring group of friends who were closer to salvation than the rest. The two decided that, if they remained on the shore day and night, perhaps God would provide them with a way of making the crossing.

By the grace of God, a ship that had been blown off course by the wind and waves was driven within sight of the shore. As it sailed close to land, the crew saw the two men standing on the shore and altered course. They agreed to Asal's request to take Hayy and himself aboard and a fair wind carried the ship to the island in no time at all.

The two disembarked and made their way into the city, where Asal's friends flocked to meet him. He introduced them to Hayy Ibn Yaqdhan, whom they greeted enthusiastically and treated with much respect and deference. Asal advised Hayy that this was the group closest to understanding and wisdom among the entire population and that, if he was unable to teach them, he would have even less success in instructing the masses. The island was now governed by Asal's old friend, Salaman, who believed in engagement with society and had argued in favor of outlawing asceticism.

Hayy began to teach and spread the secrets of his wisdom but had progressed only a little beyond the surface forms of things by describing what others had already given them to understand before they started to shut themselves off and shrink from what he had to say. In their hearts they resented him, even if they behaved towards him with courtesy out of consideration for a stranger and proper respect for their old friend, Asal. Day and night, in public and in private, Hayy tried to win them over and convince them but this only increased their disdain and aversion. They wanted what was good and genuinely desired the truth but, because of their weakness of character, they were not prepared to accept what he said or follow his example by searching for the truth in the way that he had. In fact, they only wanted to learn of the truth by conventional methods. His hopes dashed by their reluctance, he despaired of their reformation.

Hayy then considered the different classes of society and found each group satisfied with what it had. They had taken their desires for idols and their god was their passions. Desperate to amass the dross of this world, they are diverted by what they can accumulate, until they reach the grave. No counsel will avail nor good advice prevails and discussion only serves to entrench them. They have no path to wisdom and no share therein. They are soaked through with ignorance. What dominates their hearts is the profit they can make. God has laid a veil across their hearts, their ears and eyes and a terrible torment awaits them. All of them, with few exceptions, adhered only to the worldly aspect of their faith. They have thrown away and sold for a trivial price the good they did, thinking it worthless and slight. Business and commerce have distracted them from the word of God and they fear not a day when hearts and minds will be turned inwards.

Realizing this, it became perfectly clear that speaking to them publicly was impossible. Any of his attempts to impose a higher task on them was bound to fail.

When he understood the condition of mankind, and that the greatest part of them were like brute beasts, he knew that all wisdom, direction and good success, consisted in what the messengers of god had spoken, and the divine law delivered; and that there was no other way besides this, and that there could be nothing added to it; and that there were men appointed to every work, and that every one was best capable of doing that unto which he was appointed by nature; that this was god's way of dealing with those which were gone before, and though shall find no change in his way.

Where upon returning to Salaman and his friends, he made excuses for what he had said to them, and desired to be forgiven, and told them that he had come to the same opinion with them, and had adopted their rule of conduct. And he exhorted them to stick firmly to their resolution of keeping within the bounds of law, and the performance of the external rites; and that they should not much dive into the things that did not concern them, but that in obscure matters they should give credit and yield their assent readily; and that they should abstain from novel opinions, and from their appetites, and follow the examples of their pious ancestors and forsake novelties; and that they should avoid that neglect of religious performances which was seen in the vulgar sort of men, and the love of the world, which he principally cautioned them against.

For both he and his friend Asal knew that this tractable, but defective sort of men, had no other way of salvation; and that if they should be raised above this to the realms of speculation, it would be worse with them, and they would not be able to attain to the degree of the blessed, but would waver and fall headlong, and make a bad end. But on the contrary, if they continued in that state in which they were till death overtook them, they should find safety, and stand on the right hand: but as for as those that out-went them, they should also take place of them, and be the nearest to God. So they took their leave and left them, and sought for an opportunity of returning to their island, till it pleases God to help them to a conveniency of passing. And Hayy Ibn Yaqdhan endeavored to attain to his lofty station by the same means he had sought it at first, till he recovered it; and Asal followed his steps, till he came up with him, or wanted but very little of it; and thus they continued serving God in this Island till they died.

[Ibn Tufail's concluding remarks]

And this is that (God assist you and us by his spirit) which we have received of the history of Hayy Ibn Yaqdhan, Asal and Salaman; which comprehends such choice of words as are not found in any other book, nor heard in common discourse. And it is a piece of hidden knowledge which none can receive, but those which have the knowledge of God, nor can any be ignorant of it, but those which have not. Now we have taken a contrary method to our pious ancestors as to their reservedness in this matter, and sparingness of speech. And the reason which did the more easily persuades us to divulge this secret, and tear the veil, was, because of the corrupt notions which some pretenders to philosophy in our age have broached and scattered, so that they are diffused through several countries, and the mischief which arises from thence is become epidemical. Fearing therefore lest those weak ones, who reject the authority of the prophets (of blessed memory) and make choice of that which is delivered them by fools, should imagine those corrupt notions to be that secret which ought to be hidden from the unworthy, and so should the more eagerly incline toward them; we have thought good to give them a glimpse of the secret of secrets, that we might draw them into the way of truth, and avert them from this other.

Nevertheless, we have not so delivered the secrets which are comprehended in these few leaves, as to leave them without a thin veil or cover over them, which will be easily rent by those who are worthy of it, but will be so thick to him that is unworthy to pass beyond it, that he shall not be able to get through it. And I desire those my brethren who shall see this discourse, that they would excuse me for being so careless in my exposition and so free in my demonstration; seeing I had not done so, if I had not been elevated to such heights as transcend the reach of human sight, and wished to express the matter in easy terms, that I might dispose men and raise a desire in them to enter into the right way. And I beg of God mercy and forgiveness, and that he would please to lead us to the well of the pure knowledge of himself, for he is gracious and liberal of his favors. Peace be to you my brother, whom it is my duty to assist, and the mercy and blessing of God be upon you."

[The end of the story of Hayy Ibn Yaqdhan]

CHAPTER EIGHT
8. Ibn Rushd (Averroes)

(520-595 A.H. / 1126-1198 A.D.)

1. First Question in Philosophy
The first question prince Abu Ya'qob Yusuf[261] asked Ibn Rushd was:

"Is the heaven eternal or created?" Ibn Rushd was first disturbed by this question, and of course he was very surprised. This question reflects the image of the philosophy and philosophers in the mind of the religious-political leaders. This carefulness and concern, in regard to the relationship between philosophy and religion, was not a temporary political mode, in fact it was the general state of many devoted Muslims. They were carefully observing philosophy and the phantasm of the philosophers in relation to their religious belief. There is no doubt that this case of awareness and carefulness brought by the achievement of al-Ghazali who singled out, in his celebrated book *The Incoherence of the Philosophers,* three issues (including eternity of the world) in which the philosophical endeavor was destructive to the Islamic belief, and because of which al-Ghazali charge the philosophers, in regard to these three issues, as being infidels. Although al-Ghazali's work took place in the eastern part of the Islamic culture, the western part (Spain) was not an exception.

2. The Life and Writings of Ibn Rushd
Abu al-Walid Muhammad Ibn Rushd (Averroes) was born in 1126 A.D in Cordoba. He was well educated in the fields of Qur'anic studies, jurisprudence, the principles of jurisprudence, Kalam or scholastic theology, Arabic language, and literature. He was also skilled in medicine, astronomy, mathematics, music, and zoology. He was first of all a distinguished philosopher.

---

[261] Abu Ya'qob Yusuf Abu Muhammad bin 'Abd al-Mu'men (regiend 1163-1184) one of the famous al-Muwahhed Caliph in Spain. Al-Muwahhed dynasty ruled 1145-1269 A.D.

In 1169 he held the office of judge (*qadhi*) in Seville, then in 1171 Abu
Ya'qob Yusuf brought him to Cordoba and appointed him as the chief
judge and his personal physician. Ibn Rushd intelligence manifested
itself well in medicine and philosophy. In medicine he wrote al-*Kulliyat
fi al-Tibb*, as medical encyclopedia dealing with anatomy, diagnosis,
pathology, physiology, and general therapeutics. This book was
translated in 1255 A.D. into Latin under the title "Colliget" and it was
reprinted several times.

In Philosophy he wrote about 38 philosophical works (books, short
commentaries, long commentaries, and summaries) among these books:

Tahafut al-Tahafut (The Incoherence of The Incoherence) as a reply to

al-Ghazali's book The Incoherence of the Philosophers.

Fasl al-Maqal fima Bainal Hikama wal-Shari'ah min Itsal (Decisive

Treatise on the Harmony of Riligion and Philosophy)

Mabadi' al-Falsafa (The Principles of Philosophy).

Talkis Kitab al-Jadal (Middle Commentary on Aristotle's Topics)

Rislat an-Nafs (on the Soul)

Al-Daruri fi Usul al-Fiqh (Summary of al-Ghazali's al-Mustasfa)

 Three short commentaries: on Topics, Rhetoric, Poetics

The writings of Ibn Rushd were translated into Latin in the 13th century
by Michael Scotus, and Hermannus Alemannus. Roger Bacon
acknowledged that Scotus brought the most important change to the
West by introducing the ideas of Ibn Rushd, especially his
commentaries that reflect a genuine understanding of Aristotle.

In the 13th century, group of scholars called themselves Averroeists,
the most famous of the m was Siger of Brabant, soon after Averroeism
became a distinguished philosophical school in Europe.

3. The Central Points of Ibn Rushd's Philosophy
The philosophy of Ibn Rushd revolves around two central points:
1. The relationship between philosophy and Islamic religion.
2. An authentic commentary on Aristotle.

In regard to the first part, Ibn Rushd tried to harmonize philosophy and religion. Especially that the Greek philosophical heritage presume the eternity of the world, while Islamic religion teaches creation.   Another reason was the criticism of al-Ghazali to the metaphysics of the philosophers that contradicts the Islamic creed.
Ibn Rushed thinks that both philosophy and religion are true, and to justify that they do not contradict each other, Ibn Rushd argued that truth could be comprehended on different levels. He differentiate between the philosophical understanding of truth and scripture, and the public understanding of the scripture, as a result he thought that religion express the truth in a symbolic figurative language that is easy to comprehend by the majority of the people who are not philosophers, while the philosophers understand the deeper level by logical reasoning.
His attempt of the reconciliation of philosophy and religion was well presented in his book: *Fasl al-Maqal fima baina al-Hikma wal-Shari'ah min Itisal (The Decisive treaties on the relationship between Philosophy and Religion).* In this book Ibn Rushd hold the idea that religion is true and philosophy is true too, therefore, they can easily be harmonized.

If the activity of 'philosophy' is nothing more than study of existing beings and reflection on truth, and if the Law has encouraged and urged reflection on beings and truth, then it is clear that what this name signifies is either obligatory or recommended by the Islamic Law.

Ibn Rushd supported this idea by quoting some verses from the Qur'an such as the saying of the Exalted: 'Reflect, you have vision' another example he sited from the Qur'an: 'Have they not studied the kingdom of the heavens and the earth, and whatever things God has created?'

Ibn Rushd thinks that this textual authority is not only an indication, rather it is an obligation to use intellectual reasoning, or a combination of intellectual and legal reasoning. He thinks that Qur'anic text is urging the study of the totality of beings. Ibn Rushd made an argument to rendered the study of beings by philosophy and logic as obligatory:

Since the Islamic law render the reasoning and reflection obligatory, and since reflection is nothing more than inference and drawing out of the unknown from the known, and since this is reasoning or at any rate done by reasoning, therefore we are under an obligation to carry on our study of beings by intellectual reasoning.
By this way of argumentation Ibn Rushd tried to prove that it is preferable and even necessary for anyone, who wants to understand God the Exalted and the other beings demonstratively, to have first understood the kinds of demonstration and their rules of validity. Understanding logic will help to avoid rhetorical and fallacious reasoning.

Ibn Rushd said that if someone other than Muslim scholars has already examined a philosophical topic, then it is clear that we ought to seek help towards our goal from what has been said by such a predecessor on the subject, regardless of whether this other one shares our religion or not. Ibn Rushd shares with al-Kindi the same argument of justifying the study of Greek philosophy. Al-Kindi eloquently said:
"We ought not to be embarrassed of appreciating the truth and of obtaining it wherever it comes from, even if it comes from races distant and nations different from us. Nothing should be dearer to the seeker of truth than the truth itself, and there is no devalue of the truth, nor belittling either of him who speaks it or of him who conveys it."

Ibn Rushd raised the issue that in as much as nations learn from each other in the field of medicine and mathematics, they should also learn in philosophy. But al-Ghazali had already showed that there is no harm from the logic and mathematics of the philosophers, but the harm resides in their field of metaphysics. Since it is clearly contradictory to the Islamic faith. In addition to that, Greek philosophy has no concept of God in the monotheistic sense.

Contrary to al-Ghazali, Ibn Rushd thinks that the study of ancient philosophy is obligatory by Islamic Law, "since their aim and purpose in their books is just the purpose to which the Law has urged us, and that whoever forbids the study of them to anyone who is fit to study them, i.e. anyone who, unites two qualities, (1) natural intelligence and (2) religious integrity and moral virtue, is blocking people from the door by which the Law summons them to knowledge of God, the door of theoretical study which leads to the truest knowledge of Him; and such an act is the extreme of ignorance and estrangement from God the Exalted."[262]

Ibn Rushd admits that there might be some harm resulting from the study of philosophy, but he reduced that to the minimum and considered it as an accidental effect of this field, equating it with the error that may also occur accidentally from other fields such medicine, geometry, and jurisprudence. He thinks that truth from philosophy and scriptural truth cannot conflict. In cases in which the apparent meaning of Scripture conflicts with philosophical conclusions, the Scripture must be interpreted allegorically or metaphorically.

Philosophical knowledge might lead to knowledge about a subject that is mentioned in the Scripture; then the apparent meaning of the words inevitably either accords or conflicts with the conclusions of demonstration about it. "If this meaning accords there is no argument. If it conflicts there is a call for allegorical interpretation of it. The meaning of 'allegorical interpretation' is: extension of the significance of an expression from real to metaphorical significance, without forsaking therein the standard metaphorical practices of Arabic, such as calling a thing by the name of something resembling it or a cause or consequence or accompaniment of it, or other things such as are enumerated in accounts of the kinds of metaphorical speech."[263]

---

[262] Ibn Rushd (1973): p. 27.
[263] Ibn Rushd (1973): p. 35.

Ibn Rushd thinks that all Muslims scholars agree in regard to the principle of allegorical interpretation; however, they only disagree about the extent of its application. He brought the example that the Ash'arites give an allegorical interpretation to the verse about God's directing Himself and the Tradition about His descent, while the Hanbalites take them in their apparent meaning.

Ibn Rushd thinks that the secret of Scripture having an apparent meaning and an inner meaning lies in the diversity of people's natural capacities and the difference of their innate dispositions with regard to assent. It does match with variety and levels of people's intelligence. The Qur'anic text according to Ibn Rushd fall into three kinds with respect to interpretation and error:

1. Texts which must be taken in their apparent meaning by everyone. Since the meaning can be understood plainly by demonstrative, dialectical and rhetorical methods alike, no one is excused for the error of interpreting these texts allegorically.

2. Texts which must be taken in their apparent meaning by the lower classes and interpreted allegorically by the demonstrative class. It is inexcusable for the lower classes to interpret them allegorically or for the demonstrative class to take them in their apparent meaning.

3. Texts whose classification under the previous headings is uncertain. Error in this matter by the demonstrative class is excused.

Ibn Rushd said that the unlearned classes must take such texts in their apparent meaning. The learned or scholars should not set down allegorical interpretations in popular writings, because this causes confusion among the people. Therefore allegorical interpretations ought to be set down only in demonstrative books, because if they are in demonstrative books they are encountered by no one but men of the demonstrative class. But if they are set down in other than demonstrative books and one deals with them by poetical, rhetorical or dialectical methods, then he commits an offence against the Law and against philosophy. As a result Ibn Rushd thinks that books of philosophy and demonstrative knowledge should be banned to the unqualified, but not to the learned.

"Thus people in relation to Scripture fall into three classes: One class is those who are not people of interpretation at all: these are the rhetorical class. They are the overwhelming mass, for no man of sound intellect is exempted from this kind of assent. Another class is the people of dialectical interpretation: these are the dialecticians, either by nature alone or by nature and habit. Another class is the people of certain interpretation: these are the demonstrative class, by nature and training, i.e. in the art of philosophy. This interpretation ought not to be expressed to the dialectical class, let alone to the masses."[264]

But the comprehension of the truth varies among people whom Ibn Rushd divided into three kinds:

---

[264] Ibn Rushd (1973): p. 52. Ibn Rushd explained further: When something of these allegorical interpretations is expressed to anyone unfit to receive them, especially demonstrative interpretations because of their remoteness from common knowledge both he who expresses it and he to whom it is expressed are led into unbelief. The reason for that [in the case of the latter] is that allegorical interpretation comprises two things, rejection of the apparent meaning and affirmation of the allegorical one; so that if the apparent meaning is rejected in the mind of someone who can only grasp apparent meanings, without the allegorical meaning being affirmed in his mind, the result is unbelief, if it [the text in question] concerns the principles of religion.
Allegorical interpretations, then, ought not to be expressed to the masses nor set down in rhetorical or dialectical books, i.e. books containing arguments of these two sorts. They should not be expressed to this class; and with regard to an apparent text, when there is a self-evident doubt whether it is apparent to everyone and whether knowledge of its interpretation is impossible for them, they should be told that it is ambiguous and [its meaning] known by no one except God; and that the stop should be put here in the sentence of the Exalted, 'And no one knows the interpretation thereof except God'. The same kind of answer should also be given to a question about abstruse matters, which there is no way for the masses to understand; just as the Exalted has answered in Isis saying, 'And they will ask you about the Spirit. Say, "The Spirit is by the command of my Lord; you have been given only a little knowledge" '.

The first and probably the largest in number is approachable to ideas that can be expressed by means of logic.

The second is open to to persuasion.

The third, which is few in number, seek understanding by appealing to conclusive evidence.

Ibn Rushed thought that religion is the most suitable to the masses or the simple-minded majority. While the enlightened few need a disclosed scientific truth. [265]

4. Ibn Rushd and Hayy Ibn Yaqdhan

But if this is the case then Ibn Rushd nullifies the role of philosophy and philosophers from the society. It becomes an endeavor that is restricted to the elite with no social dimension. This manifest that the task of philosophy according to Ibn Rushd is very similar to that of Ibn Baja and Ibn Tufail. The philosopher is a solitary being seeking his own intellectual felicity without caring about the "lower level" majority. Similar to that attitude of Hayy Ibn Yaqdhan who left the island of the Asal's people who learn the truth through the scripture in order to live in solitude in his island. In fact Ibn Rushd became the real manifestation of Ibn Tufail's character Hayy Ibn Yaqdhan.

---

[265] Ibn Rushd (1973): p. 52.

CONCLUSION

The Epistemological Paradigm
How did Muslim philosophers deal with Greek philosophy?

1. The following considers Islamic civilization in a concentric model (many circles with one common center).[266] This model has two important characteristics:

A- The circles are not only concentric, but all of them beyond the center may also be regarded as orbiting around the center, which is the core belief ('Aqidah), in the manner of a solar system.
B- If we consider the radiuses as representing the pull or force of gravity toward the center ('Aqidah), then the pull of gravity will be inversely proportional to the length of the radius; the shorter the radius the greater the pull of gravity and the longer the radius, the less the pull of gravity.

2. The Model of the Epistemological Structure: Five Circles
The first circle: This is the central circle. It represents the heart or the core of Islamic civilization, and it is also considered as the power of the activity and the continuation of Islamic civilization. It is also the core of all other circles.

This circle represents the Islamic belief, especially the Islamic Creed ('Aqidah) from the Qur'an and the Sunnah (the tradition) of the prophet Muhammad. The Islamic law (Shri'ah) represented in this core also affects all circles in Islamic civilization. It is like the supreme constitution influencing all aspects of the civilization. This inner circle is distinguished by a number of characteristics. It is holy and absolute; it is perfect, comprehensive, and applicable in all times and places. It is not a subject of human effort to add or modify or eliminate any part of it, but it is perfectly a subject of human understanding, reasoning, and reflection, in its effort to arrive at interpretations and judgments regarding humans in this life and in the hereafter. The Qur'an strongly encourages such efforts of thinking and knowledge in general.

---

[266] See Al-Allaf, Mashhad (1988): pp. 298-302. Dr. Yasin Khalil used this model to clarify his idea about Arabic sciences. However, the model being used here presents an Islamic approach.

The second circle: This circle is next to the core (Creed). It is where we find The Qur'anic Sciences, Hadith Sciences, Jurisprudence (Fiqh), and the foundation and principles of Jurisprudence (Usul al-Fiqh), in addition to what is related to Jurisprudence in the form of Islamic literature in the collection of Islamic legal judgment. Also in this circle are interpretations of the Holy Qur'an, understandings of the tradition of the Prophet, and the science of recitation of The Qur'an. This circle also includes the rules for purifying one's self or mysticism (Sufism). We can also find here the science dealing with the interpretation of dreams as based on Qur'an and Sunnah. The second circle is concerned with problems and difficulties in all aspects of Islamic culture: religious, social, political, and economic.

The third circle: This circle represents the sciences and studies that Muslims consider very important, such as the Arabic language and philology, in their efforts to prove the superiority of the Qur'anic language in both its meaning and its linguistic structure. We also find here the study of syntax, semantics of the Arabic language in addition to Arabic and Islamic literature. The third circle includes the history (the study of historical events), genealogy, law, management, arrangement and organization of the social and economic life of Muslims, in addition to arts in general and particularly calligraphy.

The fourth circle: This circle represents the mathematical sciences, natural science, astronomy, geometry, medicine, pharmacy, agriculture, engineering and architecture. Although it is far from the core, at the same time the fourth circle serves the core by proving what the core is calling for: understanding the laws of the universe and the miraculous phenomena of human beings is another way to understand the greatness of the Creator and the miraculous acts of creation.

Finally, the fifth circle represents theology, philosophy, ways of practicing mysticism or Sufi orders, Islamic sects, non-Islamic sects, and knowledge that is translated or transferred from other cultures. Here we not only find efforts of knowledge for things different from those in the core, but it is also knowledge that raises problems regarding the core itself. In this circle we find skepticism, interpretations, and arguments leading to problems such as those we

The Epistemological Paradigm

find in philosophy. In this circle we also find non-Abrahamic religions and controversies among religious groups. This circle sometimes provide support to the core, but it may cause problems as well, because of the instability of its nature; it becomes particularly active when the influence of the core becomes weakened and other nations and groups activate themselves in such a way that the intellectual influence of this circle becomes more noticeable socially and politically.

3. Epistemological Characteristics:
1. The central circle or the core is complete; "This day have I perfected your religion for you, completed my favor upon you, and have chosen for you Islam as your religion." *(Qur'an, 5:3)* The practicality of the Divine Law is presented in its flexibility and its application in many different cultures, in different eras.
2. The circles are not closed except for the central one. The other circles are dynamic and have vitality. They are active in opening themselves to other cultures and civilizations to interact with them, but this interaction does not occur indiscriminately. For example, the second circle is more cautious in its interaction with other civilizations because it is closer to the core, while the third opens itself to interact more freely with other cultures in a way that permits a number of non-Islamic elements to enter or infiltrate into Islamic civilization. These may include: some influence of Aristotelian logic in the study of the Arabic language, some influence of Roman administration on the Umayyad Caliphate, and some references to the influence of the Persian culture on Muslims in management and the ways of ruling in the 'Abbasid Caliphate.
3. The fourth and the fifth circles are the most open to interaction with other cultures and civilizations. The influence of the fourth circle on Muslim life is obvious, while the influence of the fifth circle on Muslim social life has been very limited. For example, Greek philosophy faced severe criticism from Muslim scholars; Al-Ghazali's book *The Incoherence of the Philosophers* is a good example of this. Later Aristotelian logic faced a similar fate with Ibn Taimia (661-728A.H./1263-1328 A.D.). Philosophy could not even enter the realm of Islamic civilization until some Muslim scholars and philosophers spent a great deal of effort to reconcile it with the core or to use it in defense of it.

Bibliography

Al-Kindi: Al-Kindi, Abu Yusuf Ya'qub bin Ishaq:

(1948) *"Kitab al-Kindi ila Al-Mu'tasim Billah fil Falsafah al-Ula"*
Edited by al-Ahwani, first edition, Cairo.

(1950) *Rasa'il al-Kindi al-falsafiyya*, ed. Muhammad 'Abd al-Hadi
Abu Rida, Dar al-fikr al-Arabi, al-juz' **(1)** 1369/1950.

(1953) *Rasa'il al-Kindi al-falsafiyya*, ed. Muhammad 'Abd al-Hadi
Abu Rida, Dar al-fikr al-Arabi, al-juz' **(2)** 1372/1953.

(1974) *Fi al-Falsafah al-Ula*, A Translation of Yaqub Ibn Ishaq al-
Kindi's Treatise *"On First Philosophy,"* In *al-Kindi's Metaphysics*, ed.
and translated by Alfred L. Ivry, New York, Albany, 1974.

Al-Razi: Al-Razi, Abu Bakr Ibn Zakariya:

(1939) *Opera Philosophica*, edited by Paul Kraus Cairo.

Al-Farabi: Al-Farabi, Abu Nasr:

(1890) *Alfarabi's philosophische* Abhandlungen, hrsg. V. Friedrich
Dieterici, Leiden.

(1890) *'Uyun al-Masa'el, (Fontes quaestionum),* in Al-Farabi (1890)
pp. 56-65.

(1895) *Maqalah fi ma'ani al-'Aql. (On the meaning of the word
"Intellect").* In *al-thamaral Mardiyya fil Risalat al-Farabiyyah*, edtied
by: Dieterici, F. Leiden,

(1907a) *Risalah fi jawab masa'il su'ila 'an-ha (Answers to Questions*

Put to Him), in collection of various treatises, edited by Muhammad Isma'il, letter number 14, first edition, Cairo.

(1907b) *Mayanbaghi Ta'alumohu qabal Ta'alum al-Falsafa (What must Precede the Study of Philosophy)*, in collection of treatises, ed. by Muhammad Ismail, letter number 3, first edition, Cairo.

(1328 A.H. / 1910 A.D.) *Mayanbaghi An Uqaddam qabal Ta'alum al-Falsafah (What must Precede the Study of Philosophy)*, in *Mabadie' al-Falsafah al-Qadimah, (Principles of Ancient Philosophy)* collection of various treatises, edited by Al-Maktabah al-Salafyyah, first letter, first edition, Al-Muayyed press,Cairo. 1328H/1910C.E.

(1938) *Risalah fi al-'Aql (AlFarabi Risalat Fi'l-'Aql)*, Arabic text with French translation by Maurice Bouyges, Beyrouth, Imprimerie Catholique.

(1964) Al-Siyasat al-Madaniyya (Mabadi' al-Mawjudat), ed. By fawzi Najjar, Bairut.

(1968) *Ihsa' al-Ulum,* edited by Uthman Amin, third edition, Cairo.

(1985) *Mabadi' ara' ahl al-madina al-fadila, (Al-Farabi On The Perfect State),* translated by Richard Walzer, Clarendon press, Oxford.

Al-Ghazali: Al-Ghazali, Abu Hamed:

(1958) *Tahafut Al-Falasifah (Incoherence of The Philosophers),* translated by Sabih Ahmad Kamali, The Pakistan Philosophical Congress, Lahore.

(1980) *Deliverance from Error (al-Munqidh min al-Dalal),* trans. by R.J.McCarthy as *Freedom and Fulfillment*, Fons Vitae, Louisville, KY.

(1987) *Ihya Ulum al-Deen*, 5 vols. Dar al-Rayyan llturath, al- Qahira.

(1408 A.H./ 1988 A.D.) *Al-Arba'een fi Usul Addeen*, Darul Jeel, Bairut.

(1997) *The Incoherence of The Philosophers*, translated by Michael E. Marmura, Brigham Young University Press, Provo, Utah.

Ibn Baja: Abu Bakr Muhammad bin Yahya, (Ibn al-Sayigh)

(1956) *Kitab al-Nafs (on The Soul)*, Pakistan Hitorical Society, Karachi.

(1973) *Rasa'el Falsafiya*, edited by Badawi, 'Abdul-Rahman, Benghazi, Libia.

(1991) *Rasa'el Ibn Baja*, edited by Majid Fakhri, Dar al-Nahar, Bairut, second edition.

Ibn Rushd: Ibn Rushd, Abul Waleed Muhammad:

(1999) *Faslul Maqal fi mabain al-Hekmah wal-Shari'ah min Itisal*, translated from the Arabic by Jim Colville, The Kegan Paul Arabian Library, Vol. Six, Kegan paul International, London.

(1976) Another translation, with introduction and notes, of Ibn Rushd's *Kitab fasl al-maqal, (On The Harmony of Religion and Philosophy)* with its appendix *(Damima)* and an extract from *Kitab al-kashf 'an manahij al-adilla,* by George F. Hourani. Messrs. Luzac & Co, London.

(1973) Fasl al-Maqal wa Taqreer ma bain al-Shari'ah wal-Hikma min al-Itisal, Dar al-Mashreq, Beirut.

Ibn Sina: Abu Ali (al-Shaykh al-Ra'is):

(1957) *Al-Isharat wal-Tanbihat*, 3 vols.edited by, Sulaiyman Dunia, al-Qahira.

(1960) *Al-Shifa'*, edited by, Ibrahim Madgor, al-Qahira.

(1985) *Kitab al-Najat*, Dar al-'Afaq al-Jadidah, Bairut.

Ibn Tufail: Abu Bakr Muhammad:

(1999) *Hay Ibn Yaqzan*, translated from the Arabic by Jim Colville, The Kegan Paul Arabian Library, Vol. Six, Kegan paul International, London.

(1400 A.H. / 1980 A.D.) *Hayy Ibn Yaqdhan*, edited by Farooq Sa'ad, third edition in Arabic Language, Dar al-Afaaq, Bairut.

(1929) *Hay Ibn Yaqzan,* translated by Simon Ockely, in 1708, Frederick A.Stockes Company Publishers, London.

Al-Allaf, Mashhad (2003): *Mirror of Realization,* IIC Classic Series, USA.

Al-Allaf, Mashhad (1988): *Dr. Yasin Khalil, His Philosophy and Scientific Works*, Baghdad, Iraq.

Alexander of Aphrodisias (1887): *De Anima* in *Commentaria in Aristotelem Graeca,Supplementum II*, Berlin.

Ariew, R. & Watkins, E (2000): *Readings in Modern Philosophy*, 2 vols. Hackett Publishing Company.

Aristotle (1941): *The Basic Works of Aristotle*, Edited by Richard McKEON, Random House, New York.

Bacon, Roger (1962): *Opus Majus,* Transl. by R.B. Burke, 2 Vols, NY.

Badawi, AbdurRahman (1961): *Mu'alafat al-Ghazali*, Cairo.

De Boer, T.J. (1965): *The History of Philosophy in Islam*, translated by Edward R. Jones, Luzac & Co, London.

Al-Farisi, 'Abdul Ghafir (1968): *Biography of Imam al-Ghazali*, in al-Subki (1968).

Farmer, Henry G. (1934): *Al-Farabi's Arabic-Latin Writings on Music*, The Civic Press Glasgow.

Gilson, E. (1929): *The Greek-Arabic Sources of Augustinism Influenced by Avicenna*, Paris, 1929.

Gohlman, William E. (1974): *The Life of Ibn Sina*, annotated translation, State University of New York, New York.

Hammond, Robert (1947): *The Philosophy of Alfarabi And Its Influence On Medieval Thought*, The Hobson Book press, New York.

Heijenoort, Jean van (1967): (Editor): *From Frege to Godel, A source book in Mathematical Logic, 1879-1931*, Harvard University press. Cambridge. Third edition.

Hilbert, David (1925): On The Infinite, in Heijenoort (1967).

Hyman, Arthur & Walsh, James J. (1973): Philosophy in the Middle Ages, Hackett Publishing Company, Indianapolis.

Kamali, M. H. (1991): *Principles of Islamic Jurisprudence*, Islamic Text Society, Cambridge.

Locke, John (1988): *An Essay Concerning Human Understanding*, edited by Peter H. Nidditch, Clarendon press, Oxford.

Mosa Ibn Maimoon (Maimonides) (No date): *Dalalt al-Ha'ereen*, edited by Husain Atai, Maktabat al-Thaqafah al-Deniyyah

Al-Razi, Fakhrud Deen (1323 H.): *Al-Muhassal fi Araa' al-Mutaqademeen wal Muta'khereen*, Cairo.

Philoponus, John (1897): *De Anima*, in *Commentaria in Aristotelem Graeca*, 15, Berlin.

Rescher, Nicholas (1964): *Al-Kindi: An Annotated Bibliography*, University of Pittsburgh Press.

Ross, Sir W.D. (1930): *Aristotle*, Methuen, 2nd edition.

Sa'ed al-Andalusi (1912): *Tabaqaat al-Umam*, Bairut.

Schweitzer, Albert (1949): *Philosophy of Civilization*, Macmillan, New York.

Al-Shahrastani (1892): *Al-Milal wal- Nehal*, London.

Sheikh, Sa'eid M. (1982): *Islamic Philosophy,* The Octagon Press, London.

Simplicius (1882): *De Anima*, in *Commentaria in Aristotelem Graeca*, 11, Berlin.

Skyrms, Brian (2000): *Choice & Chance*, an Introduction to Inductive Logic, Wadsworth.

Al-Subki (1968): *Tabaqat al-Shafe'iyyah al-Kubra*, vol. 6. Cario.

Themistius (1900): *De Anima*, in *Commentaria in Aristotelem Graeca*, 5 Berlin.

Ibn Abi Usaibe'ah (1882): *'Uyun al-Anbaa' fi Tabaqat al-Atebba'*, Cairo.

Wolter, Allan B. (1967): Roger Bacon, in the Encyclopedia of Philosophy, ed. Paul Edwards, Vol. 1. Macmillan Publishing Co., NY.

Zaidan, Abdul Karim (1987): *Al-Wajeez fi Usul al-Fiqh*, Maktabat al-Quds, Baghdad, Iraq.